STILL ON
THIS JOURNEY

STILL ON THIS JOURNEY

The Vision and Mission of Dr. Ron Daniels

Still on This Journey: The Vision and Mission of Dr. Ron Daniels

This book focuses on the vision, mission, values and philosophy which have served as the driving force behind my near lifelong journey for justice and provides perspectives on the Institute of the Black World 21st Century (IBW) as the culminating project, my legacy endeavor.

Library of Congress Control Number: ISBN 978-0-578-41427-0

Printed in the United States
First Printing, 2019

Cover design by Kyle Pennerman
Text design by Alan Bell

Publisher's Cataloging-In-Publication Data
(Provided by Five Rainbows Cataloging Services)

Names: Daniels, Ron, Dr., author.
Title: Still on this journey : the vision and mission of Dr. Ron Daniels / Dr. Ron Daniels.
Description: New York : State of the Black World Press, 2019.
Identifiers: ISBN 978-0-578-41427-0 (paperback)
Subjects: LCSH: African Americans—History. | African Americans—Reparations. | African Americans—Social conditions. | Blacks—History. | Pan-Africanism. | Civil rights. | Social justice. | BISAC: SOCIAL SCIENCE / Ethnic Studies / African American Studies. | HISTORY / African American. | SOCIAL SCIENCE / Discrimination & Race Relations. | POLITICAL SCIENCE / Civil Rights.
Classification: LCC E185.86 .D36 2019 (print) | DDC 305.896/073—dc23.

Table of Contents

STILL ON
THIS JOURNEY

The Prologue:
It's Been a Long Time Coming

As the legendary Rhythm and Blues singer Sam Cooke might declare, "it's been a long time coming," but eventually it was imperative that "the book," this initial volume get done. Urged on by family, allies and friends, for decades I have been contemplating writing a book or books as part of my duty/responsibility as a social and political activist to share reflections on my work and lessons learned with this and future generations. All too often social and political activists are too immersed, consumed and overwhelmed by the "struggle," the "movement" to take time to write. Such has been my plight, my predicament.

Ever since a memorable night in a rat and roach infested tenement in an impoverished section of August Wilson's Hill District of Pittsburgh when I stared into the stars and said to myself, "people should not have to live like this," I have been on a journey for justice; a spiritual calling to engage in civic work and civil and human rights advocacy to see that people do not have to live as my beloved

Mother and four children did to survive/subsist in one of America's "dark ghettos." From the Cadet Corps and NAACP Youth Chapter in my teens to the formation of Freedom, Inc. in Youngstown, Ohio, to the Mid-West Regional Coalition, Federation of Pan African Education Institutions, Ohio Black Political Assembly, Ohio Institute for Practical Politics, National Black Political Assembly, Federation of Nationalist and Pan African Organizations, African Liberation Day, National Committee for Independent Politics, National Black Independent Political Party, National Rainbow Coalition, Jesse Jackson for President Campaign, 1988, African American Progressive Action Network, National Malcolm X Commemoration Commission, State of the Race Conferences, African American Institute for Research and Empowerment, Ron Daniels for President, 1992, Independent Progressive National Convention, Campaign for a New Tomorrow, Haiti Support Project, Million Man March and Day of Absence, State of the Black World Conferences, the Institute of the Black World 21st Century and all the projects, programs, campaigns and initiatives associated with these and other endeavors not mentioned, I have been passionately, persistently and consistently pursuing this mission, this journey.

The journey has not been without its casualties and consequences. It has sometimes been undertaken with too little attention to the impact on family and the kind of self-development that could have contributed to maintaining family and enhancing the capacity to engage the struggle from a position of greater economic stability. Writing "the book" has been another casualty. As noted above, my plight in this regard is not unusual. The heavy lift required to build movements and institutions sometimes makes it incredibly difficult to pause to write major manuscripts in the heat of battle.

When I embarked on an independent campaign for President

of the United States, an article in *The New York City Sun* newspaper dubbed me the "guts and faith" candidate, suggesting an effort that was bold in vision/mission/purpose but short on resources. Historically and up to the present, most of the movements, institutions and initiatives I have undertaken have been on "guts and faith," requiring maximum personal sweat equity. I have never been a movement prima donna. If necessary, I am willing to type the memos, design the flyers (if ever so basic), lick the stamps, stuff envelopes and multi-task at an insane level to ensure success. Moreover, I have a penchant for not waiting for resources before launching initiatives. Where there is a need that should be addressed, my tendency is to move forward, confident that if the cause is righteous, resources, even if insufficient, will follow. If there is a need, I seldom approach it by saying "if" we had the resources, we would act. I prefer to act, create the program, project or initiative and present our record of work to the people, funders, whomever in hopes that resources will be forthcoming.

Much of what I have managed to accomplish in collaboration with key allies, friends and supporters has been on "guts and faith." Of necessity, this approach has required the expenditure of an incredible amount of time in the trenches doing tasks that, in the broader scheme of things, have not necessarily been the best use of my experience and skills. I have never refused to launch an initiative or allow one to fail for lack of the paid staff/personnel needed to perform the day to day tasks that often make the difference between success and failure. I roll up my sleeves and with dedicated teams of volunteers work like hell to make the improbable possible. It is not an approach that I would recommend to aspiring activists and organizers, but it is the approach I have felt compelled to utilize in sometimes "willing" success in this journey for justice.

This hands-on approach has meant postponing, delaying and

setting aside "the book." But it does not mean that I have not been writing; I just haven't been able to pause to pen a substantial manuscript of ideas in a single volume. Indeed, as I sought to find a way to get my ideas/views out to Black people and to achieve a following, I decided to write a weekly column for distribution via the National Newspaper Publishers Association, the Trade Association for more than 300 hundred Black newspapers across the country. I wanted to write articles on critical issues of concern to Black people in a popular, readable, understandable style to develop a national constituency. This was the vision for *Vantage Point,* Articles and Essays by Ron Daniels. William Ellis, Senior and his son Bill, Jr., Editors/Producers of the Akron Reporter Newspaper were the first to publish *Vantage Point* articles. They also put in a good word with other Black Newspapers to do likewise. For almost a decade, I wrote fifty-two articles a year and personally mailed them out to more than 100 selected Black Newspapers.

The strategy was successful. Black people from across the country came to know Ron Daniels because they read *Vantage Point* in their local newspapers or *The Final Call,* the national newspaper of the Nation of Islam. On various occasions, I ran into readers who informed me that they clipped my articles and compiled them in folders because they were informative, readable and provided perspectives with which they agreed. So, in lieu of authoring books, I became a prolific essayist and utilized *Vantage Point* as a vehicle to advance the movements, institutions, projects, programs and initiatives I was promoting as an "activist/scholar."

In reality, I was writing "the book" week by week, article by article, essay by essay. As I began to think about writing a book, I planned to follow the path of Dr. Manning Marable, one of the preeminent scholars of the last half century, whose very first book, *From the Grassroots,* was simply a compilation of his weekly columns. It seemed simple enough to catalogue a number of my articles and essays thematically, write a forward and introduction to each section and, voila, there would be the book. As a component of my Doctoral work at Union Institute and Universities, I actually compiled a series of articles and essays for that purpose but never got around to writing the forward or the introductions to sections.

In the meantime, I contributed essays to several books including: "Racism: Looking Forward, Looking Backward," in *Race and Resistance,* edited by Herb Boyd; "The Crisis of Police Brutality and Misconduct in America: The Causes and the Cure," in *Police Brutality, an Anthology* edited by Jill Nelson; "Institutions for Black Empowerment," in *State of the Race, an Anthology* edited by Dr. Jemadari Kamara and Tony Van Der Meer; "The Rebellion in Los Angeles: The Crisis of Capitalism," in *Why L.A. Happened: Implications for the '92 Rebellion,* edited by Haki Madhubuti; and, "The Million Man March: From Patriarchy to Partnership," in *Million Man March/Day of Absence: A Commemorative Anthology,* edited by Haki Madhubuti; and, I served as an Editor of *By Any Means Necessary: Malcolm X, Real Not Reinvented,* along with Herb Boyd, Dr. Maulana Karenga and Haki Madhubuti. While these contributions were gratifying, they are not "the book."

Haki Madhubuti, Founder, Editor/Publisher of Third Word Press has stayed on my case, constantly urging me to write the book with the assurance that Third World Press would publish it. Prior to the expiration of President Obama's term in office, I fantasied about writing a book entitled: "Black Politics in the Age of Obama." Same formula—collect the articles and essays written during the Obama presidency, write an introduction with a contextual framework and go to press. I never got around to writing the framework and the fantasy proved to be just that, a fantasy. Time and time again, the movement, the struggle, the day to day grind of activism and organizing has gotten in the way of writing "the book." It's been a long time coming but, alas change is going to come!

Now in the year of my 77th birthday (it was actually supposed to be the year of my 75th birthday), more than three quarters of a century on this planet, more than a half century of activism and organizing and in the winter of this journey, I am determined to make time, to pause to pen this long overdue volume, "the book," *Still on This Journey: The Vision and Mission of Dr. Ron Daniels*. This book will focus on the vision, mission, values and philosophy which have served as the driving force behind this near lifelong journey and provide perspectives on the Institute of the Black World 21st Century (IBW) as the culminating project, my legacy endeavor. The medium for accomplishing this will largely be through articles and essays published via *Vantage Point*, which helped to build a following of supporters for my work over these many years and a concluding section on IBW.

Having finally "gutted" out "the book," God and the Ancestors willing, hopefully this will be the beginning of a series of writings that shed information and knowledge about other dimensions of this journey. It's been a long time coming but the first book is here at last!

Note: A special shout-out to Earl Ofari Hutchinson, a prolific author, who came to the rescue at a critical moment in the completion of "the book" to provide much needed encouragement and a virtual primer on how to cross the finish line!

Autobiographical
Acknowledgements

"The book" has been a long time coming, so the litany of persons to be noted and thanked is far too lengthy. But, I don't believe one achieves the modest things I have accomplished without meaningful contributions and help from family, friends, allies and the village. As I look back, reflecting on the people who have influenced my life and work, the list kept growing and growing day by day. I am so blessed to have had so many folks who parented, mentored, informed, encouraged and inspired me along this journey. I owe a debt of gratitude to all of them, those who will be named here, and others who may be omitted by lapse of memory. Much of my life has been dedicated to paying that debt, to honoring the confidence and trust so many have placed in me as I have pursued this journey. And, so in the African tradition of pouring Libations, as a sacred expression of gratitude, I am obligated to call out their names, the living and those who are ancestors, some now and others in subsequent volumes.

As I have occasionally noted in my speeches and writings, I am the son of a coal miner and a coal miner's daughter. First and foremost, I am deeply indebted to my mother, Wealtha Marie White, the coal miner's daughter, who grew up in the coalfields around Beckley, West Virginia, during the Great Depression. She was a brilliant woman whose education was cut short by circumstances, a griot who shared stories about the hardships of the Great Depression as a way of encouraging her four children to be strong, self-sufficient and to make something out of nothing if necessary. We watched her struggle, dream and endure as a single mom in the Hill District of Pittsburgh after the unfortunate divorce from my father, trials and tribulations that eventually led to a nervous breakdown. But, through it all, and for me most of all, she always saw something in me, believed in me, encouraged me and gave me the freedom to spread my wings and fly. She was always a source of comfort and inspiration as I navigated the obstacles along this journey.

My father, William (Bill) Daniel, the coal miner, was 20 years my mother's senior, which was eventually the source of incompatibilities that led to the divorce. Frankly, early on he did not see in me what my mother saw; but, nonetheless, he was an incredible source and resource of values and knowledge which left an indelible imprint on me. He was also a griot, even more so than my mother. Born in Talbot County, Georgia, we grew up repeatedly listening to stories about Africans in America surviving under southern apartheid. He took us once to a tree where a family member was lynched, related how family members and other Blacks defended themselves against the threats of the Klan or had reputations such that the White folks didn't mess with them. He was a stanch member of the NAACP because he recalled the vital work the organization did in the South during his younger years. It was from my father that I learned how much Black people in the South respected Booker T. Washington and Tuskegee Institute. He also shared stories about the efforts of Blacks to organize businesses and other institutions like insurance companies which, grew out of mutual aid societies. My Grandpa Dave Daniel is buried in Mutual Aid Cemetery. He had great regard for Dr. Benjamin Mays, the venerable President of Morehouse, and attended the graduation ceremony of his nephew (my cousin) Dr. Samuel DuBois Cook in 1948. That class included none other than Dr. Martin Luther King, Jr. Indeed, Dr. Cook, who made his transition as I was penning this volume, was a friend of the King family.

Bill Daniel was also a union man. He was Shop Steward for the United Mineworkers of America and a great admirer of its founder and long- time President John L. Lewis. He recounted the bloody battles between miners and owners in the early days of organizing the Union or during strikes, one of which may have been the infamous massacre at Matewan. After leaving the coalfields of West Virginia for the steel town of Youngstown, Ohio, he became a stanch member of the United Steel Workers of America. He also saved up enough money for my mother and him to open a business, Daniel's Grocery and Confection, "the Colored Store" at 708 Park Avenue. Bill Daniel was a strict disciplinarian who believed that your word is your bond, pay your bills on time, attend church, pay your dues and do right by neighbors and all human beings. He was an amazing man. Though he initially doubted I would amount to much, he later became a stanch supporter!

In the prologue, I reference my life altering experience in the Hill District of Pittsburgh, a "dark ghetto" with problems and dysfunctions but also strengths for a "man child in the promised land" like me. It was to the Hill District that my mother eventually took up refuge after a separation and divorce when I was nine years old. My aunt, Reba Cannon, a free-spirited, party-going, rambunctious, loving, caring woman initially took us in at her home—1716 Wylie

Avenue. Prior to taking up residence in Pittsburgh, when we wanted to have a good time, we would often pile into a car with my Aunt Virginia and her husband Ernest to journey from Youngstown to visit with Aunt Reba. I have fond memories of Aunt Reba and 1716 Wylie Avenue. She never had children, but my mother could always count on her in times of trouble. Aunt Reba was special.

After a brief stay with Aunt Reba, my mother found a permanent home. The section in the Hill District where we landed was rough. But, it was also a village where there were no motherless or fatherless children because neighbors, no matter their station or status in life, tended to look after the children. It was a kind of unwritten or unspoken code of community obligation. I can't remember their names, but I say thanks to the community parents of 6 Shipton Street and the surrounding neighborhood.

There were also caring, nurturing, lifesaving institutions in the Hill District like schools, churches and community centers. As a bright but troubled student, it took dedicated, loving teachers at McKelvey Elementary and Herron Hill Junior High, Richardson, Thomas, Boer and Shrinko to invest that extra attention needed to encourage me to believe in myself and the prospects of a brighter future beyond the confines of my family's impoverished circumstances.

I was baptized at Ebenezer Baptist Church when I was 12 years old. I give praise to the one-armed lady, the strict taskmaster in Sunday School, who insisted that we pay attention to our lessons. I learned well. There was a weekly contest at the Baptist Young People's Union (BYPU) sessions on Sunday evening with a small monetary prize. I won virtually every Sunday. At 12 years old, I was also the youngest person at the time ever to be elected a delegate to the State Baptist Convention—which was held in Philadelphia.

There were several community centers in the lower Hill

District— Ammon Recreational Center, Kay Boys Club, Irene Kaufman Center and the Elks. But, it was Hill City, a community center right around the block from Shipton Street, that had a lasting impact on my life. This was because of devoted social workers who served as surrogate parents and guardians of the community youth/young people. Mr. Ford and Mr. McKinney are two who come to mind. But, it was Carl Redwood, Sr. who took to me, embraced me and kept encouraging me to keep on the path toward a better life. Carl Redwood, Sr. was a lifesaver.

And, then there was Archie, a young man who returned from the Marine Corps to volunteer at Hill City, apparently because this vital community center had also contributed to his salvation. One day he posted a note on the Center's bulletin board, challenging all young boys who wanted to become men to report to a meeting with him to become members of the Cadet Corps. I reported for duty, and it was a turning point in my life. As it turned out, the Cadet Corps was Archie's idea of the kind of drill team (drill teams, especially boogie drill teams and drum and bugle corps were very popular in those days) that would teach discipline, team work, civic engagement and responsibility to what we would call "at risk" youth today. He was an incredible leader/teacher who created an incredible model and gave us/me an invaluable experience, one which I would later take with me to Youngstown and replicate by creating a Cadet Corps, a paramilitary youth organization, which showcased my leadership potential and laid the foundation for my eventual rise as a civil rights/social justice scholar/activist/leader. Oh, how I lament never having been able to find Archie to tell him the immeasurable influence/impact he has had on my life. But, at least I can whisper … thank you Archie, and perhaps he will hear it in the ancestor realm!

As my readers might have discerned, the story of the early

evolution and the development of Dr. Ron Daniels is largely a "tale of two cities," both steel cities, Pittsburgh (the Hill District) and Youngstown, Ohio. After five harsh, difficult years, the task of raising four children, with extremely limited resources and opportunities in Pittsburgh and after a nervous breakdown, my mother abandoned the dream of making a home in the ramshackle, roach and rat-infested tenement at 6 Shipton Street. After a brief attempt to start anew in Wilkinsburg, a suburb of Pittsburgh, she decided to send my brother David and me to our father in Youngstown and take the two younger children, Eddie and Patricia, fathered by Eddie Stuckey, our beloved but deceased stepfather, to Indianapolis where her younger sister Aunt Oretha, and brother, Uncle John, resided.

I dreaded this decision and separation of siblings, but it was the best mother could figure out under the dire conditions with which she was coping. I dreaded having to return to a father who had warned my mother that I had too much freedom in Pittsburgh and was going to become a little hoodlum if not reined in. He brutally laid down the law on the very first day of our return and declared that I would not have the same kind of unbridled freedom mother had afforded me in Pittsburgh. I was terrified, stressed and depressed.

But, all was not lost. The redeeming grace was to be found in family, neighbors, community institutions, church, teachers, surrogate parents and the Cadet Corps. I am forever indebted to my "half-sister," Wylene Ballard, who essentially sacrificed the most promising years of her life to come to Youngstown, to help Bill Daniel run the Colored Store and help raise her two "half-brothers." For me she was a lifesaver, a source of solace and inspiration. She believed in me in a manner similar to my mother.

A strong believer in the extended family, my father opened our cramped little home to the children his sister, Aunt Mary. The

Cook family nieces and nephews would journey from Georgia during summers for a respite and more importantly to secure jobs in the steel mill. Cousin Peyton Cook was one of them. He was my favorite cousin on the Cook side. He was a very kind and caring person who would eventually follow in the footsteps of his father, Rev. Manuel E. Cook, to become a minister. Rev. Peyton Cook served as Chaplain at Milledgeville Hospital in Milledgeville, Georgia for many years. He too witnessed the trials and tribulations I was suffering and encouraged, urged, me to be patient, that there was light at the end of the ordeal, if I just believed and persevered. I needed these words to maintain my sanity. I call out the names of Wylene Ballard and Peyton Cook for helping me keep the faith!

Like 6 Shipton Street in Pittsburgh, the village surrounding 708 Park Avenue in Youngstown also watched out for and collectively reared the children. We sometimes resented it, but the watchful, sometimes intrusive but caring and protective eyes of the neighbors were indispensable to our upbringing. I remember most, if not all of them, from the nosey Terri family across the street to Pearson, Stennis, Thomas, Gibson and Hill, Buckins, Harris families in the immediate neighborhood to the Phiffer, Cousin, Minor, Ziegler and Wilcox (Preston Wilcox's family) families on nearby streets. They were the extended family of the village. I call out their names in remembrance and gratitude. And, I call out the name of Emory "Bulldog" Williams, my sister's friend, graduate of Morris Brown University where he played football, for taking time to patiently develop my football and baseball skills, counsel and comfort me in those trying times.

Community centers like Lexington Settlement/Hagstrom House in the Associated Neighborhood Centers, Camp Lexington and the West Federal YMCA (the Colored Y in de facto segregated Youngstown) also had leaders and mentors who helped guide me in my early formative years. Jim Oliver, Program Director at Hagstrom House, deserves special mention because he was the inspirational coach for the McCullough Williams Junior League football team. I played fullback for the team. Jim was a great mentor and father figure who took special interest in me and offered constant encouragement. He would later become a key advisor and supporter of my work as a civil rights/human rights leader. Charles A. Smith, Jim Lottier and Bill Huff (whom I will comment on later) were also outstanding mentors and counselors at these vital community centers.

And, like Pittsburgh, there were dedicated/committed teachers at Hayes Junior High School and The Rayen School: Carney, Fizzy Kale, Beers, Pickering and Lee who challenged an underachieving student to climb to higher heights. At Youngstown State University it was G.A. Dobbert, a hard-nosed, demanding professor, that most students avoided, who captured my imagination with his use of the Socratic Method, insistence on qualitative/critical thinking and teaching history in an inter-disciplinary manner that brought to light revelations that were virtually impossible to understand when buried under mountains of quantitative facts, dates and detailed minutia. G.A. Dobbert emphatically helped me to become the Professor I am today!

I owe much to Tabernacle Baptist Church for discovering and honing my skills as a speaker/lecturer. From the Junior Usher Board, to BYPU, Junior Church and the obligatory attendance at Sunday School, Tabernacle helped nourish and groom me for leadership in later years. I am especially indebted to an unlettered man of the cloth, Rev. Lawson Booker, Superintendent of Sunday School, who constantly encouraged and insisted that a shaky, insecure young man stand before the assembled Sunday School Classes to review the lesson. He didn't even have a high school diploma, spoke broken English, but he saw a future in the young Ron Daniels and time and time again pushed me to stand before the assembly to review those lessons. Over the past decades, I have addressed audiences small and large all over the world and been interviewed on network radio and television stations—without fear. I thank Rev. Lawson Booker for his belief in me!

As referenced above, it was the Cadet Corps that served as the incubator for what was to become a lifelong dedication to social justice, civil rights/human rights. Modeled after the organization created by Archie in Pittsburgh, I expanded the concept to include camping, boxing, first aid and community engagement. However, crack military and boogie drill was the centerpiece of the organization just as it had been under Archie in Pittsburgh. About 30 teen-aged young men, 13-15 years old, were recruited from the neighborhood to form the Cadet Corps. Precision, disciplined drill was the Cadet Corps calling card. This was special because a group called the Legionaries was already on the scene. They were strictly a boogie drill team that was extremely popular in the community. The Cadet Corps stressed learning traditional military drill as a pre-condition for performing boogie drill. This approach was initially ridiculed as "square" by the Legionaries and their followers. We were determined to do it our way, the way Archie had prescribed in Pittsburgh.

And, we succeeded. We developed a crack drill team that successfully competed with the Legionaries and groups from around the State of Ohio in parades and drill exhibitions. We appeared on television shows in Cleveland, Akron and Youngstown. In addition, we conducted annual camping trips on our own, supervising ourselves under my leadership as the Commander. And, unlike the Legionaries, who were sponsored by the Elks Lodge, the Cadets did not have a sponsor. What we had was a dedicated group of mostly mothers, Cadet mothers who took us under their wings, taught us how to organize fish fries and chicken dinner sales to raise our own money to buy drill team uniforms, camping and first aid equipment. The Cadet mothers trained us to prepare and market our product like a science. They, along with a couple of fathers, were the backbone of the Cadet Corps.

As teenagers, the Cadet Corps had an account with the Army-Navy Store where we could purchase up to $1,000 of equipment on our signature/name as young men. The Cadet Corps was an amazing organization which received rave reviews, accolades and support from neighbors and the community. Folks took note of the young man who could effectively command such a disciplined, dedicated and accomplished group of young men, a young man that some said might one day be the first Black President, Ron Daniels. Even Bill Daniel, my father, began to come around after so many people complimented him on his son's leadership and accomplishments in the community via the Cadets. He began to accept what my mother always saw, the potential for exceptional leadership and service. In later years, offshoots of the Cadet Corps would develop in the city and a similar group was organized in Elizabeth, New Jersey, by one of our members, utilizing the core principles and methods we devised and utilized. Equally important, the Cadet Corps groomed me for entry into the civil rights movement and beyond.

Without question, the Cadet Corps and the Cadet Mothers and Fathers who supported us, helped to make me what I am today. Such is my respect and debt to these Mothers and Father that every Christmas day, without fail, I would rise early in the morning and visit each and every one of them: Mrs. Atkinson, Mrs. Brock, Mrs. Anderson, Mrs. Moore, Mrs. Reynolds, Mrs. Clinkscale, Mrs. Hill, Mrs. Sledge, Mrs. Johnson, Mrs. Watson and two couples, Mr. and Mrs. Hicks and Mr. and Mrs. Allen to thank them for helping to raise Ron Daniels (Mr. Eugene Allen, in particular, was like a surrogate father). And, when I moved the New York, I continued to call them on Christmas day. There are only two left today, but they know to expect a call from their son every Christmas without fail.

One day William "Bill" Huff approached me and a couple of the Cadets about coming to his home to listen to speeches by Dr. Martin Luther King and Malcolm X. He was Associate Director of Lexington Settlement/Hagstrom House where the Cadet Corps met and conducted drill practice. So, he was keenly aware of the talents of the group and saw an opportunity to enlist its Commander and some of its members in an important cause and organization, the Civil Rights Movement, through involvement with the NAACP Youth Division. Bill was my cousin on my father's side, an active member of Tabernacle Baptist Church and deeply committed to social justice. He had a reputation for being on the militant side.

The listening sessions at his home proved to be momentous. We were absolutely in awe of the oratory of Dr. King and Malcolm X. I was particularly impressed because it touched a nerve in me, and from that memorable night in the Hill District of Pittsburgh I decided to work for improvement in the lives of human beings. It marked another turning point when the youthful energy, enthusiasm, skill and growing experience in leading young people, in efforts for civic engagement and preventing juvenile delinquency, would be translated into the Civil Rights Movement. Bill Huff became a constant mentor and advisor in this new quest and eventually a follower of the cousin who he tapped for leadership in the "Movement." I shout out his name in profound appreciation for his life-changing engagement, mentoring and constant support.

It did not take long for me to embrace my new found calling with vigor. I listened and learned from mentors and advisors in the NAACP—Nathaniel Lee, Alice Lev, Esther Spruill, Helen Arnold and most of all, Ralph W. Clarke, who became my principal NAACP Youth Advisor. Over time, he became a devoted follower as I moved beyond the ranks of the NAACP to create organizations and institutions and led movements at the state and national levels. I had a meteoric rise in the NAACP. I was elected President of the Youngstown Youth Chapter, President of the Ohio Conference of Branches Youth Division and ultimately President of the Regional III Youth Division. I also founded the College Chapter at Youngstown State University. I was engaged in leading picket lines and boycotts of facilities that discriminated against Blacks. I remember the picket line at the local Woolworth Store conducted in support of the Sit-In Demonstrations in Greensboro and other places around the country. It was under the banner of the NAACP that I attended/participated in the March On Washington in 1963 and almost went to Selma in 1965. The NAACP provided an invaluable training ground and lessons which would serve me for a lifetime. It was only fitting that it would be so, given my father's lifelong belief in and dedication to the NAACP. We say thanks to all the aforementioned persons affiliated with the NAACP who helped mold the young Ron Daniels for decades of leadership and service in this journey.

In this tale of two cities, Youngstown, Ohio, would come to serve as a foundational and formidable base for my ascension to leadership at the state, national and international levels. When the call to Black Power exploded across the land, I was on the verge of entering the Graduate School of Public Affairs (GSPA) in Albany, New York (now the Rockefeller School of Public Affairs and Policy) to study for the Master's Degree. Always associated with the more militant wing of the NAACP, nonetheless, I initially questioned the goals/objectives and utility of the concept of Black Power. My experiences in Albany resulted in another turning point, one which would decisively shift my ideological bearing to embrace Black Power and a deeper appreciation for the struggles of ordinary people and grassroots activism. For this I am indebted to several people: Leon Van Dyke, leader of the Brothers, an organization of Black workers dedicated to ending discrimination/exclusion in the construction industry, who adopted and taught me about organizing poor and working people (I also shared my organizational knowledge and skill with them); John Gunnell, Professor at GSPA whose challenge to me, to examine more closely the call for Black Power, led to my Master's Thesis, *Black Power: An Ideology on Anvil*; Ivanhoe Donaldson, who introduced me to brothers in SNCC like Robert Fullilove, Johnny Wilson and Phil Hutchins, who schooled me on the analysis, meaning, mission, strategy and tactics of the concept of Black Power, and the master teacher, warrior woman and indefatigable advocate for reparations, Queen Mother Audley Moore, who adopted me during this transitional period as her student and son. We utter their names in appreciation.

I returned to Youngstown transformed. I left as an NAACP leader committed to its "Integrationist" approach. I returned as a devotee of Black Power with its manifestations of Black consciousness, historical/cultural awareness, institution-building and empowerment. While in Albany I drew up a chart which described the mission, structure and function of a new organization which I intended to build. The first person to review it was none other than Preston Wilcox, the son of the Wilcox family from the neighborhood, whom I had never met until my work on my Master's Degree. Preston was "Mr. Harlem" and a strong believer in Black Power. He was delighted to meet this emerging leader from his hometown, adopted me and became friend and advisor. He reviewed my chart approvingly, endorsed it and wished me well in pursuing the creation of a new organization. Preston always concluded letters or messages with "Yours in the Struggle," which I adopted and use to this very day in honor and respect for him. With his blessing, I returned to Youngstown to build Freedom, Inc., a community-based Black Power organization committed to *Unity, Cooperation and Action* among Black people!

At its height, Freedom, Inc., which evolved into a Pan African, nationalist and internationalist organization, was one of the most formidable institutions of its kind in the U.S. The Uhuru Center Cultural Education Institute founded by Freedom, Inc. was a three-building complex, which housed the Native Son Bookstore; Uhuru Center Press (printing business); Kuumba Graphics and Design; the Marcus Garvey School for African Education, which offered after-school classes in basic health/medicine, graphic design and printing, construction arts, agriculture/gardening and African Dance. And, of course, there was an African Drill Team. In addition to the buildings in the Uhuru Center Complex, Freedom, Inc. owned two large houses which were home for staff, a four-unit apartment complex, a school bus and staff car. The organization had assets in excess of a quarter of a million dollars by 1975!

The incredible work of Freedom, Inc. and its base in Youngstown propelled me into leadership positions with the Mid-West Regional Coalition, Federation of Pan African Education Institutions, Congress of African People, National Black Political Convention, African Liberation Day (of which I was one of the Founders), National Black Political Assembly and the National Black Independent Political Party. Because of Freedom, Inc., Youngstown came to be recognized as one of the strongest centers of Pan—Africanism in Black America. It was there I developed a style of work, which attracted the breadth and depth of engagement and support in the Village of Youngstown, and where it became part of my DNA as a scholar/activist, organizer, mediator and facilitator, functioning in leadership roles/positions at the national and international stage to this very moment. And, it was the body of work that would elevate me to the status of a national/international leader, recruited to become Executive Director of the National Rainbow Coalition, Deputy Campaign Manager for Rev. Jesse Jackson's 1988 presidential bid and the first African American Executive Director of the Center for Constitutional Rights.

Freedom, Inc. was where the seeds sown in the villages of the Hill District of Pittsburgh and Youngstown blossomed into full fruition! For that I am compelled to call out the names of those who contributed to fertilizing and cultivating this endeavor: Wendell Atkinson, my dearest friend, confidante and one of the founders of Freedom, Inc., along with Hank Williams, Bob Christian, E. Thaxton King, Bob Thornton, Alvin Hopkins, James Bellard, Collie Burton, Calvin Nathan as well as others who joined the Cabinet/Leadership including Raymond Yancey, Robert Beal and Richard Atkinson; Ode Aduma, whose bold Africa-centered murals graced the walls of the Uhuru Center; Eugenia Atkinson, Laura Byrd Wilson, Mercedes King, incredible warrior women who were pillars of the staff and of the organization—Rev. Georgina Thornton, Mary Christian, Roberta Bellard, Lorraine Yancey, Kiesha Malika, Nalongo Aduma, Vivian Martin and all the women who were members of the Martin Luther King Sisters—Delores "Dee" Smith, the epitome of African femininity, grace and empowerment, who formed the Au Naturelle Models as a parallel, supportive group to Freedom, Inc.

Indeed, there were many incredible supporters of Freedom, Inc. and Ron Daniels whose names must be shouted out: A. J. Carter, my father's first cousin, a fourth grade graduate from Georgia with an encyclopedic mind, a Garveyite and UNIA loyalist to the bone, and a constant source of knowledge and information; Mother Ash, devout UNIA member who loved her some Ron Daniels (I wore the red, black and green necklace she gave me for decades); Jimmy Davis, a stanch, pro-Black Union man in the mold of A. Phillip Randolph who helped mightily with construction work on the Uhuru Center; Ms. Elvie and the waitresses at Elvie's Soul Kitchen who always fed the Brothers of Freedom, Inc. so well; B. Ramsey McDuffie, a socially conscious Black professional, constant financial contributor and our honorary Chief of Protocol; Margaret Linton, an erstwhile member of the local Black elite with the "common touch," whose advocacy with James Mosely via the Black Broadcasting Coalition launched Ron Daniels as a television talk show host with Perspectives in Black on WYTV, Channel 33 on the ABC Network. Perspectives in Black and its subsequent iterations evolved into the most watched Black public-interest television program in the area over a span of 17 years (I am a radio talk show host today because I learned through OJT as a pioneer at WYTV); Howard Duncan and Jeff Piece for affording me the opportunity at WYTV; Greg Andrews, Carl Bryant, Mattie Majors, Sophia Brooks and Margo Williams, television talk show hosts who were always supportive of Freedom, Inc. and the work of Ron Daniels; Ron and Lynette Miller and the entire Davis Family, Roselyn Mahone, Sheila Jackson, Ernest Lokey, Mercedes King, Kenneth King, Mildred Delgado and the Harambee Coalition for serving as supporters of African-Cultural Weekend, the Youngstown Black Political Assembly, Kwanzaa and other Initiatives; Clarence E. Barnes, the atypical, militant Urban League leader who was a fierce proponent of social justice, an unapologetic ally, a role model and the most authentic/genuine Christian I have ever known; faith leaders Rev. Morris W. Lee, Rev. Reginald Dockins, Rev. Douglass Shamburger, Rev. Elizabeth Powell, Rev. Georgina Thornton, Rev. James Kitchen, Minister Van Muhammad, and most of all the Rev. Lonnie A. Simon, Pastor of New Bethel Baptist Church, a Black Republican in the best tradition, whose immersion among the urban poor in Chicago via the Urban Training Center for Christian Mission, under the Direction of Rev. C.T. Vivian, converted him to social activism and Black consciousness. Rev. Lonnie A. Simon became an unshakable pillar of support and devotee of Freedom, Inc. and Ron Daniels. We/I owe so much of the success of Freedom, Inc. and my leadership with other institutions and movements to Rev. Lonnie A. Simon.

Inevitably, with fading memory, I have neglected to call the names of others who are worthy of mention. Even as I pen these words, the faces of some not previously noted surface in my mind's eye: Lugenia Atkinson, Romelia Carter, Laura Lumsden, Rhoda Dotson, Emily Parkman, Odie Lee Ellis, LaVerne (Trice) Douglas, Rose McIver, Leonia McIver, Alexander G. Rotan, Frankie "Mr. Luckie" Halfacre, Dick Diehl, James Cobbin, Mrs. Ruth Squire, Evelyn Turner, Carole Gregory, Doreime Wilson, Joann Madison, James "Monk" Tillman, Big Boogie D, Bob Jennings, Herman "Pete" Starks, Bailey Barnes, Rose Brown, B.J., Larry Reed, Jim Roberts, Goldie Williams, Dr. Earnest Perry, Dr. William Johnson, Dr. James Hovell, Oliver Montgomery, Charles Street, Atty. Floyd Haynes, Jim Roberts, J.B. Williams, Robert Wigfall, Ezell Armour, John T. Smith, Frieda Evans, Sami Bahour, Abe Harshman, Bud Tamarkin, Felix Valentine, Kimberley and Anna Richards and family.... What a blessing to have had the support of and been empowered by such a multitude, named and un-named, from virtually every walk of life, class and status from the village of Youngstown, Ohio. I sincerely hope that those omitted will understand and forgive.

I would be remiss in this roll call of remembrance if I did not shout out the names of Walter Palmer, brilliant humanist/activist, organizer/leader from Philadelphia who shared his concept of the "Moral Imperative" as a philosophical approach and vision for organizing

Black people and suffering humanity. His ideas were instrumental in shaping the early political/ideological direction of Freedom, Inc. And, Makaza Kumaniyka aka Herb Callendar, a fervent believer in our organization, who worked tirelessly to secure resources for Freedom, Inc. from the General Convention Special Program of the Episcopal Church under Bishop John Hines. GCSP was a powerful faith-based funding agency formed in direct response to the call for Black Power and the rebellions that exploded in urban areas across the country in the mid 60's. It was administered by a dedicated group of activists and organizers committed to building the infra-structure/capacity of the Black Power/Nationalist/Pan-Africanist movement to liberate African people, Black people in the U.S. and the world. Leon Modeste, Howard Quander, Adeylabu Adeigbola, Viola Plummer and Makaza Kumaniyka were among the key in-house, radical activists dedicated to fulfilling this mission utilizing the resources of GCSP.

The Center for Black Education, Malcolm X Liberation University, Chad School, Federation of Pan African Education Institutions, Pan African Work Center, Lynne-Eusane Center, Freedom, Inc., Federation of Southern Farm Cooperatives, Emergency Land Fund and the Mid-West Regional Coalition were among the organizations funded via GCSP by this team of radicals. It was through this team that I was privileged to meet brothers and sisters from CORE, SNCC and other strong Pan Africanists organizations from across the country, introductions which contributed significantly to the adoption of Pan Africanism as the ideological framework for the work of Freedom, Inc. Brothers and sisters like Lincoln Lynch, John Oneal, Fran Beal, Byron Rushing, Ralph Featherstone, Jamila Jones, Owusu Sadaukai, Jimmy Garrett, Ike Reynolds, Muriel Tillinghast, Leon Moore, Courtland Cox, Charlie Cobb and Dowoli Gene Locke, with whom I would work for decades.

Having witnessed our work on the ground Makaza Kumani-yka became the strongest advocate for Freedom, Inc. and eventually the Mid-West Regional Coalition, which was headquartered with and administered by Freedom, Inc. Without his steadfast support it is doubtful that a little-known activist from the small steel town of Youngstown would ever have been noticed, let alone have garnered the resources to build one of the most formidable Pan African organizations/institutions in the country. Makaza was my brother, friend, comrade and stanch ally. It is essential that I call out his name with great respect and appreciation in this acknowledgement and libation!

As referenced earlier, the Mid-West Regional Coalition (MWRC) was administered by Freedom, Inc. It consisted of about 35 Pan Africanist organizations with a Communications Center, Training Center for Independent Schools and Economic Development Resource Center. MWRC developed into an invaluable vehicle for grassroots mobilization throughout the Mid-West for national and international initiatives like the National Black Political Convention and African Liberation Day. Two brothers, comrades and friends, stand out as solid allies in forging such an amazing region-wide formation: Rev. Gilbert Carter aka Aleem Mushindi, Founder of the Society for the Cooperative Improvement of Africans (SCIA) in Canton, Ohio. SCIA was a grassroots, community-building/institution-building organization which published *North Star* ewspaper and functioned as the Communications Center for MWRC. Michael Banks, aka Sanii Andika, was Chairman of the Peoria Organization for African Unity (POAU). He specialized in economic and entrepreneurial development. POAU served as the Financial Administrative Center for MWRC. Aleem Mushindi, Sanii Andika and I did some solid, sustained work together across many years. Their support as comrades in struggle was crucial as I emerged as a national leader within the Pan

Africanist movement and beyond. They shall forever be remembered as my brothers and friends.

Coming out of the historic Gary National Black Political Convention, the Ohio Black Political Assembly (OBPA) emerged as the strongest Chapter of the National Black Political Assembly (NBPA) and base for my eventual election as President of the National organization in 1974—succeeding Congressman Charles C. Diggs as part of the Tripartite leadership, which included Mayor Richard G. Hatcher of Gary and Amiri Baraka, poet, playwright, political activist and leader of the Congress of African People. John Warfield, a beautiful Brother, scholar/activist, Chairman of the Texas Black Political Assembly, ally and friend placed my name in nomination. I remember him with great fondness and respect.

Once again, my elevation to a position of national prominence was made possible by stalwarts who joined with me to make OBPA such a strong organization. Dean Lovelace (whom I literally just received word via email made his transition), Phyllis Lovelace, Lawrence Nelson and Ray Alexander from Dayton; Doris Rankin, Chuck Sells, Lana Mitchell, Charles and Essie Hughes and Bailey W. Turner, the master teacher/organizer also from Cincinnati (who served on my Doctoral Committee at Union Graduate School and Universities); Dr. Nick Nelson, Ako Kambon, Blanche Glover and the indefatigable Yolanda Robinson from Columbus; H.B. Williams from Toledo; John Fuller from Akron; and, Richard Gilbert from Zanesville are among the diverse collective of leaders and supporters who come to mind.

As President of NBPA and beyond, I will forever be indebted to the incomparable Dr. Mtangulizi Sanyika and the suave and brilliant Dr. Jemadari Kamara for their friendship and collaboration. Joined by Sister Mashariki Kuradisha, an urban planning specialist and driving force with the Maryland Black Political Assembly, we successfully worked to define "progressive nationalism," as an ideological school of thought that incorporated race, class and gender (not just race); a nationalism which served as a legitimate and useful framework for situating the National Black Political Assembly within the body politic of Black America and the Pan African world. Mt.—as he is affectionately known—is one of the foremost architects, theoreticians and practitioners of Community Economic Development as a theory and practice for African/Black empowerment. Dr. Kamara sacrificed resources and time to come to Youngstown to manage the Ron Daniels Mayor Campaign in 1977, the most cost-effective (less than $20,000) and successful independent campaign for Mayor in the history of that city. Both remain friends/allies to this day. As it relates to my campaign for Mayor, it is also important to call out the names of former Congressmen Walter Fauntroy and Ronald V. Dellums and legendary C.T. Vivian who took the time to come to Youngstown to campaign on my behalf. I have had deep relationships with them over these many years.

The effort to create a Black Political Party as many nationalists, Pan-africanist and social justice activists had pushed for at the Gary Black Political Convention, gained momentum in 1980 when the fourth and final Black Political Convention in New Orleans passed a resolution calling for the creation of the National Black Independent Political Party (NBIPP), as the outgrowth of the National Black Political Assembly. The Founding Convention met in Philadelphia in November of that year. It was a tumultuous, lesson-filled experience. After some internal struggles, I was elected to the Tripartite leadership of NBIPP. I am particularly moved to call out the names of the remarkable Sisters in NBIPP who trained/mentored me and the Brothers in this formation on gender equity issues. They firmly, but lovingly, kicked our behinds and compelled us to listen and learn.

And, though I am still a recovering sexist, I owe my struggle to become better to NBIPP Sisters like Dr. Elsa Barkley Brown, Ka Fluel-
len, Atty. Barbara Anrwine, Kikora Ras-Tabasimu, Zohara Simmons,
Sylvia Wright and Alicia Tee. It is important to call the names of Thad
Mathis and Butch Cottman for the incredible NBIPP.

Few people have the opportunity and privilege of serving in a
high capacity within a presidential campaign in the U.S. I was afforded that experience by the Rev. Jesse L. Jackson, one of the greatest civil rights/human rights leaders this nation has ever witnessed;
an authentic genius whose visionary, unique and electrifying campaigns for President in 1984 and 1988 were among the most remarkable and significant in American history! Rev. Jackson tapped me to
serve as Executive Director of the National Rainbow Coalition, the
concept which was the philosophical framework for his presidential
campaigns, and ultimately as Southern Regional Coordinator and
Deputy Campaign Manager for the 1988 Jackson for President Campaign. Words are simply inadequate to express the magnitude of this
once in a life time experience. I call the names of the highly revered
Jack O'Dell and Lewis Carter for being my partners in building the
base for and "rainbowing" the Rainbow Coalition; to Mrs. Jacqueline
Jackson and the family for embracing and welcoming me into their
home during this period; Badi Murphy, the producer extraordinaire,
for assisting me to organize the incredible welcome for Rev. Jackson
at Piedmont Park in Atlanta when he arrived for the Democratic National Convention; and , last but not least, Joe Beasley, whom I have
designated "Ambassador to the Black World," who used his vast network of contacts, resources and personal credibility to mightily assist
our team to establish a functioning Regional Office with volunteers
and community support. He is simply an awesome African man who
has become a reliable friend and ally. I am forever indebted to Rev.

Jesse L. Jackson, a global icon, for this life altering experience!

I launched an Independent Campaign for President in 1992 because of my profound disappointment that the Jackson for President Campaigns failed to achieve the potential of the National Rainbow Coalition to become a mass-based, independent, third force in American politics; a people-based, visionary organization capable of effectively advancing a progressive agenda. Mounting an independent campaign was also consistent with my role as a torch-bearer for the politics of social transformation envisioned in the Preamble National Black Political Agenda, adopted at the 1972 National Black Political Convention. And, in a way it fulfilled the promise of the folks in Youngstown, that the young Commander of the Cadet Corps just might be the first Black President. Winning the presidency was obviously not the goal of Campaign for a New Tomorrow (CNT), the organization established to advance the campaign. Fulfilling the potential of the Rainbow Coalition was the vision and mission of the Ron Daniels for President Campaign.

It was an arduous undertaking which would not have been possible without the sacrificial and energetic support of far too many folks to name, many of whom I simply don't remember at this stage in life, but we utter the names of Asiba Tupachache, the Native American Warrior Woman who kindly consented to run as our Vice-Presidential Candidate; Janice Graham, host of the *Our Common Ground* Radio Show, who agreed to serve as Chairperson of the Campaign; Rick Adams and Dr. Claire Cohen, PA Campaign Chairperson; Roger Newell, Paul Pumphrey and Sister Lorraine, D.C. Chairperson; and Kolonji and Kupenda Olusegun, whose home was my home away from home while campaigning in D.C.; Pete Carter, Sedou Njoya, whose home was my home when campaigning in New York; Floyd Davis, Wayne and Gloria Lum; and Fred Davis; Leon Van Dyke from

Albany; Walt Dixie, Syracuse; Larry Gossett and the Rainbow activists from Washington State; Rainbow activists from Iowa; The Peace and Freedom Party in California; Howie Hawkins and Green Party activists who supported the mission of the Campaign and facilitated visits to Vermont and New Hampshire; Atty. Mtumishi St. Julian, who made sure I would be on the ballot in Louisiana (Mtumishi has been an invaluable ally and friend over the years); the "tall one," Bob Law, who provided a regular platform via his nationally syndicated radio show *Night Talk* to give consistent national exposure to the campaign; and, State Representative Dave Richardson from Philadelphia, one of the most progressive nationalist/Pan-africanist elected officials of the era, who cast his ballot for Ron Daniels during the roll call for President at the 1992 Democratic Convention; a symbolic but meaningful gesture that alerted the world to my candidacy and his respect for independent Black politics as an option for Black empowerment. I thank them all, named and unnamed for daring to believe that we could make a significant stride towards forging a "New Covenant for a New America."

I was honored when asked to become Executive Director of the Center for Constitutional Rights (CCR) at a critical time in the evolution and development of this radical, progressive, public interest legal and educational organization. CCR's roots stem from the Mississippi Freedom Summer of 1964, when hundreds of young visionary, mostly White lawyers and activists, including Arthur Kinoy, Bill Kunstler, Morten Stavis and Ben Smith, traveled to that state to immerse themselves in the struggle of African Americans to regain the right to vote. I was aware of CCR through my work with Arthur Kinoy on independent politics, the Rainbow Coalition and Jackson for President Campaigns; Marilyn Clement long time Executive Director of CCR, who occasionally contacted Freedom, Inc. to sign on to Amicus Briefs on various cases; and. Michael Ratner, whom I knew by reputation as one of the foremost human rights lawyers in the country.

Though honored to be asked, it was a request I initially turned down because of what I perceived to be an overly burdensome gauntlet of interviews/interrogations that candidates had to endure at the hands of the CCR Board/Staff Collective. Dr. Vicki Alexander, whom I met and came to respect as a dedicated progressive and friend during the Jackson Campaign/Rainbow Coalition days and my independent campaign for President, insisted that I remain in the process. It was through her efforts allied with Arthur Kinoy, Marilyn Clement and those whom they persuaded that I was selected as the first African American Executive Director of CCR.

I took the helm at a time of crisis in CCR's history, the resolution of which would require a stressful but essential rescue operation with funders and institutional makeover. It was a productive and meaningful experience which enriched my knowledge and burnished my credentials as a leader in the progressive movement. I served as Executive Director for 12 amazing years, matching that of my predecessor and friend Marilyn Clement. The success of my tenure was the result of the collective commitment of dedicated Directors and staff like Margaret Carey, Michael Deutsch, Martha Swan, Rick Best, Carolyn Chambers, Annette Dickerson, Jaribu Hill, Robert Osborne, Bill Goodman, Kevi Brannerly, Ms. Becky and Alberto White.

My tenure at CCR opened a window to engagement in the world's first Black Republic, Haiti. Under the leadership of Michael Ratner, CCR successfully litigated the cases of Haitians who were HIV positive who were being imprisoned at the Guantanamo Naval Base in Cuba. Through that work Michael had become deeply involved in the struggle for democracy and development in Haiti and knew many of its leaders; one of whom was Chavannes Jean Baptiste, Chairman of the Peasant Movement of Papay, the largest peasant movement in Haiti. Though I had done extensive work throughout the Caribbean as a Pan-africanist, Haiti was locked down under the dread regime of Jean Claude "Popa Doc" Duvalier. Michael introduced me to Chavannes, and we developed a relationship as the result of extensive conversations about Haiti's history and its future. I was particularly interested in encouraging African Americans to identify with Haiti because of its unique history and culture. This led to an invitation by Chavannes to organize an African American fact-finding and support delegation to Haiti in June of 1995. It was absolutely an exhilarating experience as we connected with the history, culture, power and spirit of resilience of the Haitian people.

Inspired by the experience, upon our return, I founded the Haiti Support Project (HSP) to build bonds of solidarity with our sisters and brothers in Haiti, mobilize material support for the struggle for democracy and development and impact U.S. policy. Michael Ratner made the first donation to launch HSP. Hadley Grosbeck and Robin Lloyd were also major supporters. Over the past two decades HSP has emerged as the leading organization *building a constituency for Haiti in the U.S.* among African Americans in collaboration with Haitian Americans. We obviously thank Chavannes Jean Baptiste, who has remained a friend, for the experience that led to the formation of HSP.

Many others deserve mention: Bazlais Jean Baptiste, Marx Aristide, Peggy Regis, Myrtha Wroy, Mawiyah Duperval, Jan Mapou, Rico Dupuy, Jean Jean Pierre, Yves Rose Green, Jocelyn Mayas, Erna Letemps and the Voices of Haiti, Mayrse Kedar, Leslie Voltaire, Raymond Jeanty, Dr. Joseph Baptiste, Alex Baptiste, Madame Dauguste, Gabriel Verrette, Johnny McCalla, Marc Prou, Judge Lionel Jean Baptiste, Dr. Serge and Dr. May Parisien, Lionel Delatour, Patrick Delatour, Alex Georges, Alex Cantave, Marie St. Fleur, Zenobia Lewis,

Eddie Harris, Ambassador Raymond Joseph, Lisa Llutoff-Perlo, President Rene Preval for his support of the Model City Initiative in Milot and warm reception of our delegations at the Presidential Palace; Congressman Gregory Meeks, the first Member of the Congressional Black Caucus to make the Pilgrimage to the Citadel with HSP, and, " The Chairman," Congressman John Conyers, CBC Champion for Haiti with whom HSP collaborated to convene influential Conferences on the Future of Democracy and Development in Haiti at critical junctures.

Above all my gratitude to the Local Development Committee of Milot and Lionel Pressoir, the enlightened, indomitable visionary entrepreneur, developer and true believer in the promise of a bright future of Haiti and the Haitian people, who has been HSP's indispensable partner on the ground. Lionel and his sons embody the future of Haiti. We cannot thank him enough for his undying faith in HSP and the prospects of African Americans partnering with Haitians to restore Haiti to its rightful place as a beacon of hope for people of African descent everywhere! And, I must call out the name of Emily Moore, a remarkable woman who has trained hundreds of African Americans to play tennis through a family academy she and her sister established; a dedicated social/political activist who fell in love with Haiti on her first pilgrimage with HSP and subsequently has become the single largest individual donor to HSP projects and initiatives!

Though my tenure at CCR was enriching and rewarding, the persistent, unrelenting crises in Black America, particularly in the urban inner- cities, seriously tugged at my heart, soul and head to "return to the source," to re-center myself among my people, to culminate my life's journey deeply immersed in the struggle for African/ Black liberation/freedom, self-determination, just and wholesome families, communities and nations. So, in 2005, I departed CCR in the "autumn of my advocacy" to devote more time and energy to pursuing the mission of building the Institute of the Black World 21st Century. I stepped out on faith without a job in hand (CCR did provide a generous severance package) and no funding, determined that a revised version of IBW would be my legacy project.

It was/is a daunting task, but I had come this far by faith and the incredible assistance/help of legions of friends, allies and supporters who saw something in the vision and work of a "man child in the promised land," raised up from the Hill District of Pittsburgh, PA and the lower Northside of Youngstown, Ohio. I have shared the names of a multitude these persons, known and not so well known, ancestors and those who still labor amongst us, but I have yet to proclaim the names of Dr. Edward Crosby and Dr. James Turner, two formidable scholar/activists and institution-builders who pulled a battered and bruised activist/scholar in from the battlefield time and time again to offer refuge and respite from the struggle, to retool and refuel to continue this arduous struggle.

Dr. Edward Crosby, founder of the Department of Pan African Studies (DPAS) at Kent State University is one of the great institution-builders of our time. He has received far too little recognition for his monumental accomplishment of building DPAS into one of the most comprehensive centers of African- centered pedagogy and praxis in the Pan African world. I had the privilege of contributing to this process when Dr. Crosby reached out to me to become an Instructor for the Institute for African American Affairs, which was the precursor to DPAS. He was aware of my work as Chairman of Freedom, Inc. and called upon me to help define this new discipline of Black Studies via OJT (on the job training). I knew nothing about African Cosmology or the Black Experience, the courses I was assigned to teach, but my academic training under Professors like G.A. Dobbert and John

Gunnell, coupled with my wide-ranging experiences as a social and political activist equipped me to take on the task of learning while teaching. Dr. Crosby and his wife/partner Shirley Crosby worked tirelessly to build a citadel of African/Black knowledge at KSU, and I was privileged to play a small part. But, more importantly, Crosby and the DPAS family created space for me to return, to come in from the cold to retool whenever I was in a time of fiscal/financial crisis or suffering from battle fatigue. There is no question that I have reached this far along this road because of Dr. Edward Crosby!

Dr. James Turner is one of the founders, the architects, of the Black Studies Movement. A brilliant and devout "race man," whom the students at Cornell University selected as Director of what was to become the world-renowned Africana Studies and Research Center (ASRC). It was from this perch in Ithaca, NY, situated in the icy cold environs of the Finger Lake Region, that Dr. James Turner utilized his position to become one of the great scholar/activists and contributors to the global struggle of African people of our time. ASRC emerged as an epicenter of African-centered scholarship, local, national and international activism. Under Dr. Turner's leadership the intellectual and material resources of ASRC were put at the disposal of the community, Black America and the Pan African world in a manner that was principled and defensible within the academy. And, ASRC was a space where weary warriors like Ron Daniels were brought in from the cold to share real life experiences with students, while retooling and refueling. I learned so much during my tenures as a Professor at Cornell, but the greatest gift was the unbreakable bond of friendship which we developed. No one has been more influential along this journey than my friend, comrade and brother Dr. James Turner. We are kindred spirits. At every crucial juncture, twist and turn in the movement, where I had to make a critical decision, he was/is always there to provide advice and counsel. He has been and continues to be a source of constant encouragement, inspiration and a solid pillar of support. He is my brother forever!

It took twenty years for me to finally obtain a doctoral degree, a lapse in time which cost precious resources in terms of personal and family security. I was simply too swamped with the day to day work of the "movement" of the "struggle" to expeditiously secure the doctorate. I say finish, because I enrolled in the Union Graduate School (UGS), a highly innovative, experienced based, degree-awarding institution around 1976 in its second year of operation. I could have completed the required course work, and equivalent of the dissertation in 12 months at a cost of about $3,000. But, due to financial constraints, I fell behind on tuition payments and became delinquent. I elected to run for Mayor of Youngstown as an independent candidate in 1977. Thereafter, the priority of achieving the doctorate receded in importance in the face of ongoing organizing and activism.

Though I have made mistakes along this journey, the failure to seize the moment and find the time and resources to complete the doctorate was the single biggest mistake of my life's work. It was not just about the degree; it was about the financial resources which come with the advanced degree that would have created greater family and personal stability and even enabled me to contribute more to causes I cared about from a position of enhanced personal capacity. As the years dragged on, the period for reinstatement at UGS expired and the cost of tuition increased as this experimental institution grew in stature. Consequently, it seemed highly unlikely that I would ever obtain the doctoral degree.

Dr. Jean Thomas Griffin, Core Faculty Member of my Doctoral Committee, wasn't having it. I initially selected Dr. Griffin without knowing that her daughter Lillian Thomas was one of my students during my tenure at Hiram College. Indeed, Lillian was one of the finest students I have taught during my career as a university professor. Dr. Griffin never gave up on the possibility that I might re-enroll and complete the Doctorate at UGS. She followed my work and would periodically inquire about when I was going to apply for reinstatement. She stayed on my case, encouraging, exhorting, pleading with me TO finish the task. Finally, she took the unusual step of going to the Dean of the University, and demanded that my delinquency be removed and that I be readmitted without having to start the process from scratch! Her argument was that my life's achievements as a social and political activist and scholar were exactly what the University was created to validate. The Dean was persuaded and consented to readmit me without penalty and with the prospect of completing the degree in 18 months. Unbelievable, the impossible was made possible by the mother of one of my finest students who took my destiny into her hands!

It took about three years to complete the work. What would have cost around $3,000 if I had completed the program in the 60s would eventually cost me close to $20,000. That notwithstanding, on a momentous day, my committee which was comprised of Dr. James Turner, Baily W. Turner, Dr. Edward Crosby (who joined by phone) and Dr. Jemadari Kamara convened in a conference room at the Center for Constitutional Rights and approved my composite work, including the Project Demonstrating Excellence as the major degree requirement. I was a Ph.D. at last due to unflinching belief and conviction of Dr. Jean Thomas Griffin! What a blessing! God and the ancestors are good!

Dr. Haki Madhubuti, is not only one of the greatest poets and authors of our time, he is undoubtedly one of the great institution-builders of our time. Blessed to have a gifted wife/partner, in the person of Safisha Madhubuti, together they relentlessly focused on planting and nurturing the seeds of education for liberation via schools and a publishing house. These institutional seeds have blossomed full blown into an entire city block which today houses Third World Press, Institute for Positive Education/New Concept Development Center and the Betty Shabazz International Charter School. Their work and contribution to African people/Black people is one of the triumphs of nationalist/Pan-Africanist movement of the 20th and 21st centuries.

I am not quite sure when and how we bonded. I remember being in awe of his poetic brilliance as he would recite on stages with the likes of Sonia Sanchez and Amiri Baraka. We served together on the Executive Committee of the Congress of African People, were co-founders of African Liberation Day and partnered in the quest to declare the birthday of Malcolm X a National African American Day of Commemoration by act of self-determination. We have become brothers and comrades through struggle. He has always been there, on call whenever I've needed him. And, as much as anyone, he has constantly pushed me to write "the book" the promise that it would bear the seal and sanction of Third World Press. Though I have fallen short in that regard, fortunately, Haki has included my essays in two edited works: "The Rebellion in Los Angeles: The Crisis of Capitalism," in *Why L.A. Happened: Implications for the '92 Rebellion*; "The Million Man March: From Patriarchy to Partnership," in *Million Man March/Day of Absence: A Commemorative Anthology*. And, he afforded me the opportunity to be Co-Editor with him of *By Any Means Necessary: Malcolm X, Real, Not Reinvented* along with Herb Boyd and Dr. Maulana Karenga.

When I was awarded the Doctorate, I was simply going to continue to be just plain Ron Daniels. Haki Madhubuti who said to me,

"You've earned the right to be called Dr. Ron Daniels. So, carry that title with pride and dignity." And, so it is that I "be" Dr. Ron Daniels!

When I stepped out on faith to return to the source and re-center my work in Black America and the Pan African World, the effort to build the Institute of the Black World 21st Century as the legacy project was already in progress. The Initiative is rooted in the decision by a little-known formation called the African American Progressive Action Network (AAPAN), which I convened after leaving the National Rainbow Coalition post and the Jesse Jackson for President Campaign in 1988. This amazing collective of activists and organizers agreed to accomplish three tasks: To declare 1990 "The Year of Malcolm X" to commemorate his 50th birthday; to resurrect the concept of State of Black America Conferences which had been focal points for national deliberations and action in the era of the 60s; and, to create a progressive Black Think Tank.

In one of the most remarkable feats of organizing I have been involved with, all three tasks were achieved. The year 1990 witnessed an explosion of organizing around the 50th birthday of Malcolm X, culminating with a major celebration in Omaha, Nebraska, where May 19th was proclaimed a National African American Day of Commemoration; in 1994 and 1997 State of the Race Conferences were convened at Sojourner Douglass College in Baltimore; and, AAPAN created the African American Institute for Research and Empowerment (AAIFRE) to fulfill the goal of building an African-centered, progressive think tank. The seed for what was to become the new IBW was planted. AAIFRE conducted successful organizer training and leadership development sessions at the State of the Race Conferences in 1994 and 1997, but it was not until 2001 at the first State of the Black World Conference in Atlanta that the idea of a progressive Black Think Tank received mass support.

Not completely satisfied with the progress of AAIFRE, prior to the Atlanta Conference, we reviewed the history and work of the original Institute of the Black World, which was defunct, and decided after consultation with some original founders, that a revised version of IBW could make an important contribution to the Black Freedom Struggle in this era. "Twenty-first Century (21st)" was added to the name to distinguish the new IBW from the original. The *Atlanta Declaration* from State of the Black Conference embraced the idea of the creation of the Institute of the Black World 21st Century and set a timetable of April 2002 for the formal launch. With that, we set about the task of building an institute that would be worthy of the original through its contributions to the liberation of Black people in these times.

I cite this background because the process of building the new IBW as an instrument for global Black empowerment had been underway since 1989, and it is integrally linked to the convening of State of the Race and State of the Black World Conferences. I also cite this history as the predicate for calling the names of many of the persons and institutions who have contributed to this project largely at my behest: Dr. Charles Simmons, President of Sojourner Douglass College (SDC), who graciously agreed to host State of the Race Conferences I and II because he viewed them as consistent with the mission of the college; Kareem Aziz, a friend and supporter dating back to my days as President of the Ohio Black Assembly, who took on the huge task of being the on the ground liaison for SDC and principal Coordinator. He bore the brunt of the work of two successful State of the Race Conferences.

Seemingly out of no-where, this amazing Sister was called in by Greg Akili to help with the logistics and arrangements, training, anything and everything for State of the Race Conference I in Baltimore.

She arrived; she contributed and has continued to contribute to IBW through thick and thin ever since. I shout praises to the high heavens for Makani Themba; Carolyn McClair and Rev. Wayne Stokeling have been an irreplaceable, invaluable part of the team since 1994, offering their services at every State of the Race and State of the Black World Conference and other notable events over these many years; true believers in this project without whom we would not have progressed this far.

The Honorable Minister Louis Farrakhan has participated or sent a representative to every State of the Race and Black World Conference since 1994 and provided resources at critical moments to ensure the continuation of this project; Our beloved Sister Susan Taylor has never hesitated to heed the call to be at our side for State of the Black World Conferences and other IBW activities. If she's available, we know she will show up; Danny Glover has been the Chairman of every Pan African Institute at State of the Black World Conference since 2008 and consistently lent his name or participated in other IBW events and initiatives such as the National African American Reparations Commission; the multi-talented Atty. Nkechi Taifa, has graciously agreed to moderate forum after forum on criminal justice issues and is a true believer and supporter of the Mission of IBW; Dr. Julianne Malveaux, Black America's leading political economist, has never refused our invitation to participate at State of the Black World Conferences or other IBW initiatives and events; James Early, one of the sharpest thinkers on the planet is a Brother who has quietly and unpretentiously been supportive for many years; and, the "amazing" George Fraser not only shows up at State of the Black World Conferences and related Initiatives, he ensures that IBW always has exposure at his awesome Power Networking Conference as a way of embracing and enhancing the project.

Bev Smith, the inimitable "Queen of Night Time Talk Radio," has been a stanch supporter for years, always making *The Bev Smith Show* available to visibly support Dr. Ron Daniels and the vision/mission of IBW; George Curry, Black America's premier journalist was always available to speak at IBW forums and events and continually found ways to give visibility to our work; Dr. Conrad Worrill, the rough and gruff, expletive spewing former, long time Chairman of the National Black United Front, has been an invaluable friend and partner on many Initiatives as I have traversed this journey; Marc Morial, one of Black America's pre-eminent Civil Rights Leaders, has been a constant friend, participant and supporter as an expression of confidence in this project; and, last but not least Gregory Griffin, an obscure but very conscious and committed Brother from Baltimore, has contributed $10.00 a month to IBW since 2002 as a true-believer and sustainer of this project. His contribution epitomizes what is required to build and sustain Black institutions in Black America and the Pan African World! To these many stalwarts, these blessings personified, I say thank you, thank you, thank you!

Stepping out on faith to pursue my vision without a job in sight was a very risky proposition. But, I had faith that my long history of service would be rewarded by an opportunity opening up that would enable me to move forward with some measure of security. "We've Come This Far by Faith" is one of my favorite gospel songs. That faith paid off when New York City Councilman Charles Barron, Chairman of the Higher Education Committee, stepped up to recommend to Senior Vice-President of the City University of New York (CUNY), Jay Hershenson, that I be considered for employment as a Distinguished Lecturer at one of the CUNY Colleges/Universities. The position of Distinguished Lecturer is primarily based on significant life experiences and achievements that can bring added value to the classroom and campus community. The meeting Councilman Barron arranged with SVC Hershenson went extremely well. He was very impressed with my long record of service and accomplishments, including that fact that I had the Ph.D. He wrote letters to the Presidents of City College, Medgar Evers College and York College requesting that they consider interviewing me for a position as Distinguished Lecturer. My preference was for York College because it located in Jamaica, Queens, not far from our home in East Elmhurst. Besides, I felt in my gut that if I were appointed at York, it would turn out to be a wonderful fit and experience.

My feelings were validated. With words of support from community leaders like Dr. Karl Rodney, Editor/Publisher, New York Carib News, Roy Hastick, President/CEO, Caribbean American Chamber of Commerce and Industry, Congressman Gregory Meeks, Ron Thomas, a Vice-President at York College, and a very warm interview with President Marcia Keizs, where we connected, she agreed to appoint Dr. Ron Daniels as the first Distinguished Lecturer at York College. However, first, I had to pass muster with faculty of the Behavioral Sciences Department, where the Political Science Discipline is housed. My vast experiences were also an asset as I met with my future colleagues, many of whom knew of me through my work at the Center for Constitutional Rights, National Rainbow Coalition and Jackson for President Campaign.

Serving as York College's first Distinguished Lecturer, at the pleasure of my President, Dr. Marcia Keizs and acceptance of my colleagues and the campus community has been a joy beyond belief. Equally important, the work has been complementary and supportive of my mission of building the Institute of the Black World 21st Century. It has been absolutely crucial to pushing this legacy project forward. Therefore, I am honored to call out the names of Charles

Barron, President Marcia Keizs and all those who intervened to make this providential appointment possible!

There are so, so many more sisters, brothers and friends who in ways small and large have in some measure touched my life and pushed me along this path. We will inevitably miss many but pause here to add to this Libation the names of Dudley Thompson, Eusi Kwyana, Tim Hector, Bill Rivera, Rosie Douglas, Atherton Martin, Ozzie Liburd, Winston Carroo, Dessima Williams, Babatunde Olatunji, Dinizulu, Dr. Vincent Harding, Howard Dodson, Bill Strickland, Pat Daly, Dr. Walter Lomax, Congresswoman Barbara Lee, Dr. C. Delores Tucker, Dr. E. Faye Williams, Phillip Carter, Charles Stephenson, Carlotta Scott, State Senator Bill Owens, Hulbert James, Mzee Leonard Tate, Letetia Daniels, Linda Brown, Dr. Ramona Edelin, Bill Lucy, Atty. Derrick Humphries, Dr. Elsie Scott, Keenan Keller, Cynthia Martin, Rev. JoAnn Watson, Atty. L. Londell McMillan, State Representative Bill Crawford, Dr. C. Delores Tucker, Van Jones, Junette Pinkney, Atty. Jill Sofiyah Elijah, Walt Bremond, Bill Merritt, Kermit Eady, Ed Vaughn, Bernard Parker, Dr. Julius Garvey, Dr. Leonard Jeffries, Dr. Maulana Karenga, Chokwe Lumumba, Jonita Scott-Obadele, Jitu Weusi, Dr. Waldaba Stewart, Esmeralda Brown, Henry Nicolas, Bruce Richard, Estela Vazquez, Rev. Dr. Herbert Daughtry, Imam Talib Abdur- Rashid, Rev. Dennis Dillon, Rev. Dr. Tyrone Pitts, Rollie Kimbrough, Rev. Dr. Joseph Evans, Debra Fraser-Howze, Yolande Cadore, Asha Bandele, Jim Dunn, Ron Chisom, Rev. F.D. Kirkpatrick, Father A.J. McKnight, Wendall Paris, Doris Darby, Rev. Mack Charles Jones, Faya Rose Toure, Senator Hank Sanders, Sandino Thompson, Brother Arif, Nancy Wright and Ricardo Wright, Dr. Peter Agho, Esailama Diouf, Betty Dopson, Imhotep Gary Byrd, Adriene Gaines, Cody Anderson, Kerney Anderson, Jerry Lopes, Rene Bishop, Bernard White, Verna Avery Brown, Mark

Thompson, Warren Ballentine, Carl Nelson, Wanique Shabazz, Earl Ofari Hutchinson, Danny Bakewell, Rick Caffey, Jean Ross, Nick Taliaferro, Fatiyn Muhammad, Robert Pickett and the Open Line Crew, Sid Trommer, Anne Braden, Mike Albert and Lydia Sargent, Berthold Reimers and Tony Bates, Hazel Trice-Edney, Richard Muhammad.........There is a story behind every one of these names. I shout them out in appreciation for their contributions and support.

While the vision of IBW is my legacy project, it is a collective project; one that cannot succeed without the dedication of a core of true believers committed to ultimately achieving the scope and scale required for IBW to have meaningful impact on the fate and future of Africans in America and the Pan African world. The reality is that much that we have accomplished since the launch of IBW in 2002 has been done on "guts and faith." During my independent run for President, the highly regarded New York City Sun Newspaper dubbed me the "guts and faith candidate," suggesting that I was seeking to achieve a major breakthrough with meager resources. Of course, this was/is not unusual for me because it is how my beloved mother raised us to make something out of nothing, to not be deterred because of the odds, to press forward with confidence that" if you can conceive it, you can achieve it." For better or worse, this has become the mantra of IBW. A dedicated band of true believers has been at my side, determined to actualize the vision and mission of IBW!

And, so it is that I praise the name of Rick Adams, IBW Board Chair and much more, a veteran social and political activist and educator who has been a stanch supporter, partner and friend collaborating on numerous Initiatives and Projects over the past 40 years. His service to IBW as an experienced, resourceful and dedicated non-compensated staff has been foundational to the progress we have made this far.

Baba Leonard Dunston is a giant in the Black Freedom Struggle, an uncompromising race man who is one of the most respected Brothers I know. He was the highest ranking African American in the administration of Governor Mario Cuomo, and he served with distinction as President of the National Association of Black Social Workers. His vast experience, networks and relationships have contributed mightily to IBW's success, particularly in coordinating the Black Family Summit as another non-compensated staffer.

Don Rojas is one of the most respected revolutionaries of our time. He was Press Secretary for Prime Minister Maurice Bishop of the People's Revolutionary Government of Grenada, the most progressive, powerful and influential government in the English-speaking Caribbean to date. Don's decision to join forces with IBW as Director of Communications and contribute his enormous talent, expertise and access to progressive leaders and institutions in the Caribbean, Central and South America and the Pan African world has definitively elevated IBW's stature in the Pan African world.

Gloria Rosaline Preudhomme is a proud Bajan Woman from Barbados who springs from a rich family tradition of social justice activism. A deeply spiritual person, she is possessed of amazing administrative, management and interpersonal skills. And, she's African-centered to the bone, always bringing a sense of appropriate African décor to IBW meetings, symposia and conferences. She has bestowed these gifts to IBW as our organizational Executive Assistant. Engaging Roz as our "taskmaster" was a pivotal decision in moving this project forward. She has been the behind-the-scenes driving force, the rock undergirding IBW's evolution and development. We also call the name of her husband, George Preudhomme, who not only has lent her to us, but has become a sustaining contributor to the work in the process. Though many have contributed to IBW's success as board and staff (some are mentioned in other sections of the narrative), this is the dedicated core of true believers who have and continue to be at the center of the day to day work sustaining and maintaining this project by "guts and faith."

Just as there is a Core Group at the National level, it would be a major omission not to call out the names of the New York-based Ujima Support Committee Volunteers, the local folks who have been pillars of support for State of the Black World Forums, State of the Black World Conferences, Pilgrimages to Haiti, the Pan African Unity Dialogue, whatever and whenever called upon to serve. Scores of persons committed to Volunteer as we were building a strong IBW base of support and presence in the greater New York area. Most faded, as volunteers are prone to do by virtue of the ebb and flow of life's circumstances. But, a dedicated few have survived and committed themselves to advancing the vision and mission of IBW through thick and thin: Minister Afiya Dawson (also an IBW Board Member), Brenda Blot, George Turner, Gwendolyn Budd, JoAnn Johnson, George Nathan, Jacqueline Volant, Gwendolyn Bethea, Freddy Fitzhugh, Jamil Debe, Chris Coleman, Claude Jourdain. The selfless commitment of these unheralded sisters and brothers is the real stuff of history. I salute them for the dedication to this project!

Families are often the casualties of social movements and institution-building. The personal energy, time and sacrifices required sometimes create anxieties, stresses and strains that can tear at the fabric of families. Far too little attention is devoted to studying this question. When Black Power, Black Nationalism and Pan-Africanism exploded onto the scene in the era of the sixties, it provoked internal tensions between the converted, the reluctant and the unconverted, even within families. Moreover, if you are a leader, a public figure in "the movement," particularly the advocate for a controversial ideology, it is virtually impossible to shield one's family from the spotlight. The entire family must bear the burden of your advocacy, whether totally shared or not.

My first wife, Mary Jane Daniels and children Malik, Sundiata and Jeanette carried that burden as Ron Daniels emerged as the most visible and controversial spokesman and leader for a new movement in Youngstown, Ohio based on Black consciousness, African identity and the articulation and practice of Black Power, Black Nationalism and Pan Africanism. So, I call their names with regrets for any pain and suffering they endured but also for their love, support and engagement as they saw fit. Each in their own way has contributed to this journey and for that I am thankful.

Mary France Daniels is my wife and partner on this journey and quest to leave a lasting legacy, an institutional reflection of my life's work for future generations. She is a profoundly spiritual/religious person, educator and longtime social justice advocate in her own right. She was the New York Coordinator of the Ron Daniels for President Campaign and ran for Governor as an independent candidate. We have much in common, and this led to us hooking up to become husband and wife and partners in the struggle.

I shall never forget preparing to leave to go to Chicago for a meeting hosted by Haki Madhubuti. As I was discussing plans for the trip, she asked "you're not taking me?" I was stunned because I hadn't realized she wanted to become that deeply involved in the work I was pursuing. But, that sealed the deal. She packed her bags, and we went off to the meeting together. From that day on we have been partners. No article, essay, major paper I write escapes the sharp scrutiny of her English Major eyes. She is my Editor-in-Chief. As the First Lady of IBW, Mary France Daniels is deeply involved in the programmatic work. Equally, important I have become "Pops D" and "Papa D" to three new daughters, Tracey, Michele, Kim and sons Richard and George, Jr. who have embraced me as well as Sundiata, Malik, Jeanette and their mother Mary. It would be impossible to sustain the extraordinary level of effort required on this project without the love of my life, my wife/partner, my baby love, Mary France Daniels. I will be forever grateful for a match made in heaven!

These autobiographical acknowledgements, this special Libation for those who have joined the ancestors and those who are still among us is a testimony to enormous blessings that have been bestowed upon me; blessings without which the myriad successes achieved on this journey would not have been possible. But, it is an unfinished journey. There is yet a legacy to be completed. And, at this quarter-century mark, I feel I am standing for four awesome friends, advisors, co-partners and comrades who walked with me and shared in the struggles, adversity, accomplishments and triumphs of this unfinished journey:

Damu Smith, was one of the greatest organizers of our time, a brilliant thinker, strategist who contributed to the success of multiple movements. As an environmental and social justice activist, he helped define "environmental racism" and helped build a unified and effective Environmental Justice Movement. We were kindred spirits, brothers who locked arms and worked together on the National Black Political Assembly, African Liberation Day, National Black Independent Political Party, African American Progressive Action Network and much more. We were so close that I always had a key to his apartment in D.C. And, we shared an interest in food, eating, dining. We kept notes on our favorite eateries in cities and towns across the country. Damu was also full of life, the go to person for an incredible party! This remarkable brother left us too soon. But, his spirit lives in my/our collective remembrance of him and our commitment to continue the work. Institutionally, we will continue to work to make the Damu Smith Organizer Training and Leadership Development Institute a functioning reality. I am standing for my Brother Damu Smith.

Dr. Ronald Walters was undoubtedly the pre-eminent Black political scientist of the last half-century. A prolific author, essayist and radical scholar/activist, Ron emerged as a trusted advisor to a wide range of Black social and political movements, institutions and organizations. He played an instrumental role in the National Black Political Convention in Gary, served as the key strategist and policy adviser for Rev. Jackson's 1984 Campaign for President and was a founding member of the African Heritage Studies Association. He was also in the midst of every one of the movements previously cited with Damu and me. He was dedicated to using his intellectual gifts, his scholarship and skills as an organizer to benefit Black people in the U.S. and the Pan African world. We collaborated on so many projects and initiatives that folks sometimes mistook us for each other. Even now, people come up to me thinking I'm my Brother Dr. Ron Walters. We used to laugh about this, as I offered to trade places with him as the far more accomplished author and scholar. Indeed, I often tell folks we were both scholar/activists but Ron was more scholar than activist and I have been more activist than scholar. Perhaps, that's why we worked together so well. Ron also enjoyed eating/dining. For a period of time, whenever I came to D.C., we would meet at the famous Florida Grill to debrief, plot and plan. I miss this incredibly talented and committed Brother. Institutionally, Dr. Ron Walters will always be listed as the Honorary Chairman of the Shirley Chisholm Presidential Accountability Commission when it is activated. I am standing for Dr. Ron Walters.

Dr. Charshee Charlotte-McIntyre was a remarkable scholar/

activist, author, organizer, warrior woman. Our paths crossed via numerous movements, projects and initiatives but especially through the African Heritage Studies Association (AHSA). I attended AHSA's Annual Conference almost every year where the venerable Dr. John Henrik Clarke would hold court with his spellbinding lectures. I think it was at a conference in Atlanta that I first took note of Charsee. What a personality, warm, kind, generous, sharing, caring… We took to each other and forged an unbreakable bond of friendship. A tireless African-centered scholar and activist, Charsee was the first woman to serve as President of AHSA. She lectured on the importance of African identity, while never forsaking the Native American side of her ancestry—and encouraged all who would listen to do likewise. In fact, one of the most memorable lessons I learned from her wisdom and teachings was that "culture and ethnicity are far more important than skin color." By that, she meant that Black skin in and of itself was not a unifying factor on the African continent; that African people identify first by ethnicity, e.g., Yoruba, Hausa, Fulani, Zulu and particular culture. She stressed the importance of taking these factors into account when promoting unity and Pan Africanism among African people. Invaluable lesson! Charsee's milestone book *Criminalizing a Race* in many respects foreshadowed Michelle Alexander's seminal work *The New Jim Crow* in documenting the longstanding and deliberate disproportionate incarceration of Africans in America. Charsee was a bad sister.

When I traveled to New York she and her husband Makanda Ken McInytre opened their home to me. I was like family. Charsee loved to dance and I do too. So, at AHSA and other gatherings we were always dancing partners. Most importantly, Charsee was my friend, advisor and counselor, constantly supporting my movement and institution-building work and relentlessly pushing me to complete my doctoral degree as a scholar on my Doctoral Committee. Besides Dr. Jean Thomas-Griffin who opened the door for my reinstatement at UGS, Charshee was the one who was determined to drag me kicking and screaming across the doctoral finish line if necessary. One of my greatest regrets is that the Lupus she suffered from all her adult life, took her from us before I completed the degree. She made her transition a few months before I finished. I owe much to her for finally, finally, fulfilling the task of becoming Dr. Ron Daniels. Institutionally, I have requested that we memorialize Charshee's legacy by naming IBW's Research Consortium after her. I am standing for my beloved Sister Dr. Charshee McIntyre.

I met Wayne Thompson in my capacity as Southern Regional Coordinator and Deputy Campaign Manager for the 1988 Jesse Jackson for President Campaign. Oklahoma was one of the states for which I had direct responsibility. Having no real contacts there, it was fortuitous to meet Wayne Thompson, who over the span of a decade would become my brother, best friend and "running partner" on this journey. He is the least known of the comrades whom I cite in this concluding portion of this Libation, but he was an amazing Brother; a revolutionary whose roots were in the Black Panther Party; a Pan Africanist and internationalist, accomplished entrepreneur, environmental and health care proponent; skilled and pragmatic political leader, who along with his partners Opio Toure and John Bowman (both former Panthers) could effectively navigate the conservative terrain of Oklahoma electoral politics to deliver for Black people!

As a Black Panther, he once had to undertake a mission to rescue a group of his comrades who had been detained and were being tortured in a New Orleans jail; an experience which left an indelible imprint on his consciousness. Throughout his life he remained totally committed to freeing all political prisoners and prisoners of war, and worked tirelessly to achieve that goal. Similarly, he was deeply committed to mobilizing/organizing formerly incarcerated persons as a constituency for social justice and social change. He and John Bowman were co-founders along with Dorsey Nunn of *All of Us or None*, a powerful organization dedicated to the empowerment of formerly incarcerated persons. I wear an old, worn, *All of Us or None* hat given to me by John Bowman to remind the world of the Oklahoma connection to this essential organization. Wayne also had great confidence in the ability of young people to be a powerful force for change. As a Seminole Black Freedman, he championed the cause of the Seminole and Cherokee Freedman to protect their legitimate rights to full citizenship and benefits in these Native American Nations. You get the picture. Wayne Thompson was an extremely talented and committed brother.

As I gathered friends and comrades from around the country to form the African American Progressive Action Network (AAPAN), post the 1988 Jackson for President Campaign, one of the brothers I reached for was Wayne Thompson. That was a providential decision. From that moment on Wayne Thompson, and the Oklahoma base he brought to the table via the Oklahoma Health Care Center and circles of supporters, became an indispensable base of support for every phase of the evolution and development of the Institute of the Black World 21st Century. As part of the relationship-building process, on at least two occasions, I was invited to be the Keynote Speaker for the Annual Oklahoma City Martin Luther King Holiday Observance. I was also a Keynote Speaker for a major conference on the Endangered Black Male and Oklahoma State NAACP's Annual Freedom Fund Dinner.

Oklahoma became like a second home with a second family headed by my new-found brother in the struggle, Wayne Thompson.

Though his contribution to IBW was invaluable on a number of fronts, our closest collaboration was around the work of the Haiti Support Project (HSP) where he became my right-hand man, the go to person in terms of coordinating various initiatives, whether it was mobilizing developmental assistance, evaluating economic development/business ventures, organizing Pilgrimages to the Citadel or engaging in mediation and conflict resolution sessions with various organizations and parties on the ground in Haiti. Without question the highlight of this incredible experience was the two of us negotiating the release of Prime Minister Yvon Neptune, who was imprisoned after the ouster of President Jean Bertrand Aristide. The Associated Press announced his release via a pending flight to the Dominican Republic and on to New York City, but at the last moment Mr. Neptune refused to depart Port Au Prince due to dissatisfaction with some of the provisions of his release. He was/is a proud man!

Wayne and I were, what we used to call "bosom buddies" back in the day. We talked by phone or email almost every day about everything, the trials, tribulations and triumphs of the struggle, family, health, our aspirations in life, everything. And, oh how sisters loved them some Wayne Thompson, "that gorgeous, chocolate brown Black man" as Bev Smith affectionately described him. Sisters loved them some Wayne Thompson and we talked about that too.

Wayne fervently believed in the vision and mission of IBW and had great confidence in my leadership. I used to say to him, "I'm in the second-tier of Black leadership in America," to which he would respond something like, "Stop it. There is nothing second-tier about your leadership, Ronnie." Though my full name is Ronald, I have always preferred to be called Ron and never let anyone call me Ronnie, except Wayne. That's how close we were. Wayne's untimely transition left a hole in my soul, a sense of loss of a vital part of one's self. And, his contributions are sorely missed within IBW. Institutionally, those who complete courses in the Damu Smith Institute will receive the Wayne C. Thompson Certificate of Achievement.

Moreover, his spirit lives on in the work, the journey, the quest to fulfill the legacy of building IBW to the "scope and scale" to have significant impact on the lives of people of African descent in the U.S. and the Pan African World. This is the legacy to which I aspire as I stand for Damu Smith, Dr. Ronald Walters, Dr. Charshee McIntyre and, yes, Wayne Thompson who looks down on me encouragingly every day from the smiling photo I have of him above my desk. And, so we close this Special Libation determined to press forward. There is no other choice. Those whose names I have called, the living and those in the ancestor realm would be deeply disappointed and dismayed if I/we abandoned this essential endeavor. And, so Aluta Continua, the struggle continues.

We turn now to the Articles and Essays that are reflective of the background, ideological underpinnings, analyses, perspectives and prescriptions for change that I have articulated on this journey toward the fulfillment of a lasting legacy.

Background and Introduction to Vantage Point Articles and Essays

The articles and essays in section reflect my perspectives, analyses and prescriptions for action on a range of topics and issues of vital concern to people of African descent, Black people, in the U.S. and the world. They are selected from among hundreds of articles and essays I have written of the past twenty-five years. Though there are interrelationships between them, I have elected categorize and present the articles and essays in six thematic areas: *The Crises of Black America*; *History, Culture, Consciousness and Ideology*; *Resistance and Calls to Action*; *Forty Acres and A Mule: The Movement for Reparations*; *The Quest for Pan Africanism*; and, *Africans in America: Engaging the U.S. Political System*.

As I reviewed the materials for this section, I was struck by the consistency of my perspective and analysis over these many years and the persistence, intractability of white supremacy, structural/

institutional racism. While the conditions facing Africans in America and the world have certainly changed dramatically over the past half century, it is clear that white supremacy is a malignancy that continues to morph into maladies that afflict Black people in a myriad of ways. Hence, the Black Freedom Struggle must necessarily continue until Black Lives Matter!

For me this suggests the need for constant analysis of the Black condition, past and present, revisiting the essential vision and values which must undergird our struggle and the articulation and evaluation of strategy, tactics and prescriptions for action required to press forward. In this regard, the articles and essays in *The Crises of Black America* focus on the ongoing oppression, exploitation and marginalization of Black people, particularly young people, the working class and the Black poor. Indeed, you will note the repeated assertion that there is a "State of Emergency" for Black people confined to America's "dark ghettos."

In terms of solutions, Dr. Maulana Karenga contends that the "key crisis in black life is the cultural crisis," the imperative that people of African descent grapple with and embrace a positive sense of self and identity as a basis for internal organization and waging successful struggles for survival and development. Therefore, the articles and essays on *History, Culture, Consciousness and Ideology* embody my best thinking on ways to address this "crisis."

Frederick Douglass famously warned that "power concedes nothing without a struggle, it never has and it never will." Having culture and consciousness is meaningless for an oppressed people unless there is a commitment to engage the struggle to transform one's condition. Accordingly, including articles and essays on *Resistance and Calls to Action* was of paramount importance.

In that vein, the demand for reparations is a recurring theme since the MAAFA, the holocaust of enslavement. Having been adopted and mentored by Queen Mother Audley Moore, I have been a steadfast advocate for reparations for most of my adult life. The articles under *Forty Acres and A Mule: The Movement for Reparations* share my fundamental perspectives and conviction on this crucial issue.

I am also a devoted Pan Africanist. I am convinced that any program and call to action for Black liberation must ultimately be grounded in a commitment to Pan Africanism. *The Quest for Pan Africanism* presents articles with my views on this subject with a heavy emphasis on the importance of supporting democracy and development in Haiti as a "Pan African Project."

Finally, much of my life's work has been dedicated to exploring strategies for Black empowerment through engagement with and the effort to transform the U.S. political system. I am passionate about the urgent need for the development of a progressive Black politics that can serve as the anchor for a broader progressive movement dedicated to advancing a politics of social transformation. *Africans In America: Engaging the U.S. Political System* has a range of articles which express my views on this topic, including a number that provide my assessment of the administration of President Barrack Obama.

As I suggest in the Prologue, Articles and Essays by Dr. Ron Daniels encapsulate the vision, values, strategies and calls to action which are very much embodied in the work of the Institute of the Black World 21st Century as my legacy project. Enjoy!

SECTION I

The Crises
of Black America

The Emancipation Proclamation: From 3/5 Human to Second Class Citizenship

January 2, 2012

When I first became active in the Civil Rights Movement as a teenager in Youngstown, Ohio, January 1st was always a very important day in the Black community—not because it was the first day of a new year, but it was Emancipation Day. Every year the Interdenominational Ministerial Alliance and the local Chapter of the NAACP would host a major program commemorating the signing of the *Emancipation Proclamation* by President Abraham Lincoln on January 1, 1863. This was celebrated as a momentous occasion because with a stroke of a pen, President Lincoln freed enslaved Africans from bondage. Certainly a just cause for celebration! What was never noted in the Emancipation Day Programs was that the Proclamation did not "free" all of the 4 million enslaved Africans.

For Lincoln, the man the imminent historian Lerone Bennett, Jr. has called the "reluctant emancipator," the Emancipation Proclamation was much more an economic and military strategy than a statement of moral and political principle. The hard fact is that enslaved Africans were emancipating themselves in droves and flocking to the camps of Union Generals like Benjamin "Beast" Butler in New Orleans. Generals like Butler and radical Republicans like Congressman Thaddeus Stephens urged Lincoln to formally/officially free the enslaved Africans to strike a devastating blow to the economy of the South and, equally important, recruit them as soldiers to bolster the fortunes of an increasingly unpopular war in the North (by some estimates, more than 200,000 Blacks joined the Union Army). Accordingly, Lincoln carefully crafted a Proclamation which would have maximum economic and military impact. It freed enslaved Africans in those states that were in "rebellion" against the Union. If you were a slave in a state which had not seceded or declared war against the union—Missouri, Kentucky, Delaware or Maryland—you were still a slave after the pronouncement of the Proclamation. The Emancipation Proclamation left nearly a million Africans in bondage. This is why the 13th Amendment to the Constitution was necessary!

As Lerone Bennett, Jr. argues persuasively in his provocative book *Forced Into Glory: Abraham Lincoln's White Dream*, Lincoln did not primarily prosecute the war to end slavery but to save the Union by whatever means necessary. And, while he no doubt found slavery morally repugnant, he was also convinced that Africans were inferior to Europeans and could not co-exist with them in the U.S. as equals. He essentially viewed enslaved Africans as unfortunate captives who should be "emancipated" from bondage and protected from being oppressed by superior beings. This view was shared by most "abolitionists" of the day. It's similar to the way animal rights activists view cats and dogs. This disposition was also consistent with the infamous 3/5 Compromise which the drafters of the Constitution adopted to persuade the southern slaveholding states to join the new Federal Government. The Compromise provided that enslaved Africans, the chattel/property of southerners, could be counted as 3/5 of a person/human being for the purpose of determining taxation and representation in the House of Representatives. It was also consistent with the Dred Scott Decision which decreed that enslaved Africans were "private property" and therefore could not be granted citizenship.

Though the signing of the Emancipation Proclamation and

subsequent adoption of the 13th, 14th, 15th Amendments were welcome news, at best they moved the status of Africans in America from
3/5 of a human being to "second class citizenship." Deeply ingrained
perceptions of Africans as chattel and inferior human beings per-
sisted, thereby severely limiting the definition of "emancipation" for
formerly enslaved Africans in the South and their "quasi-free" Black
kin in the North.

At the end of the Civil War, there were 4.5 million Africans
in America, 4 million formerly enslaved Africans in the South and
500,000 "free Blacks" mostly in the North. For the most part, the 4
million Blacks in the South were woefully unprepared for their new
found "freedom." And, while the Freedman's Bureau and other programs were put in place to provide training for the formerly enslaved
Africans to enter society, they were insufficient in scale and largely
ineffective. But, the greatest handicap of all was the failure of the federal government to provide the "forty acres and a mule" which would
have given them a stake in the American Capitalist political economy.
Not only were reparations repealed, as Claud Anderson documents in
his brilliant treatise *Black Labor White Wealth*, Blacks were deprived
of an opportunity to participate in the Homestead Act and other "affirmative action" programs which benefited Euro-ethnic farmers and
major business interests like the railroads. As a consequence, the vast
majority of formerly enslaved Africans were forced into a new form
of peonage/quasi-slavery as sharecroppers, tenant farmers and agricultural laborers where it was virtually impossible to achieve self-
sufficiency or accumulate wealth.

Moreover, under southern Jim Crow Laws, certain jobs in the
non-agriculture sector were "set aside" for Whites and in all instances
Whites were paid more than Blacks for doing the same jobs. To add
insult to injury, as Harold Barron documents in his excellent essay

Demand for Black Labor, in the period after the Civil War until the turn of the century, the U.S. granted access to some 13 million European immigrants who quickly gained employment/jobs in the factories, foundries and mines in the North as the industrial revolution took hold. These workers were ruthlessly exploited, often laboring long hours in unsafe conditions for very low wages. However, millions of Blacks were confined to the South, laboring for no wages as sharecroppers and tenant farmers. As bad as conditions were for the Euro-ethnics exploited in northern work places, their condition was infinitely better than Africans subsisting under quasi-slave conditions in the South. The fruits of their anemic wages could be passed on inter-generationally, creating a passage to a better life for their progeny. The condition of Blacks in the South constituted an intergenerational deficit for sons and daughters whose future was not much brighter than their parents. Euro-ethnic immigrations would have a leg up on eventually achieving the "American dream." For formerly enslaved Africans in the South, the future was bleak, a perpetual nightmare.

When "Johnny" went marching off to World War I, things changed. Desperate to fill the void created by White men fighting the War, industrial bosses held their noses and vigorously recruited "darkies" from the South to man the jobs left open by Johnny's departure for the frontlines in Europe. Finally, hundreds of thousands of Blacks would enter northern labor markets as "wage earners" for the first time. Leaving the South for the North was like entering the "promised land." But, when Johnny came marching home, many of these Blacks lost their jobs, a pattern that soon came to be known as "last hired, first fired." Indeed life in the "promised land" was less frightening but far from the full freedom the immigrants from the South had expected. Blacks "up South" were supposedly "free," but they were actually victimized by discrimination under a system of "de facto" segregation. Despite the absence of Black Codes and Jim Crow Laws, in fact Blacks were confined to certain neighborhoods, limited to working "Negro jobs" (menial, dirty and dangerous tasks) or constrained by a "white ceiling" on jobs which only permitted them to be promoted to a certain level. The high echelon jobs were "set aside" for Euro-ethnics. The differential in wages and opportunities between Blacks and Whites in the labor market in the North is another case where Euro-ethnics had the advantage in terms of passing on accumulated benefits and opportunities to the next generation. Once again, Africans in America bore the burden of intergenerational deficits, compared to their European counterparts.

While many in White America and some Blacks would like to dismiss these factors as irrelevant to the current crises facing Africans in America, it is impossible to understand the wealth gap between Blacks and Whites and the relative underdevelopment of Black America without acknowledging this history. From the 3/5 Compromise to the Emancipation Proclamation, Reconstruction Amendments and Civil Rights Acts of the 60's, Africans in America have suffered from the perception of inferiority and deprived of access and opportunities which severely limited our progress as "second class citizens." It is an inescapable conclusion that the State of Emergency in Black America is in large measure due to ongoing intergenerational deficits resulting from our treatment as less than full citizens in these United States of America. As we seek to heal our families and communities, we must be sober about the fact that even with a Black man in the White House, there is a significant minority of Whites who still view Blacks as less than equal. More importantly, institutional/structural racism de facto remains a barrier to achieving full civil and human rights in this country. Faced with this reality, Africans in America must mobilize our internal capacity/power to shatter the psycho-cultural, economic and political walls of white supremacy once and for all. "We who believe in freedom cannot rest until we've won!"

The Fragile State of Black Progress in America

May, 2004

With the election of Barack Obama, as the first Black President of the United States, there has been an open debate about whether this historic feat is the climax of the Black freedom struggle, minimizing the need for government to address issues of concern to Black people. Indeed, despite persistent disparities in income, employment, health, education and wealth between Blacks and Whites, with a Black President in the White House, there are a considerable number of people, including some in the Black community, who believe that race is no longer a major barrier to Black progress. A recent Poll in the *New York Times* revealed that Blacks and Whites feel more optimistic about race relations in the country. Blacks and Whites also expressed a new openness to communicating and associating with each other. The question is whether this optimism about race relations will translate into racial justice as it relates to finishing what might be termed the unfinished civil rights/human rights agenda for Black people.

No one can deny that African Americans have made substantial progress in the last 50 years in shattering the walls of legal and de facto segregation and achieving meaningful breakthroughs in virtually every aspect of life in this country. With greater access to opportunity, the Black middle and upper classes have dramatically expanded. Blacks can be found at the highest levels of numerous professions, including heads of major U.S. corporations. Some of the most visible and high paid artists, athletes and entertainers are African Americans, and thousands of Blacks now hold public office from city council members, school board representatives to President of the United States.

This "progress" is the direct result of generations of struggle which compelled a reluctant nation to re-dedicate itself to adhering to the principles of the 13th, 14th and 15th Amendments to the Constitution by enacting laws like the Civil Rights Act of 1964 and the Voting Rights Act of 1965. In addition, executive, legislative and judicial branches of government were persuaded to affirmatively utilize race-based remedies to overcome the devastating intergenerational impact of centuries of enslavement and apartheid. If it was determined that custom, practice, policy or law had a "disparate impact" or "discriminatory effect" on the life chances of Blacks, race-based remedies or targeted initiatives could be employed to ameliorate the impact or effect. It was in this spirit that a broad range of "affirmative action" measures were embraced to advance Black progress, from scholarships designated for minorities in education, set asides for minority businesses and contractors to consent decrees that mandated processes which ensured greater minority hiring in public agencies like police and fire departments. Taken together these measures helped to produce greater opportunity and a better standard of living for growing numbers of African Americans.

However, while impressive, Black progress has always been fragile and insufficient, particularly as it relates to the working class and the poor. As Martin Luther King predicted, a "White backlash" developed which fueled resistance to the newly won gains of the Civil Rights/Black Power era. Capitalizing on White resentment, Republican conservatives seized the initiative to launch a major legislative and legal assault calculated to nullify or reverse these gains, arguing that

Black progress was achieved by infringing on the rights of Whites. Nothing epitomized this assault on Black progress more than the rhetoric and policy initiatives of President Ronald Reagan. It was Reagan who skillfully injected terms like "Black racism" and "reverse discrimination" into the political discourse of the time. Moreover, he cleverly suggested that welfare, food stamps, the War on Poverty and other social programs were essentially designed to help Blacks, thereby constituting an undue burden on White taxpayers.

The "Reagan Revolution" was a counter-revolution which set the stage for the steady erosion of the legislative and legal foundations of Black progress. With the rise to hegemony of the conservatives in electoral politics, social programs which ameliorated the conditions of poor and working people of all races were drastically downsized or dismantled in the name of "reducing the burden of government" on the American people. And, with more conservatives on the Supreme Court and in the federal judiciary, race-based remedies, including virtually every form of affirmative action, have increasingly been ruled unconstitutional. Hence, tools that were once used to address current and longstanding Black inequality have been effectively shelved.

Though structural racism remains the most plausible explanation for the kinds of disparities consistently documented by the National Urban League's State of Black America Report, conservatives have been successful in persuading a majority of Americans that whatever problems exist in Black America are due to cultural defects and a lack of "personal responsibility." Accordingly, it follows that legislative action and judicial decisions should be "colorblind" or "race neutral" irrespective of data which indicates that race still matters in American society.

At President Obama's prime time news conference to mark his first 100 days in office, a BET reporter asked him whether targeted programs might be needed to address situations like the massive un-employment of Black and Latino men in New York City. The President refused to take the opportunity to embrace race-based remedies as a means of dealing with depression level employment in the Black community, indicating instead that the overall success of his Stimulus Program will be the rising tide that lifts all boats. What this suggests is that we have a Black President who may well have embraced the race-neutral approach of the conservatives. If this is true, then the fragile progress that Blacks have gained could be in danger even with a Black President in the White House. In that event, optimism about better race-relations will be irrelevant to the real issue of achieving racial equity, parity and justice!

New Orleans After Katrina: The Ethnic Cleansing of a "Chocolate City"

August, 2010

The observances, commemorations and analyses are underway. Five years ago, America and the world witnessed a massive natural and man-made disaster when Hurricane Katrina struck Louisiana and the Gulf Coast with devastating fury. The toll in loss of human life and destruction of property was horrific. Vast sections of New Orleans, one of America's storied centers of culture and commerce, were underwater and in ruins. But what much of the world remembers are the searing images of thousands of people stranded on rooftops, waving American flags, pleading for help. Thousands more were packed into the Superdome and Convention Center like cattle with little food, water or attention from their government. These were the thousands of mostly poor and Black people left behind to bear the brunt of the disaster because they lacked the means to flee the coming storm like the more affluent residents of the city. In one of the most morally repugnant chapters in the history of this nation, thousands of mostly Black poor people were abandoned with virtually no lifeline from the Bush administration and the federal government; a fact that prompted Rapper Kanye West to spontaneously blurt out in a ceremony, "George Bush doesn't like Black people."

If there ever was a textbook case of "institutional or structural racism" in America, the impact of Katrina on Blacks in New Orleans is it. The lower Ninth Ward, home for thousands of working class and poor Blacks for generations, was decimated. New Orleans East and Pontchartrain Park, well-heeled middle class Black neighborhoods, were also in shambles. When the federal, state and local governments finally got their act together, thousands of Black people were relocated to Baton Rouge, Dallas, Houston, Atlanta and far flung places like New York, Washington, D.C. and Ogden, Utah as part of a mandatory evacuation. Katrina had a "disparate impact" and "discriminatory effect" on Blacks in New Orleans. Therefore, the obvious question was what would happen to displaced residents of the city once the rebuilding process began? Would the reconstruction plan and process be designed to facilitate the return of Black poor, working class and middle class folks, or would Katrina be viewed as an opportunity to reinvent New Orleans with a much smaller Black population?

Mayor Ray Nagin provoked a firestorm of criticism when he suggested that New Orleans should remain a "chocolate city." His statement captured the fear held by many Blacks that there were schemes afoot to transform New Orleans into a different kind of city. Indeed, the intensity of the reaction to the Mayor's remarks may well have been an indicator that the fix was on for a de facto ethnic cleansing to dramatically reduce the Black population and change the social, economic and political landscape of post-Katrina New Orleans. And, despite some of the glowing reports about the resurgence of the City, viewed through the eyes of the Black majority that once made New Orleans the most African city in the country, their suspicions have been validated. New Orleans is no longer a Chocolate City and it is clear that the powers that be never want it to ever be a majority Black city again.

The Superdome and Convention Center have been rebuilt better than before the storm. The French Quarter is all the way live again and business is bustling in the central business district. Most of the predominantly White areas have been rebuilt or restored, and the residents have returned to live the good life in the "city that care forgot." By some estimates, 90% of White residents have returned compared to about 65% of Blacks. With rare exceptions, the lower 9th Ward remains abandoned and desolate. New Orleans is back, but large numbers of displaced Black people are not.

Katrina provided the pretext for business interests and developers to achieve what would never have been possible prior to the storm; ridding the city of thousands of poor Black people. Not only was the Black population dispersed/displaced, the "road home" was made difficult by a gauntlet of bureaucratic barriers and procedures that only the most determined residents would muster the resolve to navigate. Moreover, a large percentage of displaced Blacks were renters, and yet under pressure from the Department of Housing and Urban Development (HUD) and to the delight of developers, the City agreed to demolish hundreds of usable public housing units to "de-concentrate" poverty. In fact, one suspects that public housing developments like the historic St. Bernard and Lafitte Projects were destroyed because they were too close to the French Quarter and central business district. There was a need to remove poor Black people from proximity of the tourist playgrounds of the City.

The net effect of the demolition of public housing and the failure to build sufficient affordable units to replace them has been a dramatic rise in rents. Units that once rented for $400 now command $750 to $1,000, putting them far out of reach of the majority of renters displaced by Katrina. A recent Brookings Institution Study touted the fact that the poverty rate in New Orleans has declined. However, it also revealed that this reduction is due to the fact that many of the displaced poor and working class Blacks are unable to return to the city because of the high rents. The refusal to re-open Charity Hospital, which largely served poor people, is another example of the scheme to push out the dispossessed to make room for more affluent residents.

New Orleans is on the rise again, but it is not being rebuilt to accommodate the Black poor and working class people who comprised the base of New Orleans famed culture. As I predicted, New Orleans is being transformed into a Disneyland like city where tourists can come to sample a culture largely created by Black people without having to deal with the "problems" associated with the Black poor. New Orleans is no longer a chocolate city. It has a White Mayor for the first time in decades and a 5-2 White majority City Council. These dramatic changes were unthinkable as long as Blacks were the decisive majority in the city. Katrina changed that. The de facto ethnic cleansing of the African population means that the New Orleans we once knew is not likely to ever be again. The story of Katrina and its aftermath is a shameful chapter in America's history.

But, there is another painful side of this tragedy. In the face of one of the most egregious indignities ever heaped on our people, we were unable to translate our anger and indignation into the collective power necessary to prevent the ethnic cleansing and gentrification of New Orleans. And, it is even more tragic because chocolate cities across the country are vanishing in the face of the onslaught of gentrification, and we appear utterly impotent to combat and reverse the tide. The ultimate lesson of post-Katrina New Orleans may well be reflected in the words of Frederick Douglass: "Find out just what a people will submit to, and you have found the exact amount of injustice and wrong which will be imposed on them; and these will continue until they are resisted with either words or blows, or with both."

Black America: A State of Emergency Without Urgency

June, 2010

I have participated in several meetings and events lately which have led me to the disturbing conclusion that there is little urgency, spark, movement to protest, counter or overcome the "State of Emergency" in the urban centers of Black America. There is an awareness that large numbers of Black people are suffering, but that awareness appears not to have provoked a common, coordinated and effective response from Black leaders and organizations or an uprising from the masses. It is a source of great concern because if we are incapable or unwilling to mount an offensive to combat the condition of the least among us, we cannot count on empathy and support from others. The key to the rescue of our communities is in our hands—but only if we have a sense of urgency and the collective will to mobilize/organize/fight to uplift our people.

I recently wrote about my exhilarating experience at George Fraser's Power Networking Conference in Atlanta. Thousands of Black business and professional leaders gathered to share information, expertise and skills related to the mission of economic empowerment. It was an awesome gathering, but it received little media attention, so it is unlikely that vast numbers of Black people from around the country heard about it. The next week, I attended Rev. Jesse Jackson's Rainbow/PUSH Convention in Chicago which commemorated the 50th Anniversary of the dramatic sit-in by four students at a lunch counter in Greensboro, NC, an event which helped to spark the civil rights revolt of the 60's. It was a well-attended Conference, loaded with valuable information. Time and time again, Rev. Jackson used the term "State of Emergency" to describe the multiple crises currently afflicting Black communities. And, he unveiled initiatives designed to compel corporate America to reinvest in Black America as a strategy to overcome persistent economic underdevelopment affecting our people.

One of the most poignant moments at the Conference was when Congresswoman Maxine Waters angrily denounced an Editorial in the *Wall Street Journal* that called on the Senate to eliminate an amendment to financial reform legislation that would provide greater access to procurement of contracts by women and minority businesses. Congresswoman Waters, who sponsored the amendment in the House, urged the participants to act immediately to block the machinations of the Wall Street lobbyists. Frankly, I wondered whether the NAACP, Urban League, National Action Network or radio talk show hosts were even aware of the amendment, let alone the effort by Wall Street to eliminate it.

Rev. Jackson's Conference was very impressive, but I came away wondering what was/is the connection between the economic empowerment thrust of Fraser Net and Rainbow/PUSH, particularly in terms of spreading the good news to a broader audience and mobilizing massive numbers of people to confront corporate America to reinvest in Black communities. Equally important, Congresswoman Waters was correct to issue a warning about Wall Street's effort to marginalize minority and women businesses. However, there was very little media at the Conference and few mechanisms to get the message to Black folks that the bosses and bankers on Wall Street are lobbying against Black interests.

June 18th on Capitol Hill in Washington, D.C., the Institute of the Black World 21st Century (IBW) launched the Shirley Chisholm Presidential Accountability Commission to monitor presidential response to issues of concern to Black America. In addition to tributes to Congresswoman Shirley Chisholm by members of the Congressional Black Caucus and CBC Foundation, Inc, the Inaugural meeting of the Commission featured a Symposium entitled Black America: The Economic State of Emergency, which focused on the growing crisis of unemployment and joblessness in Black communities nationwide. Of particular note to this conversation, Congresswoman Yvette Clarke, a member of the Sub-Committee on Small Business, expressed outrage that Blacks are virtually being locked out of the procurement process. She angrily noted that Blacks are not getting anywhere near a fair share of federal contracts. Obviously frustrated with the manner in which Black economic interests are being circumvented or ignored, Congresswoman Clarke said, "we need a breakthrough." She asked, "Are we willing to sacrifice to achieve a breakthrough?" Put another way, are Blacks willing to fight to promote and protect our interests? We had two Congress Members at different settings calling for action on matters of vital importance to Black people with little response.

The last distressing revelation came during our IBW Board meeting following the launch of the Chisholm Commission. It's about the 2010 Census. IBW is part of the Unity Diaspora Coalition, under the leadership of Melanie Campbell, President of the National Coalition for Black Civic Participation. The Coalition has worked strenuously to motivate Blacks to sign the Census forms in order to receive a fair share of federal resources. In addition, an accurate count will affect Black political power by maximizing the number of districts that have the potential to elect Blacks to public office. A fair count is the prerequisite to getting a fair share of resources and electoral political power.

That message has been hammered home for weeks through various media, community meetings and door to door, person to person contact. The robust effort notwithstanding, veteran social-political activist and strategist Hulbert James reported that Blacks lag significantly behind Whites, Latinos and Asians in responding to the Census—so much so that we may well lose seats in state legislatures and Congress in the coming years. Desperately needed resources may be lost and our electoral political power is in danger of being diluted.

There is a State of Emergency in Black America without urgency. As I pen this article, the news is that 53 people were shot in Chicago over the weekend, with eight killed. While the crisis in Chicago has captured headlines, the phenomenon of violence and fratricide is a gruesome fact of life in "dark ghettos" across the land. There is a disconnect between an upward mobile Black middle class which has migrated to the outer-city and suburbs and the millions of the less fortunate, the have nots, left behind in neighborhoods where gainful employment has almost vanished. I suspect that the lack of response to the Census is not only due to a distrust of government but a growing disillusionment that Blacks who have been elected to serve in government have not delivered meaningful change. No matter how many radio advertisements proclaim that responding to the Census will bring vitally needed resources to the community, large numbers of Black people just don't believe the hype. Moreover, there is an absence of a culture of participation in our community. There is no sustained effort by faith, civic, labor, political and community-based leaders to engage residents in discussions about the nature of the crises they face and what agenda of issues, initiatives and programs community people believe will result in significant change. Young Black men, the source of much of the violence, fratricide and incarceration in the inner-cities are among the least engaged in the struggle to transform distressed communities.

In the meantime, our national organizations and leaders are not only disconnected from the most disadvantaged neighborhoods, the places where the "emergency" exists, they are not sufficiently connected to each other. While there is collaboration between Marc Morial, President of the National Urban League, Benjamin Jealous, President of the NAACP and Rev. Al Sharpton, President of the National Action Network (NAN), it appears to lack a compelling common thrust calculated to galvanize Blacks from every strata to combat the State of Emergency. And, unfortunately, there are even rivalries, quiet and not so quiet competition for the position of premier leader/paramount chief of Black America—a sport that the media contributes to and feeds on as it anoints and abandons Black leaders at will. There were very few cameras and news media at Rev. Jackson's Rainbow/PUSH Convention because he has been relegated to irrelevancy by the pundits (and some in Black America) despite the extraordinary substance of his work. In contrast, the media was all over Rev. Al Sharpton's National Action Network Convention, providing wire to wire coverage. Rev. Sharpton has certainly emerged as one of Black America's foremost leaders in his own right, but it is also clear that the establishment media now favors him as the leadership flavor of the moment. The

Honorable Minister Louis Farrakhan, the only leader that has mobilized millions to march on the nation's capital, is barely mentioned in the media at all except in efforts to brand him as a problem or pariah.

There is a State of Emergency in Black America without urgency. What we urgently need is consistent communication, collaboration and coordination among our national leaders, organizations, institutions and initiatives—a united front where individual and organizational egos are set aside in order to mobilize a massive response to the State of Emergency. We must work to devise vehicles and practices to overcome the "disconnects" identified above in order to actualize our potential power. The mobilization must also include those who are most affected by the State of Emergency. A concerted effort must be made to identify and engage grassroots/community-based leaders from across the country, particularly young people and leaders of the hip hop generation.

Finally, if we are serious about combating the State of Emergency in Black America, it cannot be demonstrations, marches and rallies as usual. As Congressman John Lewis eloquently puts it, we urgently need a movement that "gets in the way." The Greensboro four got in the way when they sat in at the lunch counter. If the locked out and left out are in a State of Emergency, then it will take dramatic steps to bring attention to their plight. We urgently need to utilize strikes, boycotts, civil disobedience, disruption; we have to "get in the way" if we expect the government and corporate America to take us seriously. When those who feel abandoned in the inner-cities witness leaders and followers speaking truth to power and confronting the powers that be, perhaps the fratricide and violence will subside because a real movement for change will engender hope that a better future is possible. If there is a sense of urgency about the State of Emergency in Black America, our brothers and sisters imprisoned in America's dark ghettos who are turning on each other will turn to each other and join the fight to transform their lives and our communities!

A National Disgrace:
Joblessness and Fratricide in
America's "Dark Ghettos"

May, 2013

The Institute of the Black World 21st Century (IBW) is gearing up for a Day of Direct Action June 17th in Washington, D.C. to demand an end to the War on Drugs and mass incarceration and call on President Obama to invest in marginalized urban inner-city Black communities across the nation. While ending the war on drugs as a devastating racially-biased policy is essential, we in IBW have always insisted that overcoming joblessness and economic underdevelopment is ultimately the key to combating the crime, violence, fratricide and mass incarceration that have become the scourge of America›s «dark ghettos.» According to a study by the Community Service Society, «the unemployment rate for African-American men in New York, age 16 to 24, was 33.5» at the height of the Great Recession. That figure is likely closer to 50% when young Black men who are no longer looking for work are included. What is true of New York is true of virtually every urban inner-city area in this country.

In a recent *New York Times* Editorial Opinion article, Jared Bernstein, Senior Fellow at the Center for Budget and Policy Priorities, lamented the fact that chronic unemployment has emerged as a major problem for Americans in general with "11.7 million looking for work" as of the last job report and "about eight million more stuck in underemployment." But, as William Julius Wilson has pointed out, the problem of joblessness is much more severe in Black communities where work has simply "disappeared" because of massive disinvestment in urban areas and structural factors like deindustrialization. Therefore, there are disastrous, depression levels of joblessness in Black communities—levels which would not be tolerated in White communities.

There is a direct link between the depression levels of joblessness and the horrific violence and fratricide that plague Black communities. It is said that "idle hands are the devil's workshop." The mere absence of jobs and economic opportunity alone contribute to destructive behavior among young people, particularly Black males. However, in the absence of "legitimate" jobs/work, an illicit economy and new "employer" have become a reality of life in America's dark ghettos—the trafficking of illegal drugs. Africans in America are only bit players in a multi-billion-dollar global enterprise dominated by huge transnational cartels. But, the fierce and deadly competition to share in and control a lucrative piece of the action has had a devastating impact—turf wars, chronic crime, violence, fratricide, targeted, paramilitary policing and mass incarceration.

The gun violence and fratricide in urban Black inner-city neighborhoods is beyond belief. Every week there is the equivalent of a Newtown massacre in some Black community in this country. Data compiled from a variety of sources by Dr. Zachary Williams of IBW's Research Consortium paint a painful picture in terms of the magnitude of the carnage:

• Blacks in the United States are disproportionately affected by homicide. For the year 2009, Blacks represented 13% of the nation's population, yet accounted for 47% of all homicide victims.

• In that same year, the homicide rate for Black male victims was 32.14 per 100,000 ... For White male homicide victims, it was 4.26 per 100,000.

- 82% of Black victims were shot and killed with guns—74% ...were killed with handguns.

The depression levels of joblessness and horrific scale of fratricide in America's dark ghettos is a national disgrace, a moral and political crisis which all Americans should be concerned with. But, there is no national outcry, no outrage because the affected people are Black: "the wrong complexion to get the protection." Who would have believed that 50 years after the March on Washington, where Martin Luther King talked about the "Promissory Note," that continues to come back "marked insufficient funds," that a State of Emergency would exist in Black urban inner-city neighborhoods? President Obama must have the "audacity," the courage to act on this crisis.

As a general proposition in his *New York Times* article, Jared Bernstein strongly recommends that, as a matter of principle, liberals/progressives resurface and reaffirm the goal of a full employment economy as reflected in the Humphrey-Hawkins Act of 1978 [an idea which I have been advocating for years]. Under the provisions of the Act the Government would become the employer of last resort when unemployment rises above 5%, utilizing public sector jobs as a short-term remedy. As it relates to the catastrophe in distressed Black communities, a direct, targeted public sector jobs program with a priority on employing formerly incarcerated persons would have amazing results. Decent jobs with good wages and benefits are the best anti-crime, anti-violence, anti-fratricide and anti-mass incarceration program that this administration and the nation could embrace to address the disgraceful conditions in America's dark ghettos.

As we approach the 50th Anniversary of the March on Washington, it's time for President Obama to do more than reference Martin Luther King and the "Moses generation" as if the civil rights/human rights agenda is a fait accompli, a thing of the past. Black people who are suffering from the debilitating effects of the War on Drugs, joblessness, fratricide and mass incarceration need more than symbolism and the benefits that indirectly accrue to our communities from decent policies like the Affordable Health Care Act. We need President Obama to declare the conditions in Black America a moral and political crisis and call for direct action to heal distressed Black communities. On June 17th a contingent of «Drum Majors for Justice» will be at the gates of the White House to plead our case. Groups of jobless young people and representatives of anti-violence organizations should join IBW in this urgent endeavor!

Dispossessed Are "Sick and Tired of Being Sick and Tired": Pressure Mounting on Obama to Address Black Joblessness

December, 2009

In describing her attitude toward the system of apartheid in the South, Fannie Lou Hamer once remarked: "I'm sick and tired of being sick and tired." Obviously this incredible warrior woman/ freedom fighter was committed to engaging the struggle to produce change, including creating the Mississippi Freedom Democratic Party as an alternative to an unresponsive local and national Democratic Party. Much has changed in the decades since Fannie Lou Hamer uttered these words and put her life on the line to bring down the walls of apartheid in the South. As a result of the civil rights/human rights/ Black Power struggles of the 60s and 70s, large numbers of Blacks have entered the middle class and enjoy a measure of prosperity far beyond the fondest dreams of their forebears. Blacks now hold prominent positions in virtually every facet of American society. And, of course Blacks occupy elected and appointed offices at every level in local, state and national government right up to the President of the United States.

But "the more things change, the more they stay the same." As the Institute of the Black World 21st Century articulates in the Martin Luther King/Malcolm X Community Revitalization Initiative, there are now two Black Americas, largely "separate and unequal," one relatively affluent/well off and the other Black America that is mired in chronic poverty, unemployment, underemployment and afflicted by inferior education, health disparities, poor housing, crime, violence, fratricide, police brutality and jails/prisons. While large numbers of Blacks have moved up, large numbers have also been left behind and locked up—abandoned, disinherited, dispossessed. Tragically, large numbers of the dispossessed in Black America are youth/young people, many of whom see the "American dream" as a cruel hoax and nightmare. Certainly the dispossessed and those who work on their behalf have every right to proclaim "we're sick and tired of being sick and tired."

Barack Hussein Obama's campaign for President of the United States offered a ray of hope that the decades of benign and blatant neglect under Democratic and Republican administrations would end, that a Black man in the White House who had worked as a community organizer among the dispossessed on the South Side of Chicago would understand their plight and act to "change" their condition. This is the same faith that Blacks have invested in the Democratic Party since John F. Kennedy called Martin Luther King while he was in jail cell in Birmingham. Blacks deliver their votes to the Democratic Party as its most loyal constituency, providing the margin of difference in elections from Congress to the White House but are never rewarded in proportion to our support of the Democrats or in proportion to needs of the dispossessed. With Obama in the White House, the hope was, "this time it would be different."

Spearheaded by a dramatic increase in younger voters, Blacks turned out in record numbers to give Barack Obama 97% of the Black vote. Though Obama deftly avoided raising Black issues and grievances or directly responding to a "Black agenda," Black people across the board were willing to trust that once in the White House, the first Black President would remember those left behind on Chicago's South Side and the lessons he learned at the activist-oriented Trinity United Church of Christ under the leadership of Rev. Jeremiah Wright.

Nearly a year into his presidency, however, there are few signs that President Obama is prepared to directly address the plight of the dispossessed in Black America. And, there is evidence that members of the Congressional Black Caucus and other Black leaders are getting "sick and tired" of huge bailouts of the Banks and financial sector and the auto industry while there is Depression level unemployment in Black communities across the country. In a recent interview, Congressman Elijah Cummings of Maryland revealed the shocking statistic that more than 50% of Blacks are unemployed in inner-city Baltimore. In New York City, the highly respected Community Service Society published a report a few years ago indicating that unemployment among Black men was in excess of 50%. It is highly doubtful that this figure has improved during the current economic downturn. And, while I do not have statistics for other urban inner-city areas, there is no reason to believe that these locales are not suffering horrific levels of unemployment especially during the present economic collapse. As Vernon Jordan once put it: "When White America catches a cold, Black America gets pneumonia."

To be fair, the crisis in Black America is not new. Chronic unemployment in the inner-cities has been a major problem for decades. During the Nixon years, the late Senator Patrick Moynihan suggested that a policy of "benign neglect" be adopted to avoid allocating resources to address the crises in America's "dark ghettos." Ronald Reagan unapologetically shredded the social safety net, selling White America on the idea that government programs were largely benefiting Blacks to the detriment of Whites. Despite his reputation as the "first Black President," Bill Clinton focused on debt and deficit reduction as opposed to an urban policy to aid Blacks, people of color and the poor. And, though economic growth under Clinton did lift some of the boats at the bottom, absent a targeted urban strategy to address chronic unemployment and poverty, vast numbers of Blacks remained at the bottom. Needless to say, the eight years of the Bush-Cheney regime was also devoid of any semblance of an urban policy to address the lingering and festering problems of the inner-cities in Black America.

With Barack Obama in office, Black America, particularly the dispossessed believed that we were in store for "change we could believe in." Political analysts thought that Obama's pledge to create an office of Urban Affairs would finally mean the formulation and implementation of an aggressive urban policy. Thus far Obama has adopted a race-neutral posture in terms of policy prescriptions to address the myriad crises in Black America. When questioned about the needs of Black America, time and time again he has said that whatever polices work for other Americans should work for Black people. This stance is not acceptable under any administration, but it is particularly egregious with a Black President who has not taken the same position with other people of color ethnic groups. As the venerable Dr. Ronald Walters points out in a recent column, "If it is a 'mistake' to think about ethnic segments of the country in his governance, then why did he sign an executive order mandating that heads of executive agencies affect consultation with Indian tribal governments, or sign an executive order mandating the increased participation of Asians and Pacific Islanders in federal programs, or say in a speech to the Hispanic Caucus this year that when their unemployment number reached over 10% that was not just a problem for Hispanics, 'it was a problem for the nation.' No such statement has been made by the

White House about the 15.7% rate of official black unemployment."

Just like other Democratic administrations, it appears that President Obama has decided to cater to and appease other groups to hold them in the ranks while ignoring the issues and concerns of the Party's most loyal constituency—Black voters. Like Fannie Lou Hamer, there are ominous signs that Black leaders are "sick and tired of being sick and tired." Symbols without substance will not fulfill the needs and dreams of the dispossessed. It's time to relentlessly pressure President Obama to address the crisis of chronic joblessness and poverty devastating Black communities across this country.

The George Zimmerman Verdict: A Travesty in "Post Racial" America

July 15, 2013

B lack America and people of goodwill of all races watched in utter dismay as the jury in the George Zimmerman Trial issued its verdict of not guilty in the murder of Trayvon Martin. Once the case finally surfaced (after inexplicably being buried with no arrest of the killer for weeks), it was absolutely clear that Trayvon Martin was "racially" profiled as a "dangerous looking" Black man by a wannabe cop turned self-appointed vigilante named George Zimmerman. But, in "post racial" America, apparently this was not at all clear to the policing authorities in Sanford, Florida, who would have never arrested and charged Zimmerman had it not been for the massive national outcry and protests. There is absolutely no doubt in the minds of the vast majority of Africans in America that if a 28-year old Black man had pursued, confronted and killed an unarmed 17-year old White teenager, who was simply returning home after shopping at the local convenience store, that Black man would have been arrested, charged and eventually found guilty. Such is the state of race relations and racial justice in what far too many people would like to conveniently believe is "post racial" America.

From the outset, I expressed serious doubt about the prospects of Trayvon Martin's family receiving justice because Sanford, Florida is a bastion of White Republican conservatism. The selection of an all White, female jury (one of whom was a Latina) from a Jury pool in this community compounded my concerns. Moreover, the prosecution and the Martin family legal team were reluctant to introduce racial profiling as a key element in the case, choosing instead the more subtle tact of saying that Trayvon was "criminally" profiled. Virtually no one in Black America doubts that young Black boys/men are profiled as suspects simply because of their race. This is precisely why Trayvon's murder resonated with Black mothers, fathers and young people all across this country. Indeed, we must not forget that the "Stand Your Ground Law" which George Zimmerman initially used in his defense was created to defend "decent, law abiding citizens" (White people) against the "criminal elements" in our society (dangerous Black men). These specious laws propagated by the American Legislative Exchange Council (ALEC) with the backing of the rightwing, billionaire Koch brothers have spread to several states. They are part of a calculated strategy to guard against the menacing criminal hordes.

Racial profiling and Trayvon Martin's right to "stand his ground" to defend himself from a "creepy looking cracker" who was following him, despite being told by the 911 Police Dispatcher not to do so, should have been the heart of the case against George Zimmerman. Instead, the Prosecution chose to take race off the table and focus on whose voice was heard screaming on the tapes and who was on top in what should have been characterized as a "fist fight" where the aggressor had a gun. It is entirely possible that a frightened Trayvon Martin defended himself against a "creepy cracker" and was frantically administering a good old fashioned whipping on Zimmerman before he pulled his gun and killed Trayvon. How is it that in a fist fight, which was precipitated by Zimmerman's unnecessary and unauthorized pursuit of Trayvon, can he (Zimmerman) claim the right to use deadly force in self-defense? An all White Jury drawn from a predominantly White, Republican, conservative locale concluded that Zimmerman was the victim who feared for his life and therefore was not guilty of murdering Trayvon Martin.

Defense Attorney Don West even declared that it was a tragedy that could have become a travesty if George Zimmerman had been convicted. In an awkward attempt to empathize with the Martin Family, lead Defense Attorney Mark O'Mara equated Trayvon's murder to a family's loss of a son in a car accident or to cancer! The Zimmerman verdict and the post-trial gloating by the defense team demonstrate that the idea of a post-racial America is delusional. Substantial sectors of White America have no clue about what it means to be a young Black man in America whether rich, middle class or poor. The negative portrayals of Black men in the media, some of which are attributable to the War on Drugs, crime, violence and fratricide in America's "dark ghettos," has reduced all Black men to suspects. The George Zimmerman verdict was a travesty which did little to engender faith in the criminal justice system.

Recent Supreme Court verdicts further limiting Affirmative Action and gutting the Voting Rights Act of 1965 further illustrate the degree to which conservatives and a fair number of Whites of all political persuasions are convinced that race no longer matters as a major impediment to Black progress. These decisions coupled with the George Zimmerman verdict have produced widespread frustration and anger in Black America. But, this frustration and anger will be for naught unless Blacks and people of goodwill mobilize/organize to advance an agenda to finish the unfinished civil rights/human rights agenda for equality and opportunity in this nation. Those systems and institutions which commit injustices against our people must feel some pain! For example, the Stand Your Ground Law in Florida must be changed. That will require that Blacks, Latinos, Asians and progressive Whites register and march on ballot boxes with a vengeance to change the composition of the state legislature. Simultaneously, perhaps, a National Coalition of Conscience should declare an economic boycott against Florida (the NAACP National Convention is occurring in Orlando at this very moment, pumping millions of dollars into Florida's economy) until the Stand Your Ground Law is changed—GREEN POWER will produce policy change. The highly successful Moral Mondays organized by Rev. Dr. William J. Barber, NAACP State President in North Carolina, are also an excellent model of resistance which should be examined for possible adoption in other states.

The point is that anger without action is just anger. There are still millions of Blacks across the country who are not registered or who do not vote on Election Day. Those who are frustrated by the Zimmerman verdict can take it out at the ballot box by registering and then voting to rid this nation of the scourge of radical conservatism. We can use Black dollars as a weapon to advance an inclusive, progressive Black agenda by boycotting those states that adopt voter identification laws or Stand Your Ground Laws one at a time. As we gather for the 50th Anniversary of the March on Washington, hopefully, our national leaders will offer a concrete plan for resisting the "intolerable acts" that are being heaped on Africans in America. Frederick Douglass put it best when he said: "Find out just what any people will quietly submit to and you have found out the exact measure of injustice and wrong which will be imposed upon them, and these will continue till they are resisted with either words or blows, or with both. The limits of tyrants are prescribed by the endurance of those whom they oppress."

"State of Emergency" in Black America: The Killing of Black Men Continues: A Call to Action

August, 2014

When will it stop? The police killing of Michael Brown, an unarmed teenager in the streets of Ferguson, Missouri, coming on the heals of the killing of Eric Garner, an unarmed Black man by a policeman's choke hold in Staten Island, New York, is yet another painful, traumatic reminder of the long history of occupation, torture, abuse and killing of Black people in America, particularly Black men. Indeed, within hours of the killing of Michael Brown, Ezell Ford, an unarmed Black man with a history of mental problems, was killed in Los Angeles under suspicious circumstances. It doesn't matter that there is an African American President of the United States or that Blacks are mayors of major American cities, run Fortune 500 companies or are pace setters as high paid and adored hip hop moguls, entertainers and athletes; the killing of Black men continues.

Once again legions of Black people and people of conscience and goodwill are in the streets in Ferguson, Missouri and in solidarity rallies across the country. But, to add insult to injury, in scenes reminiscent of the brutalizing of civil rights protesters in Birmingham and Selma in the 60›s, St. Louis County Police units with sharpshooters, sniper squads, mine-resistant trucks and a «Bearcat armored truck» unleashed a ferocious assault on peaceful marchers, firing tear gas, stun bombs and rubber bullets into the ranks of terrorized protesters. The whole nation and the world witnessed this vicious onslaught against the *First Amendment* by highly militarized police that looked more like soldiers on the frontlines in Iraq and Afghanistan than the suburb of a major American city. There was «shock and awe» throughout the land.

The question of the hour is, and has been for far too long, when will the killing of Black men and the occupation of Black communities stop? For the past several years, I have been repetitively crying out that there is a State of Emergency in Black America, mostly in poor urban, inner-city areas—the "dark ghettos." The police occupation of Black communities, the abuse and killing of Black men and, yes, mass incarceration are the manifestations of this crisis. But, lest we only get caught up in the tragic particulars of the moment, we must be clear that the root cause of this crisis is the utter failure of this nation to finish the unfinished civil rights/human rights agenda for equitable inclusion of people of African descent, Black people, into the socio-economic fabric of this society. Black people continue to suffer the consequences of the «bounced check,» the promissory note,» that keeps coming back marked insufficient funds» that Dr. King poignantly pointed out on the National Mall more than a half century ago.

In a book edited by Jill Nelson in 2000 entitled *Police Brutality: An Anthology* I wrote, «The policy of more police and prisons has been used as a substitute for policies that promote social, economic, and racial justice for people of color. This formula of ill-conceived public policy and policing practices has produced a highly combustible situation in communities of color throughout the nation.» These words were penned in the wake of the police torture of Abner Louima, the police slaughter of Amadou Diallo and the killing of a number of Black and Latino young men in the greater New York area under suspicious circumstances. Nearly fifteen years since the publication of Jill Nelson's book, much has changed, but the killing of Black men continues.

As Michelle Alexander brilliantly discusses in her milestone book *The New Jim Crow*, rather than finish the unfinished civil rights/human rights agenda, this nation, including the Mayors and Police Chiefs of cities across the country, embraced the "War on Drugs" and adopted crime containment and community "pacification" tactics clearly targeting America's "dark ghettos." The media was complicit in this strategy by helping to create and popularize images of dangerous, crime-infested Black communities and the "dangerous Black man." Under Mayor Rudolph Giuliani New York led the way in instituting so called "zero tolerance" policing, based on harassing and arresting people for petty offenses, and the militarization of the police by the creation of specialized paramilitary units that conducted sweeps of Black and Brown communities. Racial profiling through the wide-spread use of Stop-and-Frisk was an integral component of a racially-biased and inflammatory policing strategy. The Giuliani method of policing became the model for the nation.

It is useful to provide this background and analysis because the police occupation of Black communities and the killing of Black men will not end until the ill-conceived policies and strategies contributing to the State of Emergency in America›s» dark ghettos» are eliminated and replaced by just and humane alternatives. Black people and people of good will must move beyond essential but episodic protest of police occupation, abuse and killings to more sustained strategies and campaigns to end racially-biased drug, criminal justice and policing policies and practices once and for all. And, these strategies and campaigns must begin at the local/county level and reach all the way to the federal government.

Black people must exercise political and economic muscle to

demand greater civilian control and oversight of the police. In Ferguson, Missouri Blacks are 67% of the population but all the political structures are dominated by Whites. This must change. Blacks and their allies must march on ballot boxes to seize the reins of power as a major step towards changing policing policies and practices in Ferguson. However, replacing White faces with Black faces in the corridors of power is not sufficient. Ultimately there must be a change in the policies and practices of the police. In local communities across the country we must demand an end to the militarization of the police, the utilization of military tactics as control mechanisms and the profiling/targeting of Black communities. We must also demand an end to the "broken windows" and "zero tolerance" strategies that insult the intelligence and infuriate Black people. Community-Policing must become the center-piece of a human-centered, holistic approach to crime prevention and public safety in Black communities.

SIRIUS/XM Radio Talk Show Host Mark Thompson has been advocating for increased community oversight of the police through the creation of Civilian Police Review Boards. This is not a new idea, but it is worthy of consideration as long as Review Boards are well funded and have independent investigatory and prosecutorial powers. In the past Fraternal Orders of Police (police unions) have fiercely opposed strong Review Boards. As a result, many of the Review Boards around the country have been like toothless tigers, defanged and incapable of effectively holding police accountable for abuse and misconduct. Rev. Heber Brown, Pastor of Pleasant Hope Baptist Church in Baltimore, is also suggesting that Black people lessen their dependence on policing authorities by instituting more self-policing structures and mechanisms in the Black community. This idea seems to be gaining resonance around the country.

Black people must also use economic sanctions/boycotts to

complement protests and political action to

achieve just and humane alternatives to police occupation and racially biased policing practices. Economic sanctions campaigns should be coupled with demands for private and public sector investment in Black communities to create jobs and develop business/economic infrastructure. Ending bad policing is not enough. Black people must struggle to revitalize Black communities. At all levels, the approach must be holistic.

To devise and implement local action agendas for change in drug, criminal justice and policing policies and practices in local communities, as Kwame Ture aka Stokely Carmichael would say, "Black people must be organized." There is an urgent need for permanent coalitional/collaborative type structures, comprised of organizations and leaders committed to working cooperatively and collectively to mobilize/organize for substantive change. The effort of the Institute of the Black World 21st Century (IBW) to build Drug and Criminal Justice Policy Collaboratives (Justice Collaboratives) in Pittsburgh, Philadelphia, Washington, D.C. and Baltimore could serve as a model for the development of these types of structures across the country.

At the national level we must demand that the federal government stop providing funding for local police departments to purchase the kind of military hard-wear the nation and world witnessed being used in the assault on peaceful protesters in that night of infamy in Ferguson, Missouri. At the direction of President Obama, Attorney General Eric Holder should decline to fund proposals for military equipment and expand funding for proposals that promote Community-Policing. There must be a strong signal from the White House and Justice Department that military policing is taboo and Community Policing is the national priority.

As the Institute of the Black World 21st Century strongly

advocates in the recently released Report Card on President Obama's Drug and Criminal Justice Policies (www.ibw21.org), the President and the Attorney General must vigorously continue dismantling the "War on Drugs" and all the damaging policies and practices related to this longstanding, racially biased strategy. President Obama should also seize the moment to convene an Emergency Summit on Policing Policy and Public Safety to identify and share best practices for building effective police/community relations. Community advocates, scholars/experts in the field, public interest legal organizations, Chiefs of Police and Presidents of Police Unions should be at the table. Though skepticism about such a Summit is warranted, it could have the effect of providing the President and the Attorney General with a high profile platform to articulate principles for a different kind of policing in this country. Indeed, Mayor Bill Di Blasio, as a self-proclaimed new progressive, would do well to convene such a summit among stakeholders in this city—since New York has been the trendsetter for the kind of racially biased policing that has been so destructive of Black communities nationally.

Finally, creating a new paradigm for policing is necessary but not sufficient to end the State of Emergency in America's "dark ghettos." The damages to Black families and communities must be repaired. Black America must stridently renew the demand for a "Domestic Marshall Plan," (IBW has created a framework entitled The Martin Luther King-Malcolm X Community Revitalization Initiative) with massive investment in jobs, economic development, housing, health and education to create safe, wholesome and just communities.

I conclude with the final passage of my essay in Jill Nelson's Anthology *Police Brutality.* "Unless and until this nation makes a firm and irreversible commitment to ensure that all people who live in this society will enjoy access to the same social and economic rights—good jobs, quality education, housing, health care, clean environment—instability, violence, and crime will continue to be problems that no amount or method of policing can contain for long. As community-based organizations, civil and human rights organizations, and public-interest advocacy groups struggle against police brutality and misconduct, the fight to create a new paradigm of policing must necessarily be seen as part of the broader struggle to create a more just and humane society. Therefore, the demand for police reform and accountability must necessarily be coupled with the demand for public policies that promote social, economic, and racial justice. Our goal must be nothing short of creating a just, humane, and peaceful society. If there is no justice, there will be no peace in these United States of America." "It's been a long time coming, but change gone come!"

Racism Kills!
The Epidemic of Violence
and Fratricide in Chicago and
America's Dark Ghettos

August, 2016

The tragic death of Nykea Aldridge, the cousin of basketball star Dwayne Wade, has once again called the nation's attention to the horrific human carnage afflicting Black neighborhoods in Chicago and across the country. Chicago has become the epicenter, the focal point of an internal epidemic of violence and murders that is causing excoriating pain, anguish and anxiety in Black America. It was the subject of Spike Lee's film *Chicrac,* and the latest version of *Barber Shop* also dealt with the issue. On the very day that Nykea Aldridge was killed, Dwayne Wade participated in an ESPN Town Hall Meeting on the crisis in Chicago and First Take with Stephen A. Smith and Max Kellerman devoted an entire show to the issue. Within 24 hours of this tragic loss, four more people were killed in Chicago and 23 others were shot.

As Marvin Gaye might put it, "what's going on" in Chicago and America's "dark ghettos?" Several times a year, after incidents like the death of Nykea Aldridge, there are momentary peaks of interest as newspapers write yet another series of reports on the issue and television networks convene panels of pundits to pontificate on the crisis and highly publicized town hall meetings are held to explore the "causes and the cures." Frankly, I am "sick and tired of being sick and tired" of the national head scratching on this life and death issue. The answer is both simple and complex Racism kills!

For years the Institute of the Black World 21st Century has persistently decried the "State of Emergency" in America's "dark ghettos," a multifaceted crisis brought on by a racist "White backlash" against the "gains" of Blacks during the Civil Rights Movement. Since the Reagan era, rightwing politicians have fueled and exploited this backlash to dismantle jobs and economic programs perceived to be of benefit to Black people. Massive federal government disinvestment shredded the safety net of social, educational and economic programs which ameliorated conditions of poverty in urban inner-city neighborhoods. Programs like the Comprehensive Employment and Training Act (CETA), that employed hundreds of thousands of Black youth in public service jobs, no longer exist. And, de-industrialization has deprived vast numbers of Black people of the opportunity to earn decent wages working in a virtually non-existent manufacturing sector. As Harvard Professor William Julius Wilson has documented, in many inner-city Black neighborhoods, "work has disappeared." Joblessness, which includes those who have given up looking for work, ranges from 30-50% among young Black men in many urban neighborhoods.

Under these circumstances an illicit economy emerged, largely engaged in by a relatively small number of residents, centered around drugs and related activities; an economy which breeds violent turf battles to protect territories and a cycle of murders and retaliation which become a way of life in some distressed urban neighborhoods. Over time an erosion of values, and what Cornel West calls a kind of "nihilism" sets in that accounts for how a few within these neighborhoods can commit senseless acts of violence and murder with no apparent conscience.

Urban inner-city neighborhoods have been deliberately neglected and abandoned by government and private institutions at the local, state and federal level. In fact, the response to the plight of America's "dark ghettos" has been to declare a "War on Drugs" and impose racially targeted police and criminal justice policies and practices that have resulted in the constant harassment, intimidation, arrest, detention and killing of Black people. Massive disinvestment, de-industrialization, the emergence of the illicit economy, "the War on Drugs" and racially biased police and criminal justice policies and practices—these are among the root causes of the crises of crime, violence and fratricide/murders in Chicago and similarly situated Black neighborhoods across the country. Racism kills!

During the discussion on First Take, Professor Michael Eric Dyson brilliantly and passionately made the case that jobs and justice would go a long way towards eradicating the epidemic of violence and fratricide. Hall of Fame basketball star Isaiah Thomas also pointed to the absence of investment in recreation and community centers in Black neighborhoods. What needs to be done is not rocket science, but America, this nation, refuses to act to heal Black families and communities. Racism kills!

It is obvious that massive resources in the form of jobs, economic development, housing and educational programs are urgently needed to address the crisis, something akin to a Domestic Marshall Plan to create safe, just and humane communities. But, while the head scratching and handwringing go on, inaction is the order of the day. If the chronic tragedies transpiring in Black communities were happening in White communities, a State of Emergency would be declared and this nation would act with dispatch to address the crisis. The crises in cities like Chicago have a "disparate impact" or "discriminatory effect" on Black people. This constitutes structural/

institutional racism. But, Black people are the "wrong complexion to get the protection." Hence, the death and destruction go on in the midst of a presidential election in the "land of the free and the home of the brave." Racism kills!

In Memory of Dr. Martin Luther King: Can We Make It to the "Promised Land?"

April, 2014

April 4th will be forty-six years since Dr. Martin Luther King Jr. was gunned down on a balcony in Memphis. Black America and people of goodwill in the nation and the world were stricken by grief, frustration and anger at the murder of this great man of justice and peace. Indeed, rebellions erupted in urban centers across the nation by people who could not fathom how an apostle of non-violence could be struck down so viciously and violently. It was clear that America was at yet another cross-road in the quest to achieve racial, economic and social justice.

Despite constant death threats, Dr. King never flinched in his determination that this nation should be made to live up to its creed. The night before he was murdered, he reluctantly mounted the podium at the Mason Temple Church in Memphis to once again urge his multitude of followers to remain hopeful, faithful and encouraged. He seemed to have a premonition of his demise, and yet he stared death in the face and proclaimed that he was not afraid. In the most memorable part of his oration he took the audience to the "mountaintop" with him and declared that he had "seen the promised land." Sensing that his life would be cut short he said, "I may not get there with you. But I want you to know tonight, that we, as a people, will get to the Promised Land."

As we reflect on King's courage and optimism in the shadow of death, the question is can we make it to the Promised Land. Clearly Dr. King was speaking to the long suffering sons and daughters of Africa in America when he referenced "we as a people," but given his fervent belief in the promise of the Declaration of Independence and Constitution, there is little doubt that he also believed that one day America as a nation must arrive at the Promised Land. King also knew that for the "promise" to be realized Black people and people of good will in the "beloved community" would have to struggle to achieve its fulfillment. There would be trials and tribulations because there were forces deeply committed to restricting economic and political democracy to an elite "few" to the exclusion of the "many" in this society.

As King peered over into the Promised Land, he saw a nation which embraced his concept of an Economic Bill of Rights modeled after Franklin D. Roosevelt's "Four Freedoms" where every human being would have a decent standard of living: a land where no one would lack for a job with a living wage or guaranteed annual income, quality affordable housing, healthcare and education. But, to get to the Promised Land, King was preparing a Poor People's Campaign to galvanize the "many" to struggle for an Economic Bill of Rights even in the face of the fierce resistance of the "few" at the commanding heights of capital and finance.

To get to the Promised Land, King also warned that the people, those who aspired to create the change must themselves undergo a change, a personal «revolution» that would translate into creating a just and humane society. Hence he proclaimed, "I am convinced that if we are to get on the right side of the world revolution, we as a nation must undergo a radical revolution of values. We must rapidly begin the shift from a 'thing-oriented' society to a 'person-oriented' society. When machines and computers, profit motives and property rights are considered more important than people, the giant triplets of racism, materialism and militarism are incapable of being conquered."

The people must create a "moral movement" to get to the Promised Land and that movement cannot countenance a system incompatible with "person-oriented" values. Therefore, those who would get to the Promised Land must challenge and change systems of oppression and exploitation; they must advance a politics of social transformation. As King put it, "True compassion is more than flinging a coin to a beggar; it comes to see that the edifice which produces beggars needs restructuring."

As we witness the calculated, mean-spirited assault on Blacks, labor, women and poor and working people by rightwing extremists, the explosive growth in mass incarceration within the prison-jail industrial complex and the ever increasing concentration of wealth in the hands of the few, we must continue to be inspired by King's view from the mountaintop. Black people in particular must be dedicated to leading ourselves and the downtrodden/dispossessed to the Promised Land.

The Moral Monday Movement led by Rev. Dr. William Barber, President of the North Carolina NAACP embodies the spirit of Dr. Martin Luther King's vision of the Promised Land and the road we must trod to get there. If King could stare death in the face and still keep his eye on the prize, then we desecrate his memory and violate his spirit if we shrink in the face of the current roadblocks and obstacles to the Promised Land. Too many of our ancestors suffered, struggled, bled, triumphed and passed the baton for this generation to succumb to hopelessness, apathy and indifference in the midst of a State of Emergency in America's "dark ghettos"—and the extremists' immoral assault on poor and working people.

As we memorialize the life of Dr. Martin Luther King, let us remember him on the mountaintop, looking over into the Promised Land, knowing that he would not get there, but courageously exhorting and inspiring us to continue the arduous but ultimately rewarding journey toward full freedom. We may not get there in our lifetime, but King's message from the mountaintop was/is a clarion call for a cross-generational struggle for "a more perfect union" and the creation of the Promised Land. Our people and the "beloved community," will overcome some day!

Displacing Black People and Culture: Gentrification: The New "Negro Removal" Program: A Call for an Emergency Summit

November, 2018

Gentrification has emerged as a major threat to Black communities that have been centers for Black business/economic development, cultural and civic life for generations. Gentrification has become the watch-word for the displacement of Black people and culture. Gentrification is the "Negro Removal Program" of the 21st Century. There is an urgent need for people of African descent to mount a serious offensive to defend Black communities from this insidious onslaught.

During the Civil Rights, Black Power era, the term "Negro Removal" was virtually synonymous with "Urban Renewal," local, state and federal highway and development projects that often disconnected and destroyed stable Black communities. It was not unusual for a local highway project designed to benefit residents from the suburbs or a component of an Interstate Highway system to be routed through the center of a Black community, uprooting and displacing Black people or permanently weakening businesses, institutions, networks and relationships that bound folks together. As advocates for Black entrepreneurship correctly urge Black people to create and support Black business districts in our communities, it is useful to remember that

Urban Renewal destroyed thriving business districts in Black communities across the country in the latter part of the 20th Century. In fact, there is a historical pattern of marginalizing, subverting or outright destroying Black communities to thwart our ability to achieve full political and economic empowerment and equity in this nation. Gentrification is the latest manifestation of this pattern.

There are a multiplicity of testimonies about this destructive phenomena. The caption of a feature article in the May 2, 2018 edition of the *New York Times* captured the essence of the crisis confronting Black communities across the country—"When Home No Longer Looks the Same: Rapid Change in Durham Has Left Many Black Residents Feeling Unwelcome." The article details how the revitalization of Durham, N.C. has increasingly meant development/progress for middle and upper-income Whites, but displacement for large numbers of Black working-class and middle-class people who can no longer afford to live in certain sections of the city. An article in the October 21, 2018 Edition of the *Houston Chronicle* is also illustrative of the growing concern about gentrification in Black America: "Historic black neighborhoods disappear all the time. But they don't have to."

In Atlanta, the "Black Mecca" of the South, Vine City, the neighborhood where Dr. Martin Luther King, Jr. and civil rights and political leader Julian Bond lived, no longer exists. It was wiped-out by sports stadium projects. Public housing development after public housing development has been felled by an advancing wave of "progress." The "Sweet Auburn" District, which was once the home of major Black businesses, is now stagnant. In the face of this onslaught, a youthful group of community advocates called the Community Movement Builders have recently launched an Anti-Gentrification Campaign to mobilize community residents and their allies to address the massive displacement of Black working class and poor people from their neighborhoods. One of their slogans is: *"Stop Gentrification: Keep Residents in Place."*

"Development" in Washington, D.C., the original "Chocolate City," has displaced thousands of Black people, forcing them to move to surrounding suburban areas; the prosperous central city neighborhood and Black business district in Seattle, Washington has vanished as Blacks have been forced to flee to Tacoma and other outlying cities where housing is more affordable; in Los Angeles, the Crenshaw Subway Coalition is vigorously resisting a subway extension that would spur gentrification in one of the most storied communities in Black America; in neighborhood after neighborhood in New York City, from Brooklyn, Queens, the Bronx to Harlem, gentrification is rapidly displacing hundreds of thousands of Black people. In a few years, Harlem, the cultural-political Capital of Black America, will hardly be recognizable. A Whole Foods Store now stands were Malcolm X once held his legendary rallies!

Chocolate Cities, once the domain of Black political and economic power are vanishing as increasing numbers of Whites who in previous generations abandoned urban centers for the suburbs are now returning to establish more comfortable and convenient spaces in closer proximity to their work places. "Development" to accommodate the newcomers is driving up the cost of housing, especially rental properties in a manner that is unaffordable for large numbers of Black residents. Property taxes are also skyrocketing, putting enormous pressure on Black homeowners as well. As Blacks are displaced and replaced by newcomers, this is inevitably leading to dramatic shifts in political power from neighborhood advisory boards, to city councils and the office of Mayors. Black power is diminishing.

What is equally egregious are the attitudes of some of the

newcomers whom residents of Black communities sometimes characterize as "invaders" or "neo-colonialists." This is because some newcomers are not content to become a part of the community; they arrogantly attempt to change the rhythms, culture and character of the community. For decades it has been a well-established and accepted custom that scores of drummers gather on a designated date at a regular time in Marcus Garvey Park in Harlem to play African music. But, once a large number of "invaders" became occupants of a nearby apartment building, they began to complain to the police and petitioned local elected officials, seeking to ban this longstanding weekly ritual. In Detroit, three White women, who are newcomers to a predominately Black neighborhood, falsely accused a Black man of being a pedophile and demanded that the police file charges against him. The brother in question was starting a community garden on a vacant lot int the neighborhood and the women protested this activity taking place in "their neighborhood." Fortunately, the Judge dismissed the charges in a case of "gardening while Black!" Reports of these kinds of attitudes and behavior across the country is breeding resentment and hostility towards the "invaders."

Let me be clear, as a civil right, any person in the United States has the freedom to live wherever they choose. People of African descent have waged a relentless struggle to achieve this precious right. People also have the right to live amongst their own nationality, ethnicity of ethnic group if they choose, hence there are Irish, Italian, Polish, German and Jewish communities in this country. And, occasionally these communities change in composition. "Little Italy" in lower Manhattan in New York is now mostly shops and stores as people of Italian descent have largely chosen to migrant to other neighborhoods. Voluntary migration is one thing, forced displacement is another matter. Time and time again, Black people have faced schemes, targeted policies and outright violence, e.g., Tulsa, Rosewood, to force their removal from neighborhoods and communities they worked and invested in to "develop" as their home.

Black people believe in "development" and no reasonable person would be opposed to improvements or progress that would better their community. The crucial issue for people of African descent is not development, it is "development" that is displacing Black people and culture. Therefore, the order and challenge of the day is to achieve "development without displacement." The question is, can development strategies be devised that prioritize improving the lives of the current residents and preserving the culture and character of their communities? The answer to that question is yes. The collective brainpower, skill, experience and will exists within Black America to mount an offensive to defend Black communities against gentrification, the "Negro Removal" program of the 21st Century. Therefore, we must gather our brightest and best, the conscious and committed in our brain trust to devise plans and a policy agenda to rescue, preserve Black communities. We possess the collective genius to develop just, safe, viable, vibrant and sustainable Black communities.

To that end, the Institute of the Black World 21st Century (IBW) is issuing an urgent call for a National Emergency Summit on Gentrification to be convened in Newark, NJ, April 4-6, 2019 in conjunction with the annual commemoration of the martyrdom of our beloved Dr. Martin Luther King, Jr. Newark has been selected because the City's ambitious development plans incorporate community-based strategies designed to mitigate gentrification. IBW has requested that Ras J. Baraka, the Mayor of Newark, host the Emergency Summit. This gathering is viewed as an extension of the milestone Urban Marshal Plan and Black Economic Development Symposium convened by IBW in Newark in April of this year. We envision anti-gentrification advocates, community economic development practitioners, Mayors, urban planners, faith, civil rights, labor, business and professional leaders attending the Emergency Summit on Gentrification. The Urban Strategies Program of Faith In Action, National Urban League, Democracy Collaborative and Freedom Caucus of the Center for Community Change have already signaled a willingness to partner with IBW on this crucial undertaking.

Now is the time to act boldly and courageously to defend Black communities from the destructive forces of gentrification. "If there is no struggle, there is no progress." We must muster the collective resolve to stop gentrification from devastating Black communities, from displacing Black people and culture…and we will!

SECTION II

History, Culture, Consciousness and Ideology

The Significance of Black History in the Age of Obama

February, 2009

January 20, 2009, the day that Barack Hussein Obama took the oath of office as the 44th President of the United States of America, will forever be remembered as one of the great moments in the history of this nation and the world. Few can forget Nelson Mandela's release from prison and his subsequent journey from prisoner to president in South Africa, overcoming decades of oppression under the vicious system of apartheid. This was truly a hallmark of history. Similarly, Barack Obama's ascension to the presidency marks a triumph over centuries of denigration of Africans in America, most often under horrific conditions. No one can deny the magnificence of this moment.

From the very inception of Obama's improbable quest for the highest office of the land, however, questions surfaced about the validity and authenticity of his campaign. Early on there were questions about was he "Black enough," which to some degree was rooted in his mixed race background and lack of history in the longstanding civic rights/human rights struggle of Black people in this country. For others this question represented an earnest inquiry into the degree to which Obama was committed to responding to "Black interests." And, as his campaign gained momentum with substantial votes from Whites in state after state, the question was does Barack Obama's meteoric rise to prominence and the presidency signal the arrival of a post-racial, post-civil rights society?

For many conservatives, some liberals and a surprising number of Blacks, the answer to the latter question was affirmative; Obama's astounding victory proved that race has been rendered a minor matter, an insignificant barrier to any Black person achieving the "American dream." Consequently, as Black History Month begins, some might ask, what is the significance or value of recalling the achievements, tragedies and triumphs of African people now that a Black man and his family occupy the White House? Does the Age of Obama mean the end of Black History?

Those who would suggest devaluing the significance of Black History do so at the peril of Black people and the nation as a whole. First and foremost, it is imperative that we remember that President Obama is a product and beneficiary of Black History—the steady and unrelenting march of people of African descent from the horrors of the holocaust of enslavement and the free labor that built Wall Street and the White House, to being defined as 3/5th of a human being in the Constitution to becoming the person elected to "protect and defend the Constitution of the United States." The venerable Elder, Rev. Joseph Lowery, was courageous and correct to commence the benediction of the Inauguration with verses from the Black National Anthem, Lift Every Voice and Sing ..." God of our weary years, God of our silent tears, thou who has brought us thus far on the way..."

Fannie Lou Hamer once said something to the effect that we should always remember where we came from and honor the bridges that brought us over ... "we have come over the way that with tears has been watered. We have come treading our path through the blood of the slaughtered." The teary eyes of elderly Black folks we witnessed on the National Mall, January 20th, peering up at a son of the struggle, were consciously and sub-consciously remembering, reflecting and celebrating the tribulations and triumphs of Black History!

We must continue to study and learn from Black History because, we must understand from whence we've come and how far we have yet to travel even with a distinguished son of Africa in the White House. Malcolm X once said, "of all our studies, history is most qualified to reward all research." Like Carter G. Woodson, the father of Black History Month, Malcolm understood that knowledge of self through an awareness of history had healing power for a people battered and despised by a racist, white supremacist nation, that within our unique worldview, culture and illustrious history is to be found the strength, courage and inspiration to triumph over adversity and our adversaries. The study of Black History should never be seen as an esoteric exercise. It is about the survival, sustenance and development of a people.

As we intensify our examination of Black History during the month of February, we must recognize that Barack Obama's milestone achievement is a monumental stride forward along that path "through the blood of the slaughtered." It will most assuredly have us dismiss as folly the notion that somehow we now live in a post-racial and post-civil rights society, that with the rise to the presidency of Barack Obama, the walls of structural racism/white supremacy have come tumbling down. The gaps and disparities between Blacks and Whites in America in health, education, economic well being and wealth are well documented as are the statistics on the casualties of institutionalized racism reflected in the criminal justice system and the prison-jail industrial complex.

Therefore, while we accept and celebrate the momentous accomplishment of the election of the first Black President, now more than ever we must be encouraged, motivated and inspired to finish the course. Now more than ever we must be determined to seize the moment to challenge America and our President to realize that the attainment of "a more perfect union" means mounting an all out assault to finish the unfinished civil rights/human rights agenda of the sons and daughters of Africa whose blood, sweat, toil and tears have been the redeeming grace of this nation. Now more than ever, the study of Black History must fuel the determination to keep our minds "stayed on freedom" for Black people and all oppressed humanity!

Africans in America and the Quest for Identity

July, 2010

A s I write this article, I am just returning from my annual visit to the International African Arts Festival in Brooklyn, New York. Founded in 1971 as the African Street Festival by activists associated with the Nationalist organization The East, the four-day cultural extravaganza attracts hundreds of thousands of attendees each year. Similarly, the National Black Arts Festival in Atlanta, which also occurs in July, has grown into a huge event. Whenever I attend these festivals, I feel like I'm bathing in "blackness"—immersed in an extraordinary variety of wares from around the Pan African world, food galore, African centered edutainment, and a sea of Black people!

The festivals also cause me to reflect on the sometimes tortuous quest to find the appropriate identity to define ourselves as formerly enslaved people in this country. That quest is an integral part of "cherishing a friendly union with ourselves" as discussed in a recent article. If full freedom/liberation were a reality, a discussion of the historical quest for identity would be a mere academic exercise. But, the state of emergency afflicting Black poor and working people and youth/young people in America's "dark ghettos" renders this a very important subject. I have a sense that some of the self-destructive behavior contributing to the violence and fratricide in the inner-cities is attributable to a lack of a sense of who we are as a people and a pride in our history and heritage.

Today, Black and African identify is taken for granted. It's just a fact of life. However, historically developing a comfort level with Black/African identity was the result of intense and often painful internal struggles. More than any other ethnic group or nationality that arrived on these shores, the question /issue of identity for formerly enslaved Africans was of paramount importance. No other ethnic group/nationality had to endure a systematic effort to wipe out their history, culture and identity. Other groups, e.g., the British, Scots, Irish, Germans, Italians, Poles came with these vital elements in tact thereby, easing the process of creating new communities in a strange land. For these groups, cultural continuation was the basis for cohesion/unity that enabled them to develop an economic base in their communities and eventually begin to contest for political power as part of the process of fully integrating into American society with dignity and respect. This was not the case for people of African descent.

As the late Queen Mother Audley Moore used to teach, enslaved Africans were subjected to a sustained process of "de-Africanization" as part of a system of control imposed by the slave master. We were taught that our skin color was a mark of inferiority and our African origins, religion, music and customs a sign of savagery. Black people were uncivilized and therefore should respect their European slave masters and White people in general at all times. Moreover, it is difficult for people to understand the psycho-cultural impact of being a Black/African person in a European/White society/nation where the symbols and imagery of "white and black" re-enforce the idea of white superiority and black inferiority. In the English language white is always used to depict the positive while black virtually always denotes the negative. Dr. Martin Luther King once pointed this out in one of his speeches. You have references like the "black sheep of the family," or "behind the eight ball." "Whiteness" is a sign of purity and good. "Darkness is a sign of impurity and evil. The Angels and good people are white while one imagines the devil, villains and bad people draped in black. A "little white lie" is okay. Put the adjective "black" before anything and it intensifies the sense of the ominous, disastrous or catastrophic. Not even the food we eat escapes the black/white, positive/negative, superior/inferior dichotomy—there's "angel food cake" and "devil's food cake!"

It would be somewhat amusing if these matters were not so serious and sinister as it relates to their psychocultural impact on people of African descent and our painful quest to discover and affirm identity and culture as part of building a new community in a strange and hostile land. This question of identity was also complicated by voluntary and involuntary "race-mixing" or miscegenation. As Queen Mother Moore and other historians have noted, slave masters had free rein with African women. The consequence of this cohabitation was off-spring who were sometimes "light, bright and damn near white." Mulattoes in the race contributed to the debate among our forebears as to whether we were African, Colored or Negro.

In a real sense, however, the debate and struggle was not just about terminology; it was about how to uplift, encourage, motivate, inspire a despised people, disconnected from their ancestral homeland—many of whom had internalized the myth of White superiority and Black inferiority. This is why from our earliest days in America we find leaders like Richard Allen, Rev. David Nickens, Henry Highland Garnet, David Walker, Frederick Douglass, Bishop Henry McNeil Turner and numerous others heralding the role of Black people in the Bible, the glorious history of ancient Africa and the great empires of Ghana, Mali and Songhai. Whether African, Colored or Negro was their preferred identity, they were aware of the need to rehabilitate the self-image and self-esteem of a battered people. This was also one of the central tasks of Carter G. Woodson's seminal work, *The Miseducation of the Negro.*

The search for identity has been a persistent dimension of the Black Freedom Struggle in America—the quest to create a new community from disparate ethnic groups, build social, economic and political institutions and wage the struggle for freedom/liberation within a Euro-centric, white supremacist society. Although today to be Black/African is non-controversial, unfortunately, there are vast numbers of our people who have no clue about the history/heritage and legacy of struggle associated with their identity. To be Black/African has lost its political potency as a weapon in the Black Freedom Struggle. Indeed, the "n-word" has even resurfaced as a "term of endearment" among our youth because of their ignorance or disregard for the negative history attached to that identification.

All of this suggests that a part of the" friendly union with ourselves" must involve a renewed emphasis on mass education about what it means to be Black/African in the 21st century in terms of our struggle for full freedom/liberation. Those among us who have achieved relative success must come to view their identity as Black/African as part of a legacy of struggle that demands that they be "of the race and for the race" as it relates to connecting to and fighting for the well-being of the "have nots" in our communities. And, as we seek to educate/mobilize/organize the least among us, they must be armed with the power of positive identification with Black/African as a motivating force for social justice and social change. We must move beyond Black/African as a commonplace, cosmetic proposition to once again viewing identity as a vital element in community-building/nation-building and an indispensable weapon in the struggle for full freedom/liberation.

"We Are an African People": Identity as a Unifying Force for Liberation

March, 2010

I have been so pre-occupied of late with responding to the disaster in Haiti that I neglected to pen an article for Black History Month. But, since Black History should be a continual source of study, I am belatedly sharing some thoughts on the subject. In fact, this piece was inspired in part by a very engaging conversation I had with Rev. Willie Wilson, the visionary Pastor of Union Temple Baptist Church in Washington, during the Nation of Islam's Saviors Day Commemoration in Chicago. Rev. Wilson pointed out how "African" identity was a unifying force among the quasi-free Black leaders in the late 18th and early 19th centuries as they sought to build institutions and a new community on these hostile American shores. There was clarity about their African identity, and therefore the institutions they built bore the name of the land of their origin—most notably early Black religious denominations. The African Methodist Episcopal Church, African Methodist Episcopal Zion and African Baptist denominations became the cornerstones of the emerging new African community in America.

These African Churches spawned vital African institutions like African Free Schools, the first independent Black educational institutions, African Free Societies for charitable giving and Mutual Aid Societies, which became the seed for Black insurance companies and Black banks. As time passed, however, confusion developed about the identity of the sons and daughters of Africa in America. By the 1830's the designation "Colored" was more prevalent. The great political gatherings of leaders were called "Colored People's Conventions" and "Colored" was used widely in the writings/literature.

Perhaps, the gradual decline of "African" as a conscious identity was due to the interruption of the trans-Atlantic trade of enslaved Africans, which blocked the infusion of new members into the community with memories of Africa fresh on their minds or the rise in miscegenation, that diluted the purity of African stock thereby producing what some may have chosen to call "coloreds." No matter the origin of the confusion, the issue of identity or the quest for the appropriate designation for formerly enslaved and quasi-free people became a source of major debate and struggle.

Some might ask, what difference does it make? Why make such a fuss over what we call ourselves? It is interesting that most Euro-ethnics (as Rev. Herbert Daughtry of the House of the Lord Church in Brooklyn calls them) did not have to cope with this question. As Queen Mother Moore used to remind us, the people from Ireland who migrated to this country were clear that they were Irish. Similarly, Germans, Italians, Poles and Greeks identify with the land of their origin. Queen Mother Moore used to ask, "Where is colored, Negro or Black land?" Self-identification was not a problem for Euro-ethnics because they brought their culture to America in-tact. Unlike Africans, who were forbidden from speaking our native tongues, practicing our religion or playing our musical instruments, cultural continuity was the basis for Euro-ethnics to establish viable communities in America. Cultural continuity was the foundation for an internal economy and eventually the basis for amassing sufficient political power to become significant players in the American body-politic.

Identity matters. Malcolm X once said something to the effect that "of all the crimes committed against Africans by Europeans, the greatest crime was to take away our names." By that he meant "cultural aggression," the attempt to strip us of our original culture or as Queen Mother Moore would put it to "de-Africanize the African." Given this historical reality, Dr. Maulana Karenga has consistently taught that the "key crisis in Black life is the cultural crisis." Therefore, he argues that any ideology to address this crisis must provide "an identity, purpose and direction."

Dr. Karenga's criteria for an ideological corrective to cultural aggression are instructive. The quest for an appropriate identity is not just about a name or ethnic/national designation. It is about identifying with a source that provides a distinctive worldview, historical connection and cultural foundation that anchors a people and offers a sense of purpose and direction. This is precisely what Dr. Karenga achieved by innovating Kawaida, the Doctrine of Tradition and Reason, which articulates the Nguzo Saba, the Seven Principles of the Black Value System as a guide to Black life.

Notable African scholars have identified an overarching world view and traditional way of life that is shared by Africans of various nations and ethnicities on the continent. Whether one is an African Ibo, African Yoruba, Ashanti, Fanti, Jamaican, Haitian, Bajan or African in Europe, Canada or America, the embrace of African identity and attendant worldview, principles/values should be the foundation for the development of social, economic and political institutions and a force for the liberation of African people everywhere. As a counter to the "White" aesthetic and social domination, "Black" is an appropriate and necessary designation. However, it is insufficient inadequate in terms of linking/connecting us to an ancestral homeland, worldview, cultural commonality and history of achievement, tragedy and triumph that defines who we are as African people.

Forty years ago I wrote *A Pledge to African People* to be recited as a way of instilling and conveying the power of proclaiming "We Are an African People." Just as our forebears at the outset of our sojourn in America were clear about our African identity and used it to brand institutions that were vital to our survival and development, so we as Africans today must do likewise to create greater Pan African unity in our community as we strive to achieve liberation and righteous, global, African empowerment!

The Power of "Black Consciousness"

July, 2010

Spurred by what I perceive as a "state of emergency" in Black America, in recent weeks I have been offering prescriptions for what people of African descent can do to combat and overcome decades of benign and blatant neglect in America's "dark ghettos." The irony, even tragedy, is that this discussion is occurring despite the fact that there is a Black Family in the White House. As the old folks used to say, "we sure ain't what we wanna to be, sure ain't what we're gonna be but we sure ain't what we were." It was no accident that elders in the Black community held out such hope for the moment that Barack Hussein Obama would become the 44th President of the United States of America. As the words to the Black National Anthem attest, this moment has come at great cost and sacrifice. Unfortunately, the state of emergency which we have been describing clearly indicates that the stony road we've trod has yet to lead to the pinnacle of full freedom. There are still more rivers to cross before we reach social, economic and political equity/parity for dispossessed Black people in the "promised land."

And, we will not achieve this objective unless a critical mass among us unapologetically recommit to educating, organizing/mobilizing and empowering our people for the critical task ahead. "No one else will free us but us." Toward that end, we must heed the dictum of my long time friend/counselor/advisor Dr. James Turner to teach our people to "be of the race and for the race." The success of prior stages of the civil rights/human rights/Black liberation struggle has produced untold thousands, if not millions, of Black people in various positions of authority/influence/power and millions more who are living life better than anyone could have conceived a mere 50 years ago. The problem is that far too many of our folks are "of the race but not for the race." They suffer from historical amnesia, having lost touch with the trials, tribulations, triumphs that propelled them into a life of relative success. Far too many of our people identify themselves as African Americans, people of African descent or Black but have lost a sense of the power of Black consciousness: a substantive knowledge of our origins as a people, a positive embrace of color, culture and heritage and an unrelenting commitment to utilize our economic and political power to achieve and maintain full freedom for the totality of our community.

Throughout our history there have been creative explosions where awareness of self, culture/heritage and commitment to advance the race have flourished. The Harlem Renaissance in the 1920's was such a time; the era of the 60's was another. Much of what we take for granted today, including calling ourselves "Black" or "African," is directly attributable to the civil rights/human rights movements of the 60's, particularly the rise of Black Power, Nationalism and Pan Africanism. As it became increasingly clear that the "gains" of the civil rights movement in terms of passage of milestone legislation would not immediately cure the ills of America's dark ghettos, urban rebellions erupted across the country beginning with the insurrection in the Watts community of Los Angeles. Other major cities exploded thereafter. In an effort to provide an analysis for the lack of progress in eradicating the conditions in the urban inner-cities, frontline activists/organizers from the Student Non-Violent Coordinating Committee (SNCC) advanced the concept of Black Power. On the face of it, this concept suggested that marches, moral appeal and legislation would be insufficient to achieve liberation for the masses of Black people; what was needed was the acquisition of power to advance the interests and aspirations of Black people. Black Power became the battle cry encapsulating a range of demands from equity/parity in the American system through Black control of majority Black neighborhoods and cities, revolutionary transformation to separation and the establishment of an independent Black nation.

Most importantly, Black people (previously referred to and answering to Negro and Colored) rediscovered the power of Black consciousness. People began to reaffirm their African origins, donned dashikis and other forms of traditional African dress, cast aside straightening combs and curling irons, konkoline and Murray's hair grease to go "natural." The "Afro" and African braids became symbols of resistance to Euro-centric standards of beauty and an affirmation of "Black is Beautiful." Black was not fad or fashion, it was a political statement expressing the determination of a people to have what Dr. Maulana Karenga called "identity, purpose and direction." Black was beautiful and powerful.

Emanating from the call to Black Power, the Black consciousness movement spawned an incredible array of movements, associations, organizations and caucuses within majority organizations and institutions—the Black arts and culture movement; Black education movement which included the Black studies movement in higher education and independent education movement in elementary, secondary and higher education; creation of parallel professional organizations like the African Heritage Studies Association, National Conference of Black Lawyers, National Black Police Association, National Black Officers in Law Enforcement, National Associations of Black Social Workers, Sociologists, Psychologists, Psychiatrists,

Nurses, Architects, Engineers; Black worker/labor organizations like the Coalition of Black Trade Unionists and Revolutionary Workers Movements in Detroit and elsewhere; Black elected official organizations like the National Conference of Black Mayors, National Conference of Black State Legislators, National Black Caucus of Local Elected Officials and of course the Congressional Black Caucus. Federal government workers formed Blacks in Government (BIG). And, virtually every predominantly White Church/faith denomination had a Black Caucus. Indeed, Black caucuses within predominantly White institutions became the order of the day.

Trace the history of almost any of these "Black" organizations or caucuses and you will most likely find that they originated in the era of the 60's. What they had in common was a determination to root out racism as a deterrent to Black progress in their respective areas or institutions and a passion to pursue strategies utilizing group awareness, culture and pride as a basis for demanding improvement in the quality of life for Black people. That focus is missing today. Even though we call ourselves "Black" or "African" and have organizations, agencies and institutions that are similarly identified, the power of Black consciousness is largely absent. While most of these organizations are still on the case fighting for Black people, the fire, passion and militancy have been muted. Saying it loud, "I'm Black and I'm proud" has lost its popularity and power.

Perhaps it was inevitable that the power of Black consciousness would be diluted by popular culture and its vital élan sapped by the successes it produced for a sizeable minority of Black people. In addition, the idea of Blacks preserving a distinct community came under withering attack as "separatist" and un-American by the forces of reaction on the right. Concepts like

minority, people of color and diversity gained greater popularity because they appeared to be more inclusive and palatable. We heard less and less of Black people demanding that issues disproportionately affecting Blacks be addressed with policies targeted to the Black community. And, under the leadership of Dr. Benjamin F. Chavis, organizations like the NAACP even considered broadening their membership and concerns to include all people of color. Indeed, this troubling notion has been revived by Benjamin Todd Jealous, the current President/CEO of the NAACP.

Let me be clear that there is nothing wrong with people of African descent identifying with the oppression of other people and joining in coalitions and alliances to promote social justice and social change. In fact, Black people have generally been in the forefront of advocating for others, especially when they have lacked a voice to effectively advocate for themselves. It is for that reason that we have often been seen as the "conscious of the nation." At a personal level, I could not have served as Executive Director of the National Rainbow Coalition, Deputy Campaign Manager for Rev. Jesse Jackson's 1988 presidential campaign or Executive Director of the Center for Constitutional Rights if I did not believe in building coalitions with other oppressed people and people of goodwill. I have always been equally clear, however, that the willingness to forge coalitions does not obscure the fact that the American body politic remains a pluralistic, highly competitive system where constituency-based organizations and racial/ethnic groups identify their interests and organize to protect and promote their aspirations. Even multi-racial organizations like the NAACP and National Urban League were founded to improve the plight of a particular group—Black people.

It is entirely appropriate, even necessary, for dispossessed groups to organize their constituents to advance their interests. Last time I checked, La Raza, the League of United Latin American Citizens

(LULAC), the Asian American Legal Defense and Education Fund, American Indian Movement or American Arab Anti-Discrimination Committee are not contemplating broadening their membership and focus to include people of African descent. They are open to bi-lateral or inter-organizational relations to devise common strategies to overcome common problems. That was why the National Rainbow Coalition, as originally conceived, could have been such a powerful vehicle. However, even though most of these groups were affiliated with the Rainbow Coalition, they maintained their organizations as the primary instrument for advancing the aspirations of their base constituency.

People of African descent, Black people, should not be confused: "Charity begins at home and spreads abroad." It is perfectly okay to "love thy neighbor as thyself." The state of emergency facing millions of Black people dictates that we rediscover the power of Black consciousness, not because we are opposed to any other group but because our salvation lies in "cherishing a friendly union with ourselves." It must be "in-group identification for out-group association." We must re-instill the concept of unapologetically and uncompromisingly identifying and promoting Black interests—that which is important, advantageous, useful/helpful and essential to the survival, development and prosperity of the masses of Black people. In a pluralistic political environment where groups and constituencies are contending to advance their agenda, Africans in America had better be prepared to compete or perish. Some of us will make it, but unless we organize our collective power, millions of our sisters and brothers in distressed communities will be condemned to struggle for survival as abandoned people in the Promised Land.

We've come too far as a people to permit such a calamity to happen. What is required at this critical moment are organizations committed to restoring the power of Black consciousness in the Black community; organizations which will consistently educate and challenge our people to be "of the race and for the race" no matter what their profession, position or standing in society; organizations that will remind us of the ever present need to identify/define promote and protect Black interests as a matter of principle and first priority; organizations that will work to build the kind of unity in the community that will enable us to use our collective power to cross the final rivers to full freedom in the Promised Land. To that end, it is my fervent hope that the Institute of the Black World 21stCentury will play a leading role in facilitating the resurgence of the power of Black consciousness in Black America ... and the Pan African world!

Back in the Day: When Black "Hair" Had Meaning

November, 2009

Chris Rock's documentary film *Hair*, which explores the meaning of "good hair" among Black people, especially women, has sparked a good deal of controversy. It may have also opened up old wounds about the Black aesthetic and the definition of beauty in Black America. The controversy is rooted in the historical quest of Africans in American to define and affirm our identity in the face of the legacy of enslavement, cultural aggression and forced miscegenation in a hostile, racist society. In that regard, the internalization of the White to Black superiority to inferiority continuum has had serious consequences within the Black community. The colloquial expression "if you're White, you're alright, Yellow mellow, Brown stick around and Black get back" captured the popular understanding of how the Black/White continuum operates. Historically, if you were "light, bright and damn near white," you might be treated better than darker brothers and sisters or better yet, maybe you could "passant blanc," pass for White. There was a widespread belief in the Black community that whiteness equaled success. Some within the community were so obsessed with lightening up the race that they would forbid their sons or daughters to date a dark-skinned person— "marrying up" meant hitching your dreams for success to a lighter-skinned member of the race.

African features, those characteristics that distinguish Blacks from Euro-ethnics and other racial/ethnic groups, were considered "ugly." The dark skin, thick lips, broad nose and yes, that "nappy" hair were considered badges of inferiority! This generation may be unaware that there was a time when brothers routinely "konked" their hair, utilizing a harsh, lye-based formula to get those naps out, to straighten and wave one's coiffure to look more like Dean Martin or Tony Curtis. One of the more memorable passages in *The Autobiography of Malcolm X* is when he recounts plunging his head into the toilet to quench the burning sensation of the konkolene on his scalp. In those days Brothers proudly strutted the streets with Do Rags adorning their heads to restrain the restless, konkolene straightened naps.

For women, ever since the era of Madame C.J. Walker, the straightening comb and curling iron were the tools to tame that nappy head. And, then there were the "bleaching crèmes" to wash away the blackness, that dark complexion blocking access to the upper rungs of Black society and the White world. Nadinola Bleaching Cream was a hot commodity in the "beauty" products section of stores in my day. Indeed, I can recall lying awake with sweat rolling off my face from an abundant application of Nadinola! I never Konked my hair; I was afraid of the fire. But Murray's Hair grease coupled with hundreds of strokes with a stiff brush to wave the naps was my attempted escape from the "curse of blackness." For men and women, "good hair" and "good looks" were defined by a European/White aesthetic or standard of beauty.

Back in the day, however, in the era of Black Power and Black Consciousness, hair became a symbol of protest against the long-standing internalized acceptance of a Eurocentric aesthetic/standard of beauty, and an affirmation of African culture and beauty. With the emergence of Black Power came an emphatic rejection of European culture as that which Black people should emulate and a renewed search for identity by connecting with our African homeland. "Black is Beautiful" became a virtual battle cry, a call to arms for a people who were calling themselves Negroes and Colored, to proclaim that "Black" would not "get back." The sons and daughters of Africa, Black people, were determined to rediscover and identify with a rich culture, history and heritage. Going "natural," embracing one's features, including "kinky" hair, became a badge of defiance of European/ White culture and a fervent embrace of all things African. In Harlem, the Capital of Black America, Brother Elombe Brath helped to set the trend by sponsoring African fashion shows where models dressed in African garments and wore their hair "natural" or in "Afros." The idea spread like wild fire across Black America. The Afro, Dashiki and African garb became political symbols of a newfound Black identify.

This was an era when hair had meaning. For a time, hair became a political symbol. Brothers would routinely harangue sisters, demanding that they throw away their straightening combs, go natural and stop "looking White." Especially for sisters going natural was a political decision, requiring the conversion from a Eurocentric definition of beauty to an African-centered aesthetic/standard of beauty. In an interesting reversal, I can remember very light-skinned sisters with naturally straight hair, (some who could have passant blanc), feverishly working to tease their hair so they could have an Afro! Suddenly to be Black was beautiful and the "in" thing to be. Even James Brown cleansed his hair of Konkolene, grew an Afro and pinned a song, *"I'm Black and I'm Proud."*

The embrace of an African-centered aesthetic/standard of beauty led to an acceptance of various ways Black people could wear their hair. Though braiding had been common place in Black communities for generations, now this aesthetic form took on new meaning as a symbol of identity and pride. Extensions and dread locks also became part of a range of acceptable African-centered expressions of "good hair."

Like most things that begin as symbols, however, Afros, braids, extensions and dread locks became more fad, fashion and style than political statement. Indeed, activists and organizers watched in amazement when some brothers abruptly abandoned their Afros and adopted the long, straight-haired Superfly look made popular by the character played by Ron O'Neal in one of the early Black exploitation films. James Brown, Mr. Black and I'm Proud, was one of the first to drop the Afro for the "new" style. These shocking retrogressions precipitated questions about the real content/substance of "Blackness."

At the end of the day people came to realize that you could have leaders like Mobutu, in the Congo, who Africanized titles and symbols of the nation but was a total stooge and a corrupt, self-serving puppet of the West. There were also "leaders" in the U.S. who wore African garb and had super sized Afros but were agent provocateurs, informants or just plain sell-outs. On the other hand, there were leaders, women and men, who may not have worn Afros and Dashikis but were seriously dedicated to the liberation of Black people. The lesson learned was/is that while African-centered appearance may be preferable, the content of one's politics and commitment to the people is ultimately what matters.

Chris Rock's film is useful because it provides an opportunity to reexamine the extent to which the Black community has reverted to an unconscious acceptance of a White/Eurocentric definition of "good" hair and beauty. A positive sense of self is still an important ingredient in the struggle for Black advancement, particularly among today's youth/young people. What I can say with confidence is that the struggles waged decades ago were instrumental in opening up the range of choices Black people now enjoy in terms of hairstyles. By and large, no one blinks anymore if you show up on the job with an

Afro, braids, extensions or dreads. That was not the case in the era of the 60's. So, when you look in the mirror sisters and brothers and choose your hair style for the day, that freedom is a direct result of the Black Power, Black Consciousness, Black is Beautiful movements back in the day!

"Let Us Cherish a Friendly Union with Ourselves"

July, 2010

During the Fourth of July holiday season, I generally write something to remind Black people of the remarkable life and legacy of Frederick Douglass, particularly his great oratorical gifts and steadfast spirit of resistance as reflected in his *"What is your Fourth of July to me?"* speech delivered in Rochester, New York in 1852. Douglass' fearless leadership was a critical force as an oppressed people struggled to forge a new African community in the U.S. But, this year as I reflected on the plight of Africans in America and the state of disorganization and disarray I discussed in a recent article, I elected to focus on the words of Rev. David Nickens, a lesser known 19th century abolitionist/freedom fighter from Cincinnati, Ohio. Assessing the status/condition of approximately three and a half million enslaved and a half million quasi-free Africans prior to the Civil War, Nickens saw the need for Black people to affirm our identity, create bonds of unity and build strong structures/institutions to achieve full freedom. Hence, in a speech delivered July 5, 1832 in Chillicothe, Ohio (which was strikingly similar to Douglass' famous oration), he said, "Let us cherish a friendly union with ourselves." Nickens was not suggesting that Blacks isolate themselves from other races; he recognized the importance of internal organization, collaboration and joint effort to the process of liberation.

After decades of involvement with several national organizations and movements, along with a dedicated core of longtime friends and activists, for the past few years I have devoted my energies to building the Institute of the Black World 21st Century as a mechanism that can facilitate Africans in America (and the world) cherishing a "friendly union with ourselves." This is never an easy proposition for an oppressed people because there is a tendency to internalize one's oppression, leading to distrust, disorientation and disorganization. Moreover, the oppressor is obviously not eager to see the oppressed unified and therefore will use every possible means to sow seeds of dissension and disunity. The process of building unity in the newly emerging African community in the U.S. was particularly difficult due to the devastating consequences of cultural aggression/alienation and ruthless dehumanization under the British-American form of chattel slavery. Africans in America have had to build a new community from disparate ethnic groups against incredible odds. The struggle has been uneven, but without a doubt we have successfully bent the arch of history decisively toward total liberation. From being enshrined in the Constitution of the U.S. as 3/5 of a human being to having an African American in the White House is phenomenal progress.

And yet, large numbers of our people are still not free from the affects of racial oppression and economic degradation in American society. Therefore, we must find a way to finish the course. The formula for success in that regard is still the same as it was in the difficult times in which Rev. David Nickens lived; in the face of a state of emergency for the masses of Black poor and working people and large numbers of our young people, we must strengthen our internal capacity to fight the battles necessary to win full freedom. This will require a focus on collaboration, cooperation, operational unity and joint work among leaders, organizations, agencies and institutions at all levels.

As I traveled around the country some years ago, I was struck by the fact that in every community I visited, local organizations and leaders described the persistence of various forms of racial oppression and lamented the lack of a "movement" to overcome these conditions. However, in each of these communities, there were movements and organizations engaged in struggles to combat police brutality, the prison-jail industrial complex, educational inequities, environmental racism, etc. The problem was that the organizations and leaders engaged in these struggles from different locales had no awareness of each other. There were movements and struggles in motion in communities throughout Black America, but they were disconnected.

By and large the same condition prevails today. It is not true that we do not have a "movement," it is simply that the movements we have are not connected or in conversation with each other.

To cross the finish line to full freedom, it will simply not be enough to have a multiplicity of leaders and organizations. Black organizations and leaders must be effectively connected in order to maximize our collective power. Not only must collaboration, cooperation and operational unity become a habit, we need to focus on specialization and division of labor. For instance, rather than have scores of national organizations engaged in conducting voter registration, education and get out the vote campaigns and duplicating efforts, why can't we agree on three or four taking on that task and the rest of the organizations and leaders supporting our *national voter mobilization team*. Equally important, we must strenuously strive to connect leaders and organizations doing work in various issue areas, e.g., housing, education, police brutality, criminal justice reform, etc. The environmental justice movement is an excellent example of how leaders and organizations should collaborate and do joint work. They have demonstrated that this kind of collaboration is possible.

Some years ago, under the leadership of the late Damu Smith, the National Black Environmental Justice Network (NBEJN) was formed as an umbrella structure to function as a resource center for the environmental justice movement. Scholars, activists, policy analysts and community-based advocates from various locales were connected via NBEJN, thereby creating an effective force to challenge environmental racism anywhere in the country.

As I intimated in a previous article, we urgently need this same kind of collaboration and joint work among our major civil rights/human rights, political, labor and faith leaders in Black America. Indeed, if leaders and organizations at the local level witness national leaders and organizations collaborating on the implementation of an agenda to cope with and overcome the state of emergency afflicting distressed communities, it might encourage/inspire them to act accordingly. Failing this, however, action may have to come from the bottom up through grassroots leaders emulating the organizing process of the environmental justice movement referenced above.

From my perspective, what is absolutely essential is the need for Africans in American to seize this moment of crisis to look inward and connect, network, link-up, collaborate, mobilize/organize the capacity to overcome the state of emergency which is stalling our quest to achieve full freedom—not just for the few but for the vast majority still imprisoned in America's "dark ghettos." It's time to "cherish a friendly union with ourselves." We certainly envision the Institute of the Black World 21st Century playing a vital role in facilitating this process.

Remembering Malcolm: On the Utility of Black Nationalism

May, 2009

El Hajj Malik El Shabazz, Malcolm X, was one of the most fierce and foremost leaders in the history of Africans in America. In the era of the 60s, there is no question that Martin Luther King and Malcolm X, two religious leaders from different faiths and political persuasions, were the towering figures of the time. King was a Christian Minister from the integrationist and radical democratic political lineage of Frederick Douglass, Ida B. Wells, Paul Robeson and W.E.B. DuBois. Malcolm was a Muslim from the Black Nationalist lineage of Martin R. Delaney, Bishop Henry McNeil Turner, Marcus Garvey, Queen Mother Moore and the Honorable Elijah Muhammad.

Though both lineages have contributed substantially to the Black Freedom Struggle, Black Nationalism is often relegated to the margins as a fringe ideology. However, it is worth noting that "Garvey and Garveyism" produced the largest mass movement among Blacks in the history of this nation. It is also noteworthy that the largest demonstration in the history of the U.S., the Million Man March in 1995, was organized by the Honorable Minister Louis Farrakhan, leader of the Nation of Islam. While public intellectuals like Dr. Cornel West have frequently disparaged nationalism as counter-productive, I would argue that Black Nationalism has been and remains an essential/indispensable element in the formula for the survival and development of Africans in America.

At its most basic level, nationalism is simply a call for group unity/solidarity. Nations or groups who are oppressed, disunited or in decline may recall the glories of their history and culture as a means of creating the consciousness and solidarity necessary to revive, resurrect, restore or rebuild the nation or group. Hence, Garibaldi harkened back to the glory days of ancient Rome. In America, as Malcolm put it, "we didn't land on Plymouth Rock, Plymouth Rock landed on us."

Malcolm also said: "of all the crimes committed by Europeans against Africans, the greatest crime was to take our names." This is a profound insight because it addresses the devastating impact of cultural aggression on enslaved Africans. Black people from different/distinct African ethnic groups/nations were captured by Europeans, forbidden to practice our native religions, speak our languages, play African musical instruments and taught that our color was a mark of degradation and inferiority. The slave masters attempted to de-Africanize and dehumanize enslaved Africans as part of a process of pacification and control. The goal was to produce a "docile Negro" who would never unite to resist or rebel against enslavement.

Little wonder that the few Blacks who were freed from slavery searched the Bible and the pages of history to discover the legacy of their forebears prior to the holocaust of enslavement. The glory of ancient Egypt, Ethiopia and the great Sudanic Kingdoms of Ghana, Mali and Songhai gave the likes of Richard Allen, Absalom Jones, David Walker, Henry Highland Garnet, Alexander Crummell, Martin R. Delaney and countless other early community-builders the sense that Africans had a heritage/legacy that made them somebody! Armed with the inspiration of these insights, quasi-free Blacks began the awesome task of demanding the abolition of slavery and building and sustaining Black institutions as part of a new African community in the U.S. In the face of the damage done by cultural aggression, an appeal to racial pride and solidarity was essential to the community-building process.

Historically, however, there has always been a tension between those leaders/constituents who preferred to utilize racial solidarity to pursue incorporation/integration into the American body politic as equal citizens as the primary goal of the Black Freedom Struggle versus those who saw the latter option as one possibility in the quest for self-determination. Black Nationalists have always advocated racial solidarity and the maintenance of Black institutions as integral to achieving the goal of self-determination whether that translates into a solidified Black community with full rights inside America, an independent Black nation or repatriation to Africa. Skeptical that the oppressor will ever come to respect and treat the formerly oppressed as equals, Black Nationalists have generally had an oppositional posture towards the American government. Self-determination has been the primary goal.

Without question, Malcolm X was the most influential apostle of Black Nationalism in the latter half of the 20th century. His ideas had great impact on the architects and advocates of the Black Consciousness, Black Power and Pan Africanist movements which eclipsed the integrationist tendency within the Black Freedom struggle in the 70s and 80s. In his classic 1964 speech *Ballots or Bullets*, Malcolm articulates three basic tenets of Black Nationalism: "The political philosophy of black nationalism means that the black man should control the politics and politicians in his own community.... The economic philosophy of black nationalism...only means that we should control the economy of our community....The social philosophy of black nationalism only means that we have to get together and remove the evils, vices, alcoholism, drug addiction, and other evils that are destroying the moral fabric of our community."

In Malcolm's view the purpose of racial solidarity was to build internal capacity/power for self-development—to enhance the social, economic and political well being of Black people. As to our relation to the government, Black people must identify and pursue their own interests and amass the power to compel America to do the right thing. Failing that, Black people were not duty bound to hold allegiance to or remain second-class citizens in a racist nation. The goal was/is "freedom by any means necessary."

As a manifestation of Black Nationalism, the call to Black Power generated a renewed interest in reconnecting with our African roots and working for Pan Africanism, the global solidarity of African people everywhere. It was the call to Black Power that led to the formation of Black caucuses in virtually every predominantly White institution in America or the creation of parallel organizations, e.g., the Congressional Black Caucus, National Conference of Black State Legislators, African Heritage Studies Association, Coalition of Black Trade Unionists, National Association of Black Psychologists, National Association of Black Social Workers and Black caucuses within virtually every major religious denomination. Today we take these Black formations for granted without recognizing their Black Nationalist roots.

As we celebrate the Kuzaliwa/birthday of our "Black Shining Prince," it is important to reaffirm the value of utilizing racial consciousness and solidarity to promote Black interests and aspirations. The persistent disparities between Blacks and Whites in employment, income, wealth, health, education and housing strongly suggest that we still lack sufficient control over the politics, economics and social life of our communities. Notwithstanding the election of the first Black President, structural racism is alive and well in America. Therefore, in the face of the myth of a post-racial and post-racist society, our nationalist impulse must be to maintain an oppositional posture to so called "race neutral" or "colorblind" policy prescriptions that fail to specifically address the crises afflicting Black people. Accordingly, we must unapologetically be "of the race and for the race" in militantly advocating that the full measure of freedom for Africans in America is not privileges for the few but equity and parity for the masses of Black working class and poor people. Indeed, our revolutionary nationalist impulse must be "freedom for everybody or freedom for nobody." As we remember Malcolm, let us be clear that Black Nationalism, racial solidarity for liberation and self-determination, is still the order of the day for Africans in America!

Cultural Offensive Required to Rescue Black America's Youth January, 2009

In my most recent article, I called for an Emergency Summit on Youth Violence and Fratricide to address this malignant plague in Black America. It is important to note that not every young Black person is engaged in or affected by the destructive behavior unfolding in marginalized Black communities across the country. Indeed, millions of Black youth and students are doing just fine, staying out of trouble, graduating from high schools and colleges and making their way into the mainstream of life in the Black community and the larger society. It is a minority of Black youth/students/young people largely in marginalized Black communities, who have lost their way in a nation where structural-institutional racism and oppression kill the dreams and aspirations of human beings. Make no mistake about it, however, there is no hiding place from the cancer decimating marginalized Black communities. In one way or another, Blacks who have escaped America's "dark ghettos" as well as members of other ethnicities and nationalities will ultimately pay the price for the shameful abandonment and neglect of those locked out and left out in this nation.

As I suggested in my previous article, both external and internal prescriptions will be necessary to heal marginalized communities and the youth/young people struggling to survive within them. But the kind of destructive behavior that has become common place and accepted by many of our youth will require something more than ordinary anti-violence programs, education and jobs. What we are witnessing is the consequence of a loss of "historical memory" of who we are as people of African descent and the legacy of trials, tribulations and triumphs of mothers, fathers, grandmothers, grandfathers, our forebears. Fannie Lou Hamer once said: "Always remember where we came from and honor the bridges that brought us over."

Far too many Blacks in this generation, adults and youth, have only a faint recollection of the history and culture of African people, the legacy of struggle and resistance, values, customs and traditions— "the bridges that brought us over." While the impact of institutional/structural racism on our people cannot be denied, its most insidious affect has been robbing our people of a positive/affirmative sense of self and kind. We can readily dismiss and destroy each other because we have internalized the racist premise that to be Black is less than human. People who look like us are nothing!

Dr. Maulana Karenga, the creator of the Nguzo Saba and Kwanzaa and one of the seminal thinkers of our time has repeatedly warned/admonished us that the "key crisis in Black life is the cultural crisis." If we are unaware of or refuse to embrace our own culture, the "stuff that makes a people stick," as I often teach it, our people will forever be disoriented, disorganized and potentially self-destructive. Heeding Dr. Karenga's proposition, I am convinced that any strategy, program or initiative to combat the epidemic of youth violence and fratricide must include a healthy dose of Black history and culture as a corrective. Nothing short of what my friend Dr. Ramona Edelin has called a "Cultural Offensive" is required to rescue America's endangered Black youth.

While other methods of encouraging Black youth to stop the violence and aspire to "be somebody" might work, a Cultural Offensive will have the affect of instilling a sense of love for self, family and the need to be "of the race and for the race." We want to stop the violence and fratricide by having those who are currently caught in the grips of pathology, negativism and nihilism embrace themselves as positive, proud and productive members of the African family. Indeed, in the face of the myth of a "post racial society," all of Black America could reap positive benefits from a Cultural Offensive.

At the center/core of the Cultural Offensive must be African-centered education. We must know and our children/young people must know the history of who we are as the first human beings on this planet and the source of life and civilizing influences for all of humankind. Our young people must know about the holocaust of enslavement and the heroic resistance against our captors. They must know about the de-Africanization and dehumanization of our people under America's system of chattel slavery. They must be made aware of the amazing resistance of heroes and sheroes who rebelled against enslavement. They must hear the stories of a people who made a way out of no way to create new African communities out of disparate ethnicities in the face of apartheid, violence, lynching and police occupation/terror. They need to hear the voices of the Elders in their families rendering testimonies and giving oral histories about how we survived and made it over!

We are in a struggle for the minds, hearts and souls of endangered youth/young people in marginalized and abandoned Black communities across this country. Therefore, to be effective, the Cultural Offensive must be adopted by the broadest array of institutions and organizations in our communities—churches, fraternities, sororities, business and professional associations, community-based organizations, community centers—all segments of Black America must be engaged in this Offensive. We need to fight to have African-centered courses be part of the curriculum in every school where Black students are a majority or sizeable minority. Simultaneously, we must encourage churches and community centers to have after-school and Saturday school programs where African-centered instruction is integral to the teaching of reading, math and science. I would also like to see substantial engagement by the cultural artistic community. Perhaps, Wyclef Jean and Quincy Jones hook-up to do a "We Are the World" type stop the violence, save the youth rendition. The Cultural Offensive must be inclusive, comprehensive and relentless. Failure is not an option.

By now some of my readers are saying none of this is new. That's correct. It has all been said before. What I have elected to do at a moment of accentuated crisis is to urgently restate prescriptions and remedies which are all too familiar. The problem is not what we know will work to overcome the crisis. It is whether we have the resolve to act on what we know. We must act now or watch a significant segment of this generation's young people perish. Our ancestors will not be pleased!

SECTION III

Resistance and Calls
to Action

In the Spirit of Frederick Douglass: The Struggle Continues

July, 2009

The nation has just completed commemorating its most hallowed holiday, July fourth/Independence Day. Whenever this holiday comes around, I am always reminded of Frederick Douglass' famous oration in Rochester, New York in 1852 in which he asked "What to the American slave is your Fourth of July?" Douglass incisively and eloquently catalogued the injustices against people of African descent. One suspects that his goal was not only to condemn the hypocrisy of a wayward nation but to caution Blacks not to get caught up in the pomp and circumstance of America's holidays when the struggle for freedom was far from complete.

It is for that reason that the Institute of the Black World 21st Century generally sponsors a Forum during the Independence Day celebration entitled "Black Patriotism Is Resistance." The status of Africans in America has certainly dramatically changed since Douglass' brilliant and heartfelt denunciation of America in 1852, not the least of which is the election of the first Black President. However, there are important reasons why Black people should forever preserve the spirit of vigilance and resistance Douglass exemplified as an integral part of our character as a people.

First we must always remember/recall the blood, toil and tears, the struggle that enabled us to survive, resist enslavement and break down the walls of apartheid despite incredible odds. We have struggled to build a new African community out of the disparate ethnic groups, e.g., Ibo, Fulani, Housa, Yoruba, who were captured and transported to these hostile shores.

In the face of slavery, discrimination and segregation, visionary quasi-free African leaders like Richard Allen, Absolom Jones, Prince Hall, Samuel Cornish and John B. Russwurm created independent Black institutions like the Black Church, African Free Schools, Mutual Aid Societies, Black newspapers and fraternal organizations to enhance the capacity of the emerging African community to survive. In addition, David Walker, Henry Highland Garnet, Martin R. Delaney and Frederick Douglass relentlessly argued against and mobilized to liberate their sisters and brothers from enslavement. Blacks held Political Conventions to discuss strategy, tactics and an agenda for the Black Freedom movement, created their own abolitionist organizations and utilized the embryonic Black press to educate, agitate and organize. As Vincent Harding documents in his extraordinary book *There Is a River*, a stream of community-development, protest and resistance flows unbroken through the history of Africans in America. This legacy must always be part of our collective consciousness/memory if we are to finish the course.

And, finish the course we must. This is the second reason why it is important to keep the fire of Douglass burning in our bosoms; we are not yet free. Internally we have been working to build a new African community, but that task is incomplete. Leaders from Garvey, DuBois, Honorable Elijah Muhammad, to Malcolm and Martin have challenged us to harness our human and material resources for self-development. DuBois articulated the need for an internal, Black economy and Malcolm urged us to "control the politics, economics and social life" of our community. There is a Black man who controls the White House, but it can hardly be said that African Americans have sufficient control of the Black community, or that we have gained equity/parity with our White counterparts in terms of income and wealth. We must continue to invoke the memories of our ancestors until this task is done.

And, just as the leaders of Douglass' day utilized agitation and protest to promote and defend the interests of Black people, we must use the tools at our disposal today, marching on ballot boxes, lobbying, marches/demonstrations, economic sanctions/boycotts ... to confront the structures of white supremacy that still constrain the aspirations of our people. We must not be lulled into apathy and inaction because there's a "brother" in the White House. The fact that Indira Gandhi and Benazir Bhutto became Prime Ministers of India and Pakistan respectively did not end the unequal status for the masses of women in these developing nations. Women in these countries are still fighting for their rightful place in the sun and no doubt will continue to do so until that goal is achieved. The words of Douglass from another famous speech are instructive in this regard: "Power concedes nothing without demand. It never has and it never will." We must continue the struggle until we have achieved full socio-economic equity/parity in this land—anything less than that would be a betrayal of the struggle of our ancestors.

Finally, there is an even greater mission which Douglass' Fourth of July oration calls us to assume. We must be the conscience of this country, speaking truth to power and articulating a vision of a new society devoid of greed, corruption, hypocrisy and extremes of wealth and poverty. This was Martin Luther King's wish when he called for a "radical revolution of values" that would transform America from a "thing oriented society to a person oriented society." He went on to say that "true compassion is more than flinging a coin at a beggar, it comes to see that the edifice which produces beggars needs restructuring." Our work will not be done until we have helped to create a more just and humane society with true "liberty and justice for all."

Commemorating Frederick Douglass Day

July, 2018

Many Americans have just concluded "celebrating" a protracted July 4th, Independence Day holiday. It is a time for vacationing, picnicking, family cook-outs, parades, fireworks and lots of flag-waving during perhaps the most "patriotic" season of the year. As an African in America, when I think about the Fourth of July it conjures up the memory and spirit of Frederick Douglass' iconic oration at a gathering in Rochester, New York in 1852. Douglass was a true believer in the prospects of America but knew full well that this promise could not be fulfilled unless and until the hypocrisy of the Declaration of Independence and Constitution as it pertained to enslaved Africans was resolved. Therefore, the Fourth of July was irrelevant to Africans in America. Referring to enslaved Africans in his oration Douglass proclaimed: "To him, your celebration is a sham: your boasted liberty an unholy license, your national greatness swelling vanity; your sounds of rejoicing are empty and heartless."

Unless and until Africans in America and other oppressed people have achieved full freedom, dignity and equality, there should always be a parallel Frederick Douglass Day Commemoration during the Fourth of July holiday. For example, the spirit of Douglass would challenge us to proclaim, what does your Fourth of July mean to immigrants entering this country seeking refuge from violence whose children are being taken from them by agents of the U.S. Government? What does it mean when vicious assaults by Neo-Nazis, white supremacists and anti-Semites on peaceful demonstrators is condoned because there are currently white nationalists who are Advisors to the "Orange Man?" What does it mean when young Black men and women continue to be executed by the police with impunity and athletes who kneel during the National Anthem to protest the slaughter are viciously attacked by the present "Resident" of the White House? What does it mean when voter suppression is rampant and the rights of women, LGBTQ, workers and the poor are under assault in the name of "making America Great Again?"

Under these circumstances, the words of Douglass still ring true: "Your shouts of liberty and equality (are) hollow mockery; Your prayers and hymns, your sermons and thanksgivings, with all your religious parade and solemnity, are... mere bombast, fraud, deception, impiety and hypocrisy—a thin veil to cover crimes which would disgrace a nation of savages."

Unless and until Africans in America and other oppressed people have been liberated from these "intolerable acts" by vile personages and exploitative institutions and systems, the "Fourth of July" should actually be Frederick Douglass Day; a day dedicated to reflecting on the true meaning of political and economic democracy and "liberty and justice for all;" a day dedicated to eradicating tyranny and tyrants; a day when the progressive forces of resistance and transformation heed the admonition of Douglass: "Find out just what any people will quietly submit to and you have found out the exact measure of injustice and wrong which will be imposed upon them, and these will continue till they are resisted with either words or blows, or with both. The limits of tyrants are prescribed by the endurance of those whom they oppress." Frederick Douglass Day should be an annual time for reflection, resistance and transformation!

Time for an Emergency Summit on Youth Violence and Fratricide

October 5, 2009

The video of the brutal murder of Derrion Albert, a teenage honor student in Chicago, by other teenagers sent shock waves across the nation. How is it that a group of young people could batter and stomp one of their peers to death in the midst of a throng of teenagers? In the past several years, Chicago has emerged as the capital of student murders. But, Chicago is not the only city in Black America plagued by student murders, youth violence and fratricide. As I pen this article, young Kevin Miller was just shot in the face and killed in Cambria Heights, Queens, New York, an innocent bystander of an after school brawl that erupted among students. Chicago may lead the nation in student murders, but the phenomenon of youth fratricide is a problem in virtually every locale and region of the country. It is an epidemic that has been afflicting Black communities for years (which is periodically highlighted by the widely publicized murders of young people like Derrion Albert).

Black America has been silent about this crisis for far too long. As we approach the 14thAnniversary of the Million Man March, I believe it's time for an Emergency Summit to address the crisis of youth violence and fratricide in Black communities across the country. On the eve of the 10th Anniversary of the Million Man March and launch of the Millions More Movement, the Honorable Minister Louis Farrakhan and Leonard Dunston, President Emeritus of the National Association of Black Social Workers, convened a Black Family Summit of national organizations to discuss issues affecting Black families, including Black youth. The Black Family Summit has continued under the auspices of the Institute of the Black World 21st Century—which recently sponsored a highly successful Forum on *"Life in Post Racial America"* at the Congressional Black Caucus Annual Legislative Conference in Washington, D.C. Perhaps, Minister Farrakhan and Brother Dunston should team up again to convene the Emergency Summit on Youth Violence and Fratricide.

No matter who the sponsors may be, it is imperative that a Summit be convened as soon as possible. It is critical that leaders, organizations, agencies, community-based advocates, policy experts and elected officials come together to provide an analysis of the crisis and prescribe an agenda for action. That agenda must include actions the government should take and those programs and initiatives that should be undertaken internal to our communities. In addition, we must garner the courage to demand that corporate America reinvest in marginalized Black communities. Billions of Black dollars buttress the bottom line of corporate America. We must demand a fair return for our dollars. What is absolutely certain is that inaction is not an option. There must be a concerted, coordinated and sustained campaign to eradicate this destructive plague from our communities.

From my vantage point, the root cause of the crisis is clear. It is the bitter harvest of decades of neglect and abandonment of impoverished urban and rural Black communities in this country, resulting from structural-institutional racism. Indeed, a few years ago, the Institute of the Black World called for a *Martin Luther King-Malcolm X Community Revitalization Initiative,* a massive "Domestic Marshall Plan" type program to holistically address the myriad maladies afflicting marginalized Black communities. In calling for the MLK-MX

Initiative, we offered the following perspective: "Many urban inner-city areas are like zones of desolation and despair, plagued by chronic unemployment, under-employment, poverty, inadequate health facilities, environmental degradation, poor performing schools, the infestation of drugs, crime, gangs, the illicit economy, fear, police occupation and terror—all feeding a prison-jail industrial complex where Black and Brown people are the primary fodder."

Factor in the "gentrification" of Black communities occurring across the country, and I'm not sure there is much more one needs to add to the chemistry of destructive forces with which Black youth and students are compelled to cope. Isolated, abandoned and in the absence of a "movement" which defines and explains these phenomena, it is understandable that some youth would internalize their oppression and turn on each other rather than to each other. Unfortunately, this vacuum has also been filled by an industry hijacked form of hip hop which glorifies violence and cheapens life in the name of "realness." In my judgment, the epidemic of violence and fratricide tearing apart sectors of the Black community is a consequence of these factors.

The reality is that Black leaders urgently need to seize the moment to mount a campaign to rescue our communities and our youth. At the IBW Forum on Post Racial America, Dr. Ronald Walters, our leading Political Scientist, strongly recommended a "second stimulus" package to address the crises in marginalized Black communities. This is very much in line with IBW's call for the MLK-MX Initiative. However, there are a range of other legislative proposals that an Emergency Summit should consider—policy proposals that address various dimensions of the crisis. For example, Kenny Barnes of Washington, D.C. and Congressman Bobby Rush have proposed a bill to create anti-violence projects in targeted cities across the country.

Congress Members Rangel, Conyers, Scott and Davis also have policy proposals which would positively address the crisis. These Congress Members along with Hilary Shelton, Vice-President for Advocacy and Director of the NAACP Washington Bureau, should definitely be invited to the Summit.

As noted above, however, this crisis will not be solved by legislation or external initiatives alone. It is essential that we dig deep into the Black experience of triumph in the face of trials and tribulations to muster the collective resolve to creatively and lovingly confront and overcome the dysfunction, nihilism and callous disregard for life that has become commonplace in marginalized neighborhoods in Chicago and other locales in Black America. We must resolve to bridge the "class divide" which has resulted in the isolation and abandonment of marginalized Black neighborhoods. And, we must bring organizations and agencies that are successfully implementing projects, programs and initiatives to combat violence and fratricide among our treasured youth to the table. We must find a way to replicate these models and paradigms of possibility throughout Black America. Positive hip hop artists and cultural workers, those who have the ear of the youth, must also be front and center around the table. The future of Black youth in America is in their hands and ours. If we fail to act, we will betray the spirit of our ancestors and the Black Freedom Struggle that has enabled so many sons and daughters of Africa to achieve relative success in this hostile land. An Emergency Summit to address youth violence and fratricide is the order of the day!

End the "War on Drugs" and Mass Incarceration: Invest in America's "Dark Ghettos"

April, 2013

April 4, 1967, Dr. Martin Luther King stepped to the podium of the Riverside Church in New York to vigorously proclaim his opposition to the War in Vietnam. It was one of the most powerful orations among numerous remarkable speeches delivered during his brief but extraordinary life. In articulating a persuasive moral and practical framework for his stance, Dr. King said: "... I knew America would never invest the necessary funds or energies in rehabilitation of its poor so long as adventures like Vietnam continued to draw men and skills and money like some demonic destructive suction tube. So, I was increasingly compelled to see the war as an enemy of the poor and attack it as such." Equally disturbing for King was the disproportionate impact of the war not only on the poor but specifically young Black men. So, he went on to say: "We were taking the black young men who had been crippled by our society and sending them 8,000 miles away to guarantee liberties in Southeast Asia which they had not found in Southwest Georgia and East Harlem."

Dr. King›s decision to visibly and vocally oppose the War in Vietnam was no doubt complicated by the fact that the war was being promoted, prosecuted and defended by Lyndon Baines Johnson, the President who had courageously responded to «Bloody Sunday» and the subsequent Selma to Montgomery March by working for and signing the historic Voting Rights Act of 1965. President Johnson was viewed as a friend of civil rights and social programs favorable to poor and working people. Nonetheless, King saw the Vietnam War as an ill-conceived and immoral misadventure that would ultimately undermine the quest for social, economic and racial justice. Therefore, principle and conscience demanded that he not be silent even in opposition to a President who had signed milestone civil rights legislation.

It is in that same spirit, that on April 4, 2013, a group of social justice, drug and criminal justice policy reform advocates will intensify the demand for an end to the War on Drugs and mass incarceration and call on President Obama to invest resources to revitalize America›s «dark ghettos.» Just as Dr. King saw the War in Vietnam as wasting massive resources on an ill conceived and immoral war, drug and criminal justice reform analysts, experts and advocates have concluded that the War on Drugs is a flawed strategy complete with a contemporary "demonic suction tube" which has wasted billions of dollars that could and should have been used to invest in distressed urban communities. Equally distressing, as Michelle Alexander brilliantly documents in her classic book *The New Jim Crow*, the War on Drugs is a racially- biased policy/strategy targeting and disproportionately devastating Black and Brown communities. As the brothers and sisters in the "hood" say, "the war on drugs is a war on us!" As noted in the Petition to End the War on Drugs on the Institute of the Black World 21st Century›s website www.ibw21.org, how else can we make sense of the fact that "African Americans make up an estimated 15% of drug users, but account for 27% of those arrested on drug charges, 59% of those convicted and 74% of all drug offenders sentenced to prison." The War on Drugs is a war on Black people!

Time and time again, the Institute of the Black World 21st Century has asserted that there is a "State of Emergency" in Black

America, specifically in the «dark ghettos,» the urban inner-city neighborhoods plagued by chronic joblessness, underemployment and inferior schools; neighborhoods doomed to desolation and despair as a consequence of disinvestment by the federal government in social, economic and jobs programs and where work has disappeared because of capital flight and deindustrialization; neighborhoods where the trafficking in drugs and other «illicit» forms of making a living are viewed as viable means of survival; neighborhoods where paramilitary policing, stop-and-frisk raids, police brutality and the criminalization and incarceration of young Black men (and increasingly women) has become the order of the day; neighborhoods all across this nation where crime, violence and fratricide have become *unbearable!*

As I have said so many times, the War on Drugs, policing, criminalization and mass incarceration have become substitutes for social, economic and racial justice in America's dark ghettos. The damages to our communities have been devastating ... and it must end. As we pause to reflect on the legacy of Dr. King, the commemoration of his life has largely been reduced to ceremonies devoid of the moral and political imperative to continue the struggle for social justice and transformation. This year must be different. April 4, 1968, one year after his momentous speech at the Riverside Church, Dr. King was gunned down on a balcony of a hotel in Memphis. It is important to remember that he had come to protest the plight of sanitation workers and was in the midst of planning a Poor People's Campaign to fight for an Economic Bill of Rights to ensure that every American had a job or guaranteed income, adequate housing and a quality education as a basic human right.

As we gather in King's memory on April 4th this year, our charge must be to call on President Obama to heed the voices of so many experts, analysts, advocates, national and international commissions that have declared the War on Drugs an abysmal failure; a policy/strategy which has wreaked havoc on people, particularly people of color in this country and internationally. We must call on the President to exercise leadership by proclaiming to the nation that it is time to end the War on Drugs and treat the crisis of drugs as a public health rather than criminal justice issue—a dramatic paradigm shift which, at a minimum, will lead to decriminalization of marijuana, increased funding for drug education and treatment, and a national dialogue on the desirability and feasibility of regulating and taxing drugs. Such a paradigm shift will necessitate meaningful changes in the criminal justice system to dramatically reduce or eliminate drug offenses which have led to the disproportionate incarceration of Black and Brown people. It is time for President Obama to «break silence» and declare an end to the War on Drugs!

But, we must also call upon the President to do more. It is time for President Barack Obama to have the "audacity" to declare that the State of Emergency in urban inner-city areas, where millions of Black people are suffering and struggle to survive, a moral and political crisis which demands direct/targeted economic and social policies and programs to create wholesome, sustainable communities. The President and the nation have reacted as if there is no face to the millions who are suffering in the "dark ghettos" of this land. These millions do have a face and it is overwhelmingly BLACK. As I commented in a previous article, «we are not invisible.» And, just as the sanitation workers in Memphis carried signs declaring «I Am a Man,» Africans in America who visibly marched on ballot boxes in record numbers to help re-elect President Obama, we are also compelled to demand that the President and the nation take notice of the State of Emergency in Black America.

On April 4th, in the memory of Dr. Martin Luther King and in the spirit of his opposition to the Vietnam war and his call for an Economic Bill of Rights, the Institute of the Black World 21st Century will announce a Day of Direct Action June 17, 2013 in Washington, D.C.—to coincide with the 42nd Anniversary of the War on Drugs. On this day, like Joshua at the Walls of Jericho, drug and criminal justice reform collaboratives from Pittsburgh, Baltimore and Washington, D.C., joined by formerly incarcerated persons from around the nation, representatives of Black professional organizations associated with the Black Family Summit, faith and labor leaders will act as «drum majors for justice» marching at the gates of the White House issuing a clarion call for an end to the war on drugs and mass incarceration and demanding investment in America›s dark ghettos. On June 17th, we intend to make some noise. We hope President Obama and the nation will heed our call and the walls of ignorance, indifference, hostility, blatant and benign neglect, racial bias and injustice will come tumbling down, clearing the way for the rescue and revitalization of the urban inner-city neighborhoods/communities in this country!

Celebrating July 4th:
Towards a Season of Resistance

July, 2013

The June 17th Day of Direct Action (DODA) spearheaded by the Institute of the Black World 21st Century (IBW) is history. "Drum Majors for Justice," primarily from the Northeast where IBW has worked to form drug and criminal justice policy reform collaboratives, marched to the gates of the White House to demand that President Obama end the racially-biased and destructive "War on Drugs" that has so severely damaged Black families and communities and led to mass incarceration of Black people. Equally important, protesters demanded that the damage be repaired through the development of a massive jobs and economic development program with a priority on formerly incarcerated persons. It was heartwarming and encouraging to see so many unemployed youth, formerly incarcerated persons, victims of violence and fratricide, rap activists and young organizers/leaders engaged in "speaking truth to power."

DODA was also significant because it was the first time that large numbers of Black advocates/organizers/leaders marched on the White House to demand that President Obama directly respond to the myriad crises in distressed inner-city, predominantly Black neighborhoods—America's "dark ghettos." Apparently some major civil rights leaders were concerned that the March/Rally would reflect negatively on President Obama. DODA was never intended as an anti-Obama exercise. However, it should signal that Blacks, who marched on ballot boxes in record numbers in 2008 and 2012 to provide the margin of victory for President Obama in several key states, do expect him to directly and visibly respond to the "State of Emergency" in America's dark ghettos. At a minimum, he should declare the crises afflicting distressed Black neighborhoods a moral and political crisis and call upon the Congress and the nation to act!

DODA was not anti-Obama, nor was it about protecting his image as America's first Black President. Therefore, DODA must not simply be a one-day event. As Rev. Jesse L. Jackson remarked at the Pre-Rally at the historic Metropolitan AME Church, we must decide whether we will submit to the intolerable conditions created by the War on Drugs, mass incarceration and blatant neglect by government or we can make up our minds to resist! In that vein, as the nation, including the masses of Africans in America prepares to "celebrate" July 4th, arguably the most patriotic holiday of the year, I believe the words of Frederick Douglass' July 4, 1852 speech in Rochester, NY should reverberate throughout Black America: "What to the American slave is your Fourth of July? I answer: A day that reveals to him more than all other days in the year, the gross injustice and cruelty to which he is constant victim." Africans in America have certainly made progress since Douglass delivered these words, but we are still a distance from the "promised land."

While it is understandable and acceptable that Black people view U.S. holidays as family days and occasions to gain respite from life in a tension-filled society, it is imperative that we also use these occasions to reflect on the specific nature of our historical struggle and the challenges/barriers we must still overcome. For example, under the leadership of Rev. Dennis Dillon, Editor/Publisher, the New York Christian Times and Rev. Dr. Johnny Ray Youngblood, Pastor, Mt. Pisgah Baptist Church and creator of the world renowned Maafa Commemoration, scores of New York area-faith leaders have seized on the occasion of the commemoration of the 150th Anniversary of the Emancipation Proclamation to launch a major "economic emancipation campaign." On June 19th, Juneteenth, thousands of Black people gathered at the Riverside Church to hear calls to use the 1.2 trillion dollars in Black buying/consumer power to build a stronger Black economy. They also urged Black people to use Black dollars as a weapon to reward those banks and businesses that invest in Black communities and punish those who do not with boycotts/economic sanctions.

Similarly, in this year of commemorations, the 50th Anniversary of the March on Washington should be a major occasion to galvanize Africans in America and our allies to demand that the State of Emergency in America's dark ghettos be addressed with a massive "Marshall Plan" type program to rescue and revitalize distressed Black communities.   Black leaders should remind America of Dr. King's assertion that the "Promissory Note," the check that was to guarantee full freedom in terms of basic rights to jobs, housing, health and education under the Declaration of Independence and Constitution, kept coming back "marked insufficient funds." As Dr. Mtangulizi Sanyika, Founder of the African American Leadership Project, recently put it—after the March on Washington "a deposit was made, but the check still bounced." Hopefully, the 50th Anniversary of the March on Washington will be filled with the kind of resistance Frederick Douglass passionately called for in his July 4th oration. Frankly, given the dire condition of millions of Black people who suffer from the effects of the "bounced check," there is no time for idle, ritualistic, meaningless commemorations or exercises in "leadership profiling and enhancement."

What to your casualties of the War on Drugs, mass incarceration, chronic unemployment and abandoned Black urban inner-city residents is your Fourth of July? "A day that reveals to [them] more than all other days in the year, the gross injustice and cruelty to which [they are] constant victims." Therefore, in the spirit of Frederick Douglass, let this day, this year mark the beginning of a season of resistance!

Cultivating "Conscious" Entrepreneurs to Rescue and Restore the Race

July, 2014

Each year during the Fourth of July holiday season, I inevitably turn my attention to Frederick Douglass' extraordinary July 5, 1852 oration in Rochester, New York, in which he denounced the hypocrisy of a nation that celebrated its "independence" while millions of sons and daughters of Africa were held in bondage as slaves. He declared: "What to the American slave is your Fourth of July? I answer: A day that reveals to him more than all other days in the year, the gross injustice and cruelty to which he is the constant victim." Of course, Africans in America have come a long way since Douglass made this memorable speech. As Rev. Jesse L. Jackson might put it, "the hands that picked cotton have picked a President." Our progress notwithstanding, I like to reflect on Douglass' speech because it compels me to think about the myriad crises we still face as Black people, particularly the maladies afflicting America's "dark ghettos" (urban inner-city neighborhoods), mass incarceration, an underdeveloped internal economy and persistent wealth gap. The words of Douglass remind us that individual and institutional racism are still alive in the U.S. and remain barriers to the equitable inclusion of Black people into this society. Douglass' words inspire us to be vigilant, to resist and act to promote and defend the interests and aspirations of our people.

I have just returned from participating in Dr. George Fraser's

Power Networking Conference in Dallas. My reflection on Douglass and the season caused me to think about the significance of this annual gathering of Black entrepreneurs, business leaders and professionals as a vehicle to promote the interests and aspirations of Africans in America in the 21st century. In that regard, I thought it useful to revisit the status of the emerging, new African community in the U.S. during the time of Frederick Douglass. In 1852 some 3.5 million Africans were still enslaved while about 500,000 comprised the "quasi-free" African community. Douglass' Fourth of July oration protesting and denouncing slavery and demanding emancipation was typical of the leadership class of his day. They also protested their status as "quasi-free" Blacks who could not vote and enjoy the same privileges of their White counterparts.

What is often overlooked, however, is that this emerging Black community had another agenda—building an infrastructure of self-sufficient institutions to serve its members/constituents and to enhance its capacity/power to struggle for emancipation and civil rights. Frederick Douglass was not just a great orator and organizer, he founded The North Star newspaper to ensure that Black abolitionists had an independent voice. The North Star was part of an embryonic but growing Black press as an institution in the Black community. By 1852 Africans in America had founded an independent religious denomination, the African Methodist Episcopal Church, created African Free Schools, convened Colored People's Conventions to map strategies to achieve full freedom and built mutual aid societies to provide for the proper burial of Black people. These mutual aide societies were the precursors of Black insurance companies and banks. The point is that this newly emerging African community had a duel focus and agenda: protest to achieve emancipation, civil rights and equitable inclusion as citizens, and the development of independent

Black social, economic and political institutions to enhance the capacity/power to promote and defend Black interests. The lesson is that we should never forget this duel focus and agenda.

This is why Fraser Net and the Power Networking Conference are incredibly important as Africans in America continue the quest for full freedom in the 21st Century. While not disparaging protest, Dr. George Fraser has devoted his life to relentlessly focusing on building internal capacity/power in the Black community, especially the cultivation of "conscious" entrepreneurs and professionals. As I noted earlier, despite the fact that we have an African American President, there is a "State of Emergency" in America's dark ghettos. It is undeniable that a crucial aspect of this condition is the gross economic underdevelopment of Black communities. Hence, the urgent need for "conscious" entrepreneurs and business leaders who will contribute to the rescue and restoration of the race; not just "Capitalists," but "socially responsible" entrepreneurs committed to succeeding while giving back to and building Black communities.

For George Fraser, the process of cultivating conscious entrepreneurs and business leaders begins with culture, African culture—having an awareness of the worldview, history and heritage of forebears who were the first givers of life and civilization! Therefore, every Power Networking Conference begins with an immersion in African history and culture. As is customary, this year that immersion was led by Kwa David Whitaker, George Fraser's longtime friend and mentor. It featured a brilliant presentation by Anthony Browder, world-renowned historian, anthropologist, archeologist, author and entrepreneur. Anthony is the only African American who is currently excavating a burial site in Egypt. His presentations set the tone for the Conference. But, it was not a cultural immersion simply for the sake of an immersion; it was an immersion calculated to inspire the participants to be "conscious" of their history, cultural roots and most importantly the values and principles which must be utilized today to rescue and restore the race.

George Fraser's keynote address was consistent with this mission and the need to focus on internal capacity/power to finish the unfinished Black freedom struggle as initiated by our ancestors. His major call to action was for Africans in America to "narrow our cultural vision," to make "Black people great first." In essence, he suggested that if we focus on achieving greatness for Black people, America will be great as a consequence. In the spirit of Marcus Garvey, he was admonishing Black people to put "race first." And, in a manner that would make W.E.B. Du Bois proud, this call to action was/is intended to have Black people focus on the development of a strong internal Black economy and entrepreneurs/business leaders who can compete with and excel with entrepreneurs of any race, anywhere in the world (people forget that in the 1930's Du Bois was strongly advocating the development of a Black economic commonwealth).

The cultivation of "conscious" entrepreneurs is indispensable to the achievement of this vision/mission. Therefore, Dr. Fraser declared that we must develop the means to "ostracize" those Black people who are nurtured by our community and/or have profited from our support, who do not give back or reinvest in the Black community. He specifically cited Dr. Dre, the new billionaire, who gave millions of dollars to the University of Southern California (USC), but nothing to the United Negro College Fund or a Historically Black College or University (HBCU). He also exhorted the participants to encourage our people to "coalesce around our vision and not our pain." Our history and heritage of tragedy, trials, tribulations, but ultimately triumphs, clearly indicate that "where there is a will, there is a way." Finally, Dr. Fraser, the master teacher and networker extraordinaire, challenged the participants to "connect the dots," that the development of internal capacity/power will be the result of acting interdependently as opposed to in silos independently, that our destiny as African people is inextricably linked to the willingness of conscious entrepreneurs, professionals and business leaders to embrace each other, learn from each other and act in concert to rescue and restore the race!

It was an awesome keynote address by a visionary leader/teacher/role model. And, it was an awesome Conference. More than one thousand entrepreneurs, professionals and business leaders busied themselves with ninety-six hours of awesome workshops and mentoring sessions—which were living expressions of Ujima -- Collective Work and Responsibility and Ujamaa - Cooperative Economics. Dr. George Fraser is creating a "culture of success" and building a "community" of conscious entrepreneurs, professionals and business leaders, committed to rescuing and restoring the race. As we reflect on the meaning of this holiday season for people of African descent, I think Frederick Douglass and his contemporaries would be proud that Fraser Net and the Power Networking Conference are continuing to fulfill their vision/mission!

Toward A Season of Resistance: Buy Black on "Black Friday"

November, 2013

In my most recent article, I called upon the Black Nation and our allies to seize the X-MAS season (the commercialized, corrupted, capitalist version of Christmas) to intensify the Justice for Trayvon Martin, Economic Sanctions/Boycott Florida Campaign. This call was/is grounded in the conviction that Africans in America have been far too passive in the face of unspeakable acts of indignity heaped upon the race. I am convinced that a rekindled spirit of resistance will result in victories over the oppressive forces that seek to reverse the gains of the historic and heroic Black Freedom Struggle. Collectively Black people continue to be neglected, disrespected, disregarded and abused because we have become too tame, tolerant and even accepting of our oppression. This is not to say that there is no fight-back or resistance. The problem is that we lack a "critical mass," a much larger number of Black people, who are sufficiently enraged and outraged, to act decisively to promote and protect/defend our interests and aspirations. This is the challenge we must overcome.

The X-MAS season provides an excellent opportunity for Africans in America to engage in a season of resistance. The corporate retail establishment in this country is heavily dependent upon this season for consumers to participate in a frenzy of buying to buttress their bottom line. The unofficial kick-off of the "shop until you drop" season is the Friday after Thanksgiving—which has popularly come to be known as "Black Friday" - the day when the corporate retail giants begin an all out effort to induce, seduce, bribe and otherwise "persuade" consumers to buy enough goods to enable companies to "break into the black"—achieve profitability for the year!

Unfortunately, the sons and daughters of formerly enslaved Africans in America, who complain about the oppressive conditions of stop-and-frisk, joblessness, the War on Drugs, crime, violence, fratricide and the murder of unarmed Black men like Trayvon Martin are not immune to the seductive appeal of the X-MAS season. On Black Friday, Black consumers will lineup with liberated White folks in the reckless race to give our hard earned/precious dollars to the oppressor! We are addicted. We must educate and organize to kick the habit.

Black Friday should mark a critical point of resistance for Black people, a time when Black consumers utilize the billions of dollars in our hands as a weapon to advance the Black Freedom Struggle. I have often said if Black people would commit to "keeping Christ in Christmas," focus on the spiritual and family aspects of the season and consciously refuse to participate in the senseless buying frenzy, the White Corporate establishment would come running, asking what concessions they should make to end the economic sanctions. Black people have more than 1 trillion dollars of consumer buying power in our hands. The question is whether we have the consciousness, commitment and discipline to use it to promote and defend Black interests.

There is no better time to renew a spirit of resistance than the present. Black people all across the nation should resolve to Buy Black on "Black Friday." At a minimum, Black people should seek out Black businesses and purchase as many gifts as possible from them to bolster the Black economy. Veteran activists like Bob Law have long advocated Support Black Business Days to encourage Black consumers to shop at Black stores. He is advocating a similar campaign this year. In addition, Black communities can organize Black Expos on Black Friday where scores of Black vendors and businesses can be assembled under one roof to display their wares for sale. For example, in New York, under the visionary leadership of Rev. Dennis Dillon, the Emancipation 2013 Freedom Coalition is organizing a two day Black Friday Expo November 29th and 30th at the 69th Regiment Armory in Manhattan. This kind of Expo could become a model for Black communities nationwide. The Support Black Business Days and Black Expo events exemplify the first principle of the utilization of Black consumer power—Black dollars should be used to support Black businesses and entrepreneurs as a means of building a strong economic infrastructure to employ Black people.

The second principle of the utilization of Black consumer power is that companies/corporations that depend on Black dollars must be compelled to reinvest in Black communities!   Black dollars should be used as leverage with businesses and corporations that depend on Black consumer dollars. It is reasonable to expect and demand that businesses and corporations that we patronize reinvest dollars back into the Black community in the form of jobs, advertisement in Black media, sponsorships and contributions to worthy causes. And, we should not accept peanuts or chump change in exchange for the massive dollars we spend, enriching businesses and corporations owned by interests external to the Black community. Our inner-city neighborhoods are dying for lack of jobs and investment. Therefore, we absolutely cannot permit businesses to grow fat off our dollars without demanding reinvestment in our communities. Those who refuse to do so must face the wrath of economic sanctions—and there is no better time to target offending businesses/corporations than the X-MAS season when their profitability depends on Black dollars!

As the corporate retail establishment prepares to launch the

X-MAS season, let us transform it into a season of resistance -- Remember Trayvon Martin: Boycott Florida....Buy Black on "Black Friday!"

Remembering Trayvon Martin: Economic Sanctions Against Florida: An Idea Whose Time Has Come

July, 2013

In a recent article I called for economic sanctions against Florida to compel business and political leaders in that state to change the "Stand Your Ground Law" which provided the basis for the acquittal of George Zimmerman in the murder of Trayvon Martin. There are times when there is a convergence of ideas, a meeting of minds, such that a particular strategy has the potential to galvanize a movement to achieve a major victory. It appears that such a convergence of ideas has occurred around at least one strategy to translate the anger and frustration over the Zimmerman verdict into justice in the Trayvon Martin tragedy—Economic Sanctions/Boycott Florida. The idea is not a Ron Daniels idea or Institute of the Black World 21st Century (IBW) call but one that is on the minds of Black people all across the country.

Dr. Patricia Newton, President Emeritus, National Association of Black Psychiatrists, was so outraged by the Zimmerman verdict that she cancelled a $1 million dollar contract she was about to sign for a conference in Florida. When I asked an elderly Black professional couple I met at Penn Station in Baltimore [who were returning from a conference in Jacksonville, Florida] whether they would be going back to Florida next year... Before I could get the words out of my mouth, the wife defiantly proclaimed that they discussed the murder of Trayvon Martin at the conference and had already resolved that they would not hold another convention in that state until there is justice in this case! Then music legend Stevie Wonder issued a statement at a concert in Canada proclaiming "until the Stand Your Ground Law is abolished, I will never perform there again." Since his pronouncement, Eddie LaVert, Stephanie Mills, Dionne Warwick and Mary Mary are among the artists who have publicly come out saying they will not perform in Florida until this abhorrent law has changed. While celebrities like Stevie Wonder provide credibility for the Boycott, it will be the actions of the multitude of conscious/committed convention goers, vacationers and consumers that will make the campaign effective. Economic sanctions against Florida is an idea whose time has come.

Just as Katrina ripped the scab off and exposed the raw naked structural/institutional racism in distressed Black neighborhoods in America like those in New Orleans, the murder of Trayvon Martin has ripped the scab off the persistent phenomenon of the criminalization of young Black men, racial profiling, stop-and-frisk and the structural/institutional racism in America's criminal justice system. The problem is that despite episodic protests and periodic mobilizations, there has not been a persistent sense of urgency in Black America about these issues. The murder of Trayvon Martin may be a decisive turning point.

One week after the Zimmerman verdict, rallies and prayer vigils were held across the country to demand that the Justice Department bring criminal charges against George Zimmerman for violating Trayvon Martin's civil rights. While we agree that this is a righteous strategy, there is a high probability that the Justice Department will not find sufficient racial animus in the proceedings to justify bringing charges. However, even if the Justice Department does find sufficient cause to bring charges, I contend that the economic sanctions/boycott Florida campaign is necessary.

At the end of the day, not only must we seek a conviction of Zimmerman, we must also indict and fight to change the law that is so flawed that it would permit an armed adult to pursue an unarmed teenager deemed "suspicious" and permit a grown man to kill a kid who fearfully sought to stand his ground against a menacing stranger. Fighting to change this flawed law is about justice for Trayvon Martin, but it is also about all of the Trayvons in the state of Florida and across the nation who are victims of criminalization and racial profiling. It is about Black people consciously and collectively standing our ground against the attacks on the gains of the civil rights/human rights/Black power movements, the abandonment and disinvestment in distressed Black communities and the daily indignities we have quietly suffered for far too long. In his last speech the night before he was assassinated in Memphis, Dr. Martin Luther King urged Black people to use boycotts to achieve justice. He said, "now we must kind of redistribute the pain." As IBW said in its Press Release on this issue, "Blacks and all people of conscience and good will should inflict some non-violent pain on the state of Florida and keep inflicting it until business leaders and the politicians scream for help and plead for the economic sanctions to be lifted." But, to achieve our goal we need a targeted (not scattered/shotgun) approach to succeed.

The major component of the campaign should be to shut off tourism to Florida. This means Black organizations should not schedule conferences/conventions in that state until the law is changed. Groups that have already scheduled conferences six months to a year out should seek to cancel the agreements and notify the venues that Black people no longer feel safe to travel to Florida, particularly with their sons. An option is to hold conferences/conventions at a Black

College/University or Black owned retreat centers. In the event that your conference is already scheduled in the next few months, resolve to spend as little money/cash in the state as possible. This campaign requires that kind of discipline.

Do not schedule a vacation in Florida until victory is won. Do not travel to an amusement park in the "tragic kingdom" or golf tournament until victory is won. At the NAACP Convention, Martin Luther King III urged the delegates not to buy Florida orange juice. In conversations with Dr. Iva Carruthers, General Secretary, Samuel DeWitt Proctor Conference, and George Fraser, President/CEO, FraserNet, they advised that refusing to buy Florida orange juice is an excellent way to "democratize" the economic sanctions/Boycott Florida campaign by creating an avenue for ordinary people everywhere to participate in the effort whether they had planned to travel to Florida or not. So, here's a set of marching orders:

No Conferences/Conventions

No Vacations

No Amusement Parks or Golf Tournaments

No Florida Orange Juice

We also hope the major civil rights leaders will embrace this righteous campaign and mobilize their constituents to actively support it. The people are ready and the train is already leaving the station. IBW has posted a petition on its website www.ibw21.org where organizations, leaders and individuals can Sign a Pledge to Boycott Florida. Finally, while this campaign is spearheaded by Black people, we obviously appeal to and welcome the support of our friends and allies of all races and ethnicities who believe that "an injury to one is an injury to all," that "an injustice anywhere to anyone is an injustice to everyone everywhere." Economic sanctions against Florida is an idea whose time has come!

Beyond "Milk Toast" Martin: Preserving the Vision and Legacy of a Reformer

January, 2011

After a long, hard fought struggle, it is certainly wonderful to have an annual holiday celebrating the life of Rev. Dr. Martin Luther King, Jr. It offers an opportunity for the entire nation to reflect on the vision, trials, tribulations and triumphs of one of the greatest leaders the world has ever known. However, each year I worry that the Holiday will become a kind of touchy/feely "Kumbaya" occasion where the emphasis is on "can we all get along" rather than a focus on social justice and social change. Almost by nature, state institutions have little interest in uplifting the ideas of heroes and heroines that pose a threat to the status-quo. And, the "mainstream media" has never been a major conveyor of messages of social change. Therefore, now that he is "safely dead," selected sections of Dr. King's "I Have a Dream," speech—the call to judge people based on the "content of their character" not skin color and the hope that one day little Black boys and girls and White boys and girls, all of us, will be able to be as one in America—have become like the official anthem for the MLK Holiday.

When most Americans think of Martin Luther King, what immediately comes to mind are those selected passages from one of the most eloquent and inspiring orations in the history of this nation. The problem is that this selective view of Dr. King dilutes his vision as a committed reformer on a mission to achieve a "more perfect union" utilizing non-violent resistance as his strategy of choice. Dr. King was obviously a proponent of "the beloved community" where human beings of all races, ethnicities, cultures and religions could live in harmony and peace. However, within a society where racism and poverty plagued millions of people, the path to this panacea was through militantly confronting racial, social and economic injustice. Stripping this fundamental dimension of his vision and mission is to create a kind of "milk toast" Martin which excludes the boycotts, marches, protests and civil disobedience he employed to challenge injustice in this land; a Martin so non-threatening that even rightwing reactionaries like Glenn Beck can embrace despite the fact that his vision of America is diametrically opposed to much of what Dr. King advocated.

While the U.S. is slowly emerging from a "Great Recession" occasioned by the reckless behavior of Wall Street financial institutions, like most MLK Holidays, this year's commemoration was mostly marked by ceremonies, parades and people engaged in worthy service projects in honor of the mild-mannered Martin. Given King's vision/mission as a reformer, one would have thought that there might have been teach-ins across the nation analyzing the implications of his teachings for crafting public policy to overcome the Great Recession and chart a path toward a more wholesome society. This kind of analysis is particularly important because of the fierce ideological struggle between conservatives and liberal/progressives over the direction of this country in the wake of the Great Recession. For example, Glenn Beck has launched a relentless campaign against City College of New York Distinguished Professor Frances Fox-Piven who proposed a guaranteed annual income in the 60s. Beck and the rightwing see such proposals as part of a sinister plot to "overthrow" the capitalist system and establish socialism. If Beck had bothered to study Martin Luther King's program for change instead of blithely attempting to peddle a "milk toast" version of him to his followers, he would have discovered that a guaranteed annual income was a basic tenet of King's platform.

Dr. Martin Luther King was not some accommodationist blandly urging Americans to just get along. He was a liberal-progressive reformer who saw major flaws that must be corrected in America's capitalist political-economy. In his seldom quoted speech at the Riverside Church in New York in 1967, where he expressed his opposition to the war in Vietnam, King, the social reformer, proclaimed: "I am convinced that if we are to get on the right side of the world revolution, we as a nation must undergo a radical revolution of values. We must rapidly begin the shift from a 'thing oriented' society to a 'person oriented' society. When machines and computers, profit motives and property rights are considered more important than people, the giant triplets of racism, materialism and militarism are incapable of being conquered." How appropriate does this message seem today when the U.S. is engaged in two ill advised, resource draining wars abroad and the profiteers on Wall Street have nearly destroyed the economy of this country and the world. How well does this message resonate when inequality, the gap between rich and poor, is the worst since the 1930s. The New York City Coalition Against Hunger recently cited data indicating that there are now fifty-seven (57) billionaires in the Big Apple whose combined annual income of $232 billion is greater than that of 13 million minimum wage workers. Those at the commanding heights of capital and finance in this country are perfectly willing to "get along" so long as their kind of greed-driven, unbridled capitalism goes untouched.

It is particularly at moments of crisis when there is such an intense debate about the direction of the nation that the progressive movement should be aggressively utilizing the vision of Martin Luther King, the social reformer, as a framework to educate the American people about the urgent need to maintain and expand the "culture of rights" social movements have achieved through generations of struggle, e.g., women's suffrage, the right to organize and maintain unions, workers compensation, the minimum wage, social security, Medicare, consumer protection, environmental protection and civil rights for Blacks and other people of color. At the end of his life, Martin Luther King was planning a "Poor People's Campaign" to substantially enhance the culture of rights for workers, the middle class and poor people by advancing the concept of an Economic Bill of Rights which would provide every American with a guaranteed annual income, housing, health care and a quality education. King was proposing radical reforms rooted in the Universal Declaration of Human rights. Indeed, in the Riverside Church Speech he declared: "True compassion is more than flinging a coin to a beggar; it comes to see that the edifice which produces beggars needs restructuring."

Needless to say, we have yet to come close to realizing the reforms King was proposing when he was gunned down on a balcony in Memphis. In fact, with the "white backlash he predicted, coupled with the rise to prominence of conservatism, there has been a concerted effort to turn back the clock on civil rights and to undermine the culture of rights for workers, the middle class and poor people. This onslaught was never more evident than in the current period when the Tea Party Patriots and other rabid conservatives are hell bent on painting any proposal for an expansion of the culture of rights, e.g., health care reform, as socialist. And, frankly by clever use of propaganda, fear mongering and outright lies, the reactionaries on the right have persuaded a sizeable segment of the public to act against their own class interest. Progressives have yet to mount an effective offensive to counter the machinations of the conservatives. One of the most positive ways to combat the rise of the right, with its restrictive, property and profit oriented vision of America, is to preserve and present the vision of Martin Luther King, the social reformer. The best way to honor King's memory is to remind Americans what he stood for and work to translate his ideas into policies and practices that will "restructure the edifice," which is producing obscene levels of wealth and prosperity for a few and misery and a lack of fulfillment for so many in the United States.

A Marshall Plan and Economic Sanctions/Boycotts: Missing Elements in the MOW Commemoration Call to Action

August, 2013

I was privileged to attend the March on Washington in 1963, and count it as one of the most profound experiences of my life. The sheer outpouring of thousands of people, particularly Black people, was a testament to our aspirations and determination to win jobs, justice and freedom. The March proved to be a decisive moment in the Black Freedom Struggle and for the nation. August 24th, I was privileged to attend the Commemoration of the 50th Anniversary of the March on Washington (MOW). Indeed, this Commemoration was marked by scores of substantive and celebrative programs, including the Institute of the Black World 21stCentury's release of an Executive Summary of its Black Paper - A Deposit Was Made But the Check Still Bounced. Tens of thousands of people poured into D.C. for the massive Rally and March on the National Mall. It was especially exhilarating to see so many young people, large numbers of them wearing Justice for Trayvon Martin T-Shirts or hoisting placards with the same theme. Whenever thousands of people are motivated to gather to demand justice, it must be judged a success.

But, the thousands who journeyed to D.C. came not only to demand justice; they were looking to the "leadership" to provide a blueprint/agenda, strategy and marching orders to translate their demands into victories. The agenda of issues presented by most of the speakers was closely tied to the grievances which motivated folks to attend the Rally/March: the recent Supreme Court Decision that gutted the Voting Rights Act and "voter suppression" laws being passed in states like North Carolina and Texas; speakers called on Congress to pass legislation to fix the VRA; the demand for Justice for Trayvon Martin was addressed by calls for the passage of the "Trayvon Martin Law" in Florida and other states to change the dreaded "Stand Your Ground" laws; Trayvon Martin's parents appealed to young people to become "Trayvon Martin Voters" in order to flex electoral muscle at the ballot box; an end to stop-and-frisk and racial profiling were also mentioned; several speakers spoke to the need for Congress to pass President Obama's Jobs Bill to address depression levels of joblessness; and, comprehensive immigration reform to bring undocumented persons "out of the shadows" was addressed numerous times.

These issues are certainly pertinent and the call to address them very important. However, in my view, there were some critical omissions which may dilute the potential impact of the Commemoration. Given the "State of Emergency" in urban inner-city neighborhoods across this country—America's "dark ghettos,"—President Obama's jobs program is necessary but woefully inadequate to repair the decades of damage done by government disinvestment, capital flight and deindustrialization. Therefore, it would have been a source of inspiration if Rev. Al Sharpton as the "keynote speaker" (I'm not aware there was one in 1963) or one of the national civil rights leaders had boldly reissued the call for a "Domestic Marshall Plan" to rebuild America's dark ghettos. After the countless billions of dollars squandered in Vietnam, Iraq and Afghanistan since 1963, the gauntlet should have been thrown down for America to make a huge deposit on the "promissory note" King referenced in his speech a half century ago. How can the U.S. justify "nation-building" in Iraq and Afghanistan and refuse to do "community-building" on behalf of her long-suffering sons and daughters of Africa in America? Moreover, picking up on the vision/mission King was embarking on prior to being gunned down in Memphis, someone might have thought to restate the call for the enactment of an Economic Bill of Rights to ensure that every American is guaranteed a basic quality of life in terms of employment/income, housing, education and health care. It doesn't matter that the obstructionists would treat such bold calls for policy initiatives with disdain; what matters is the articulation of the vision/mission and a call to action to achieve it as part of the historic and heroic struggle to fully emancipate Africans in America and achieve a "more perfect union."

The final glaring omission was the absence of a call to utilize economic sanctions/boycotts as a non-violent means to change the hearts and minds of obstructionists who refuse to respond to moral appeals to do the right thing as it relates to the legitimate interests and aspirations of Black people and the oppressed. It is useful to re-call that Dr. King rose to prominence because he successfully led the Montgomery Bus Boycott. Black passengers refused to ride buses, withdrew their patronage, exacted economic sanctions, until the seg-regationist city fathers relented, had a «change of heart,» and recog-nized the right of Black people to sit wherever they chose to be seated! In his final speech in Memphis, Dr. King challenged Black people to use boycotts to «redistribute the pain» to pursue and achieve our righteous quest for social, economic and political justice.

In the face of Stevie Wonder›s courageous decision not to per-form in Florida until the Stand Your Ground law is «abolished,» and calls by IBW and numerous organizations and individuals to Boy-cott Florida, it was astonishing that not a single national Civil Rights leader endorsed the Boycott Florida Campaign. Clearly the Boycott is a people-based effort which can inflict the kind of economic pain on the tourist industry that can cause Florida business and political leaders to have a change of heart regarding the Stand Your Ground law. One wonders whether corporate contributions to our major civil rights organizations are restraining them from vigorously embracing and advocating a time tested means of mobilizing/organizing our people to achieve victories. In that vein, a victory in Florida will build momentum to target and win victories in other states.

The Commemoration of the 50th Anniversary of the March on Washington was a success, but it lacked a bold vision/mission to inspire Black people and the «beloved community» to move from a re-active to pro-active mode in the struggle to finish the unfinished civil rights/human rights agenda. And, one of the most potent nonviolent weapons for achieving justice was left off the table—economic sanctions/boycotts. However, rather than simply complain, it remains for those who make the critique to fill in the blanks by articulating a broader vision/mission and educating, mobilizing/organizing Black people to utilize Black dollars as a weapon in the Black freedom struggle. Boycott Florida! A luta continua... the struggle continues!

Remembering Malcolm:
Fifty Years Since the "Ballot
or the Bullet"

February, 2014

February 21st marks the 49th anniversary of the assassination of El Hajj Malik El Shabazz, Omawale, "our Black Shining Prince," Malcolm X. This year is also 50 years since Malcolm delivered The Ballot or the Bullet speech. Brother Malcolm made numerous speeches, and it is hard to imagine one that was not inspirational, informational and powerful. The two speeches that stand out for me are Message to the Grassroots and The Ballot or the Bullet. Frankly, nothing matches Message to the Grassroots for its conviction, searing logic, clarity, passion and power. It›s an awesome oration!

But, The Ballot or the Bullet is a milestone speech because it comes at a critical juncture in Malcolm›s political evolution and development. After his painful departure from the Nation of Islam, Malcolm is striving to assure his devoted followers that Black Nationalism is still the philosophy/ideology which guides his work. He is also setting the stage for a more active engagement in the «civil rights movement» by offering a critique of the Capitalist political economy and its dominant political parties, the Democrats and Republicans. The Ballot or the Bullet signals a transition in Malcolm›s evolution, one which witnesses him seeking to build Muslim Mosque, Inc. and the Organization of Afro-American Unity as independent structures to advance his vision of Black liberation. Tragically, Malcolm was cut-down before his vision could reach fruition. Nonetheless, it may be useful to examine the tenets articulated in this speech to assess their relevance 50 years later.

1964 was a crucial presidential election year. Expectations in Black America were very high in the wake of the historic March on Washington in August of 1963. Black leaders and their allies were pressing President Lyndon Johnson and Congress to pass substantive legislation to ensure the rights of African Americans as first class citizens in this nation. Breaking with his prior posture of non-engagement in electoral politics, a skeptical Malcolm X indicated that 1964 offered America the opportunity to prove that it was serious about guaranteeing the rights of its formerly enslaved sons and daughters. He suggested that this might be America's last chance; therefore, he declared, "This just might be the year of the ballot or the bullet."

This was an implicit warning that Blacks were not obligated to "suffer peacefully" in the face of the ongoing, unmitigated onslaught of a white supremacist system and its policies. Because he observed the virulent intransigence of southern Democrats who labeled themselves "Dixiecrats" and the reluctance of many Republicans to overtly embrace civil rights legislation, Malcolm had little faith that either Party could be trusted to promote and defend the rights of Black people over the long haul. Hence, one could infer that he preferred the stance of Fannie Lou Hamer and the freedom fighters from Mississippi who formed the Mississippi Freedom Democratic Party—an independent political organization.

Malcolm was also firm about the importance of Black Nationalism as the ideological framework for the Black Freedom Struggle. In The Ballot or the Bullet, he sought to "make it plain" by articulating the practical meaning and application of what some viewed as a controversial philosophy. In essence, Malcolm believed that Black people should control the neighborhoods/communities where we are the majority. Black people should control the politics, politicians, economics and social life (health, education, welfare) in our communities. In its most simple and practical form Black Nationalism means that Black people should control Black neighborhoods/communities to the fullest degree possible in order to maximize our freedom and self-determination.

Fifty year later, the question is how does Black progress measure up in relation to the tenets laid out in The Ballot or the Bullet? In 1964 few would have imagined that by 2008 the United States would have its first African American President. This is stunning progress by any reasonable measure and yet, as IBW has repeatedly proclaimed, there is a State of Emergency in America's "dark ghettos," neighborhoods/communities where the masses of poor and working people are "catching more hell" than ever before as Malcolm might put it. Black people are still over reliant on a Democratic Party which can afford to take us for granted because the Tea Party dominated Republican alternative is unthinkable as an option. Worse still, with the dismantling of Rev. Jesse Jackson's Rainbow Coalition as a mass-based, progressive force, Black America does not have a viable independent political organization to promote and defend Black interests based on an agenda. The Congressional Black Caucus does a reasonable job of promoting Black interests, but it is locked into the Democratic Party and has limited capacity to utilize mass protests and other non-electoral tactics to advance a Black agenda.

At the local level Malcolm would be distressed by the lack of real control of the politics and politicians in the Black community. We have more Black elected officials than ever before, but far too many of them are out of touch with the vision of the Black political leader whose primary mission is to expose the contradictions and limitations of the "system" while mobilizing/organizing to deliver the maximum goods and services to the people. In the 60s, theoreticians and Black activists advocated a politics of social transformation—engaging the system to change the system. All across the country we find large numbers of Black people who are alienated or have given up on the electoral political process because they see little relationship between their support for elected officials and substantive change in the quality of life in Black neighborhoods/communities, particularly in urban inner-city areas. This is reflected in pathetically low voter turn-out in elections. Black folks are fed-up with too many self-serving, self-aggrandizing, vision-less elected officials.

Fortunately, Malcolm would be pleased that there are a few Black political leaders who adhere to his commitment to Black empowerment. Former Detroit Council Members Kwame Kenyatta and JoAnn Watson, former Brooklyn Councilman Charles Barron (Kenyatta, Watson and Barron left office voluntarily or were term-limited), Newark Councilman and candidate for Mayor Ras Baraka and Mayor Chokwe Lumumba of Jackson, Mississippi are on the short list of Black elected officials who have consistently used their positions to empower Black and marginalized people. Indeed, prior to becoming Mayor, Chokwe Lumumba was elected to the City Council from a district where he organized a People's Assembly to "control the politics" of the community.

The "Black community" is far more dispersed today than it was in 1964 because of the flight of the Black middle class and gentrification, which has become the "Negro removal" program of the 21st Century. Vanishing «chocolate cities» are the order of the day as Black people seem powerless to «control» our neighborhoods/communities. And, in the «dark ghettos» that remain, the «Black economy» provides economic opportunities and jobs for a mere fraction of people in need. As Rev. Dennis Dillon, Editor/Publisher of The Economic

State of New York Report, details, Black New Yorkers do not control the economics of the neighborhoods in which they live. The pattern in New York is typical for Black America. At the macro-level, despite the persistent exhortations of leaders like George Fraser, Dr. Claud Anderson, Jim Clingman and Rev. Dillon, people of African descent are pathetically negligent in "controlling" the more than one trillion dollars which flows through our hands every year!

The bottom line is that 50 years after The Ballot or the Bullet, remembering Malcolm is not a nostalgic exercise. The lessons from this milestone speech are still strikingly relevant today. A healthy dose of Black Nationalism as Malcolm prescribed it is not only still in order, it's imperative!

Making the American Flag "Our Flag"

February, 2009

On Inauguration Day in Washington, D.C., there was a veritable sea of Red, White and Blue as some two million proud Americans, including hundreds of thousands of Black people, furiously waved their American Flags on the National Mall. This overt expression of affection for the American Flag was somewhat out of character for Blacks, who have been understandably ambivalent about America's sacred symbols. No doubt joining in this patriotic display was part of the pride the vast majority of Blacks felt in witnessing one of the most extraordinary "strides towards freedom" this nation has ever achieved—the swearing-in of the first Black President of the United States. But, I was not among those waving the Flag on that historic day. I am still ambivalent. I know what the Black National Anthem and the Red. Black and Green Flag mean to me, however, I don't see myself, my people, in the Red, White and Blue.

One of the most critical lessons to be learned from the study of history is that culture is often a source of resiliency, resistance and inspiration for an oppressed people. As America's most patient patriots [African Americans have fought in every one of this nation's wars], we need never apologize for any hesitancy to wave or display the Flag or to sing the National Anthem. I prefer the ambivalence and resistance toward the Flag because the trials, tribulations and triumphs of Africans in America are not imbedded in this nation's sacred symbols. The same could be said of Native Americans and other people of color. Euro-ethnics have typically had a different feeling towards the Anthem and the Flag because America was founded as a White nation, where opportunities for Whites have been far more abundant than for Africans, Native Americans, Mexicans, Asians and other people of color. As Malcolm X aptly put it in referring to the experience of Africans in America, "you didn't land on Plymouth Rock, Plymouth Rock landed on you."

I must admit that the Black vocalists who are increasingly tapped to sing the Anthem really add a lot of soul and passion to the lyrics. But, I cringe when I hear the words "And the rocket's red glare, the bombs bursting in air, gave proof through the night that our flag was still there." It's the "our flag" phrase that I find infuriating. In 1812 when Frances Scott Keyes crafted the "Star Spangled Banner," 95% of Africans in America had no flag. Our forebears were enslaved on plantations where our free labor was yielding wealth for free White men with power and privilege to enjoy. Other lines within the four verses of the Anthem are also laced with irony, contradiction and hypocrisy. In the third verse one finds the words: "No refuge could save the hirelings or slave from the terror of flight or the gloom of the grave." The fourth verse begins: "Oh, thus be it ever when free men shall stand between their loved homes and war's desolation." Most Africans in America were not "free" and their homes were the wretched slave quarters!

Let me be perfectly clear, I am willing to stand up with pride to salute the Flag and sing the National Anthem, but it must be a new flag and a new anthem. When Jean Jacque Dessalines declared Haiti the first Black Republic in the world in 1804, the Haitian freedom fighters didn't keep the French Flag. They created a new flag with white removed as an official color to signify the dawning of a new day for the new nation. When Blacks in South Africa finally triumphed over apartheid, a new flag and anthem were created to reflect the promise and prospects of the "new South Africa."

Similarly, I want the American Flag to be "our" flag, to be one that represents the history, aspirations and promise for all the people who have come to be a part of this nation. Equally important our flag must represent a nation which has apologized for the transgressions of the past and repaired the damages suffered by Native Americans, Africans and other people of color during the course of America's history. Americans must never forget that everyone who lives in this country is the beneficiary of the conquest and dispossession of the native peoples who were the original inhabitants of this land. There is still a trail of tears and broken treaties which must be acknowledged accompanied by an ungrudging policy of systematic repair of the damage done to Native Americans. Moreover, at a minimum, an acknowledgement is appropriate for the seizure of territory from Mexico in 1848 and the subsequent mistreatment of Mexicans in this country. The same is in order for the unconscionable use of quasi-slave labor, "coolies" in the construction of the railroads and other public works projects and decades of discrimination, exclusion and mistreatment of the Chinese.

Finally, Americans need to remember that the "peculiar institution" of enslavement and generations of segregation, lynching and exclusion damaged and stymied the growth and evolution of Africans in America—the effects of which are still painfully evident today. The government of the United States, expressing the will of "we the people," must have the vision and courage to affirmatively and definitely address, redress and repair the damage done to Africans in America and other peoples cited above to erase my ambivalence/resistance to embracing the Flag and Anthem.

In other words, the Flag must represent a more perfect union based on a New Covenant for a new America: a Covenant which wholeheartedly embraces the notion of the United States as a multi-cultural, multi-ethnic, multi-religious society with a system of political and economic democracy that ensures "liberty and justice for all." And, there must be new or modified sacred symbols which reflect this new America. Then and only then will I embrace the American Flag as "our flag."

In Defense of Colin Kaepernick's "Stand"

September, 2016

The uproar continues over San Francisco 49ner quarterback Colin Kaepernick's decision to sit-down, rather than stand, during the playing of the National Anthem. Kaepernick said his decision was intended to protest the continued injustices being inflicted on Black people, including police brutality and killings. Though the negative tide has turned somewhat, his protest was initially met with a torrent of criticism from various quarters. He was called everything but a child of God for refusing to "honor America" and our men and women in the armed forces. The "love it or leave it" sentiment was very strong.

Frankly, I was infuriated by these reactions. It made my blood boil. I was already upset and had spoken about the fact that social media exploded with criticism of African American gymnast Gabby Douglas when she inadvertently forgot to put her hand over her heart when the National Anthem was played during the Medal Ceremony at the Olympic Games in Rio. So, when I took to the airways for my weekly radio show Vantage Point on WBAI, 99.5 FM on the Pacifica Network in New York. I unleashed a commentary which made the following points (listen to the commentary at *www.ibw21.org*):

There is no law which states that anyone must stand during the playing of the National Anthem or the Pledge of Alliance to the Flag. It is a strongly held "custom" and societal expectation that one stand, but no law which compels it. On the contrary, Colin Kaepernick has a Constitutional Right to express his views through protest. Freedom of speech is one of the most important cornerstones of this imperfect union. It is one of the avenues through which change can be galvanized. And, Colin Kaepernick has courageously chosen to exercise his First Amendment Right to point out longstanding, persistent injustices, "intolerable acts" that are being heaped upon African Americans who are supposed to be full citizens of this nation.

Most importantly, generations of African Americans have paid the price for Colin Kaepernick and any Black person to sit during the playing of a flawed Anthem replete with hypocrisy. Every time I hear the words "that our Flag was still there" in the Anthem, I'm filled with anger/outrage. When the War of 1812 was fought some 3.5 million Africans were still enslaved and the 500,000 or so "free" Blacks could not vote and were subject to racial discrimination and violence. "Our Flag?" We didn't have a Flag. For Black folks, singing that line and most of the Anthem is ludicrous!

That notwithstanding, Blacks have spilled blood to protect and defend America even when America refused to protect and defend Black people. From Crispus Attucks, who died in the initial skirmish of the American Revolution, to the hundreds of "freedmen" whom George Washington reluctantly armed to fight in the battles of Bunkers Hill and Breed Hill, to the thousands who took up arms to fight for our own freedom in the Civil War, Black people have fought, bled and died aspiring to be free in a nation which repeatedly rewarded our military service with a failure to protect and defend us as citizens. We have been among America's most patient patriots.

Thousands of Black troops went off to fight Kaiser Wilhelm during the First World War to save democracy, only to return to the United States to be gunned down in the streets in their military uniforms in the "bloody red summer of 1919." We fought against Hitler and

Tojo in the Second World War to once again return to an America where we were not free. Soldiers fresh off the battlefields faced humiliation, intimidation, lynching/murders and police violence in the segregated South and "dark ghettos" in the North. Indeed, the hypocrisy of fighting for freedom and democracy abroad while being denied "freedom and justice for all" at home helped to fuel the civil rights, human rights, Black Power and Nationalists/Pan Africanists movements which have painstakingly pushed a reluctant nation toward a more perfect union. Up through the Korean Conflict, Vietnam, Iraq and Afghanistan, Black soldiers have bled and died in every America war.

We have paid the price for Colin Kaepernick to stand or sit, kneel, recognize or ignore a flawed Anthem and Pledge, particularly as his protest continues to illuminate the killing of Black men and women by the police in the streets of this country. Indeed, Frederick Douglas might well have whispered into the ear of Colin Kaepernick, *"Right on Brother. What to Black people is your Anthem and your Flag!"* Or Kaepernick may have been inspired by an "American icon," Jackie Robinson who reflected in his autobiography on standing for the Flag as he carried the weight of the race on his shoulders as the first African American to play Major League Baseball: "As I write this twenty years later, I cannot stand and sing the anthem. I cannot salute the flag; I know that I am a black man in a white world."

In many respects Jackie Robinson, a World War II veteran, was/is symbolic of all the men and women, the patient patriots, who paid the price for Colin Kaepernick to sit or kneel during the playing of the National Anthem and the salute to the Flag. Africans in America and people of conscience and goodwill should resolve to stand with and defend him in his righteous pursuit to end the oppression and injustice of Africans in America. No struggle, no progress!

The Red, Black and Green:
Fly the Flag and Fight for the
Exoneration of Marcus Garvey

July 27, 2015

Augus 17 will mark the 128th birthday of the Honorable Marcus
Mosiah Garvey, the visionary Jamaican-born leader who built
the Universal Negro Improvement Association and African Communities League (UNIA-ACL) into the largest mass movement for liberation in the history of Africans in America and perhaps the world!
As such, I have long advocated that August 17th, his birthday, be celebrated as Universal African Flag Day.

An unapologetic Pan-Africanist, Garvey believed that Black
people everywhere should unite and fight to liberate Africa, the motherland, from the brutal clutches of European colonialism—Africa
should be the base for global Black Power! Hence he said, "I know no
national boundary where the Negro is concerned. The whole world is
my province until Africa is free."

At a time when people of African descent were besieged, be-
littled, marginalized, exploited and oppressed everywhere, Garvey
sought to instill a sense of pride in the history and heritage of a great
people, noting that: "A people without the knowledge of their past
history, origin and culture is like a tree without roots." He declared
that "God and Nature first made us what we are, and then out of our
own created genius we make ourselves what we want to be... Let the
sky and God be our limit and Eternity our measurement."

Garvey was determined to rally a beleaguered people and mold them into a formidable force committed to self-reliance, self-determination and nationhood. The UNIA was organized like a nation in-waiting with military, economic/commercial, educational, health, religious and administrative divisions. He also created literature, music, images and symbols, designed to promote pride and unity. For example, the "Universal Ethiopian Anthem" was adopted as the official song of the organization.

But, the most powerful and lasting symbol of unity that Garvey presented and bequeathed to African people was a Flag, the Red, Black and Green. Garvey was keenly aware of the psycho-cultural value of symbols to an oppressed/battered people. The impetus to put forth a flag became even more urgent because of the white supremacist song that became very popular in the early part of the 20th century—"Every Race Has a Flag but the Coon." The Red, Black and Green was officially ratified as the Flag for African people at the 1920 UNIA Convention, which led Garvey to proclaim: "Show me the race or the nation without a flag, and I will show you a race of people without any pride. Aye! In song and mimicry, they have said, 'Every race has a flag but the coon.' How true! Aye! But that was said of us four years ago. They can't say it now...."

The colors of the Flag were meant to have significance for Black/African people globally. In the ceremonies of IBW's public events, the Flag is saluted by reciting words that embody the essence of what we believe Garvey intended to be the meaning of the colors: Red, for the blood and suffering of African people; Black for the color and culture of our people; Green, for the land stolen from us which we will reclaim to build our nation. The Red, Black and Green Flag was meant to be a symbol of Pan African Unity! Indeed, the influence of Garvey was such that the colors appear in the Flags of Malawi, Kenya and Ghana in Africa and St. Kitts and Nevis in the Caribbean.

In the era of the 60's when Black Power, Black Nationalism and Pan Africanism reemerged as a dominant force in the Black Freedom Struggle in the U.S., the Red, Black and Green was frequently in full flourish at rallies and demonstrations. And, it was common to see sisters and brothers with buttons, hats, scarves and clothing with the colors of the Flag in the design. The colors of the Black Liberation Flag, as it came to be known, were in! It was a symbol of Black pride, unity, resistance and the struggle for self-determination and independence. I shall never forget the hundreds of Flags waving in the breeze on African Liberation Day in 1972 where some 25,000 gathered in Washington, D.C. to demand the liberation of the last colonies in Africa. It was a glorious sight, one Marcus Garvey must have been pleased with from his ascendant perch with the ancestors!

It was to preserve and promote this spirit of unity, pride and resistance and to keep the legacy of Marcus Garvey alive as an impeccable model of the struggle for Black/African self-determination that I wrote an article some years ago proposing that Garvey's birthday be declared Universal African Flag Day. In the article I noted that in New York on the day of the Puerto Rican Day Parade, the Puerto Rican Flag is on prominent display throughout the City. The same applies for the Parades of Dominicans, Colombians and other Latino nationalities in New York. And, at some of the largest pro-immigration reform demonstrations a few years ago there was a sea of Mexican Flags—so much so that it provoked a backlash by opponents of reform, who labeled the demonstrators un-American.

I firmly believe that Africans in America, indeed, African people everywhere should embrace the Red, Black and Green as our Flag and fly/display it during rallies, demonstrations, public events and Black/African holidays as a unifying, Pan African symbol of self-affirmation, resistance and self-determination. And, on the birthday of Marcus Garvey, Universal African Flag Day, the Red, Black and Green should be proudly on display everywhere!

Frankly, my initial calls for Garvey's birthday to be declared Universal African Flag Day, as an act of Kujichagulia/Self-determination, did not get much traction. But, sparked by the Black Lives Matter Movement, there is a new spirit of resistance in the air. I am noticing more and more Red, Black and Green Flags at rallies and demonstrations. Therefore, encouraged by these events, the forthcoming Millions Peoples March for Justice; the urging of Dr. Segun Shabaka of the New York Chapter of the National Association of Kawaida Organizations (NAKO); and, with the blessing of Dr. Julius Garvey, the son of Marcus Garvey, I am renewing the call for August 17th to be affirmed as Universal African Flag Day.

Moreover, in this season of heightened resistance, it is only appropriate that we request that President Obama exonerate the Honorable Marcus Garvey of the trumped up charges of which he was convicted as one of the first victims of the FBI. Marcus Garvey's life and legacy matter to Black/African people. Therefore, we are obligated to fight to clear his name! So, sisters and brothers, let's do it. Fly the Flag and Fight for the Exoneration of Marcus Garvey! #FlytheRedBlackandGreenAugust17

Forty Acres and a Mule: The Struggle for Reparations

Reparations Are Imperative: The Stagnate "State of Black America"

May, 2014

I recently attended the release of the National Urban League's Annual *State of Black America Report* at the National Press Club in
Washington, D.C. The Report is an extremely important document
because it provides key indicators of Black progress in a number of
social and economic areas in relationship to White Americans. This
year's Report, *One Nation Underemployed: Jobs Rebuild America*, focuses on the critical issues of joblessness, the wealth gap and economic inequality in Black America. The data explodes the myth
that, because the United States has a Black President, we now live
in a "post-racial" society—"race still matters" in America. According
to the Report, the Median Household Income for Whites is $56,565
compared to $33,764 for Blacks; 11% of Whites live below the poverty
line, 28.1% for Blacks; unemployment among Whites is 6.5%, 13.1%
for Blacks; and, the critical "wealth-building" indicator of home ownership, Whites own their homes at a rate of 73.5% compared to 43%
for Blacks—stunning disparities for a "post racial" society.

Even more alarming is the persistence of an enormous wealth
gap between Blacks and Whites. According to a study co-authored
by Dr. Thomas Shapiro, who spoke at the release of the *State of Black
America Report*, the median wealth for White families in 2009 was
$113,149 but only $5,677 for Blacks! The study defines wealth as "what
we own minus what we owe." Not surprisingly, Dr. Shapiro and his

associates draw a direct correlation between homeownership and wealth accumulation. Obviously the gap between Black and White home ownership is a major contributing factor to the abysmally low wealth accumulation in Black America. And, for those who think race is inconsequential, as George Fraser and many Black analysts have pointed out, huge amounts of wealth was lost during the "Great Recession" when African Americans were deliberately targeted for toxic sub-prime mortgage loans. Racism in the mortgage industry led to the loss of Black wealth.

What is sobering and alarming about this data is that in relative terms it hasn't changed very much in the past decades if not generations. Though I have not taken time to do the research, I am confident that a survey of past *State of Black America Reports* would show that the status of Blacks in comparison to Whites has remained relatively the same. For example, though income has increased for both groups, it is highly likely that the gap in the median income has remained about the same. Moreover, despite an expanded upper and middle class, the astonishing wealth gap between Blacks and Whites has not changed significantly. The other startling reality is that if the Black upper and middle classes have expanded and there is still a significant gap between the races, this suggests that those stuck at the bottom in Black America (poor and working people) have not progressed but stagnated. These are the Black folks who are imprisoned in America›s «Dark Ghettos.» As Malcolm X might put it, they are catching more hell than ever before!

Though the *State of Black America Reports* are important, given the unchanging status of Blacks relative to Whites, it›s almost as if you could just say ditto on the data year after year. What accounts for the stagnate state of Black America? I believe it is the legacy of the intergenerational deficits of enslavement and the persistence of structural/institutional racism.

The cold fact is that Africans in America never received a substantial stake in terms of land or capital for the generations of free labor that produced incredible wealth for plantation owners, the shipbuilding, textile manufacturing, whiskey distilleries and a range of related industries and occupations—industries and occupations that thrived off the European slave trade and cash crop production, e.g. cotton, rice, sugar, indigo.

In addition, there was the "Jim Crow" system in the South, which "set-aside" certain jobs for Whites and paid higher wages to Whites in jobs where Blacks and Whites did the same work. These material incentives were designed to ensure that White poor and working people would always fare better than their Black counterparts. In modified form, this system of "affirmative action" for Whites existed all across the nation well into the 20th century. The benefits of «White privilege» were intended to drive a permanent wedge between Black and White poor and working people to prevent unified opposition to the manipulative, self-serving White ruling elites. By and large the system has worked well. In no small measure the relative gap between Blacks and Whites in terms of income and wealth is a legacy of enslavement and structural/institutional racism. And, large numbers of White poor and working-class people still see Blacks as enemies instead of allies in the struggle to achieve a better quality of life.

The question is, how is it possible to ever erase the income and wealth gap between Blacks and Whites without dealing with the root cause of persistent inequality—the failure to provide compensation to the formerly enslaved Africans for the centuries of free labor and cultural, spiritual and physical destruction that have severely hampered the quest for justice, socio-economic equity/parity, freedom and self-determination. The answer is clear, Reparations for the damages done to the sons and daughters in America are imperative if we are to achieve justice, equity/parity in the U.S. and the world for that matter. So, as we mobilize/organize to overcome the stagnate state of Black America, it is imperative that the demand for Reparations be an integral part of the agenda!

Reparations: Eradicating the "Badges and Incidents" of Slavery

January 2017

2015 marks the 150th Anniversary of the adoption of the 13th Amendment to the Constitution, during the Reconstruction period after the Civil War. The Amendment officially abolished slavery, completing a process begun with the "partial" Emancipation Proclamation which only "freed" enslaved Africans in those states that were at war with the Union. It would be the first of three Reconstruction Amendments which would abolish slavery, establish citizenship and grant the right to vote to the formerly enslaved Africans. The 13th Amendment is also noteworthy because of the pledge to "eradicate the badges and indications of slavery." President Obama and members of Congress hailed the Amendment as one of the great achievements of racial justice at a ceremony in the nation's Capital.

It is important to remember that while the 13th Amendment should appropriately be heralded as a milestone measure addressing the injustices of centuries of brutal bondage and exploitation of the free labor of Africans, it was a partial, an incomplete proposition. Like the Emancipation Proclamation, this Amendment contained a major exception. It applied "*except as a punishment for crime whereof the party shall have been duly convicted.*" In addition, none of the Reconstruction Amendments offered a formal apology for chattel slavery nor provided compensation to its victims. As a consequence, millions of formerly enslaved Africans were "freed" and granted political rights without social rights. The newly emancipated Africans were not provided with "forty acres and a mule," capital or an endowment to survive, thrive and compete within a Capitalist economy, incredibly enriched by centuries of free Black labor. No reparations were provided to repair the horrific damages inflicted on Africans by chattel slavery.

It was a cruel "emancipation" that left millions of Africans in a state of peonage, a kind of neo-slavery as sharecroppers, tenant farmers and agricultural laborers, in many instances trapped on the same plantations they had worked prior to being granted "freedom." Those who did not return to the plantations were often victimized by "vagrancy laws" adopted to criminalize the unattached and unemployed "freedmen." These "vagrants" were fed into the infamous convict-lease system, a collusion between prisons and private sector interests which involved hiring out convicts (mostly Blacks) to plantations and private businesses to profit from their free labor … again.

This arrangement was readily justifiable under the "exception" incorporated into the 13th Amendment. In the meantime, under the protection of their "Radical Republican" benefactors, Blacks could vote in the South, run for and hold elective offices. But, it was a highly dependent political freedom. This perilous situation would end with the Compromise of 1877 when the Republicans abandoned their Black dependents in order to retain the presidency. All federal troops were withdrawn from the South leaving Blacks vulnerable to the vicious and often violent whims of vengeful Whites.

The bottom line is that 150 years after the adoption of the 13th Amendment, the "badges and incidents" of slavery have not been eradicated. The persistent "wealth gap" between Blacks and Whites, chronic underdevelopment in distressed Black communities and mass incarceration are clear testimonies to the inability of Black America to overcome the intergenerational deficits of enslavement and post-emancipation discriminatory policies and practices. Accordingly, Africans in America must compel this nation to face the reality that reparations are imperative to eradicate the "badges and incidents of slavery" if there is to be justice, peace, reconciliation and a "more perfect union" in this land!

Passing HR 40:
Towards A Real Conversation
on Race in America

August, 2009

The infamous arrest of Harvard Professor Henry Louis Gates at his home in Cambridge momentarily brought the issue of race to the forefront in America ... again. For more than a week, the television and radio airwaves were filled with debate and acrimony over whether racial profiling and/or preconceived perceptions of criminality about Black men played a role in Professor Gates' arrest. When President Barack Obama weighed in at a White House press conference on health care reform by proclaiming that the Cambridge police acted "stupidly," the incident became the dominant story for several news cycles. The uproar, which the President's remarks provoked, demonstrated the limits of the power of a Black man in the White House in a nation that is still in denial about racism. President Obama reluctantly dialed back his rhetoric and accepted Sergeant James Crowley's suggestion that the parties meet at the White House for a beer.

With hundreds of media cameras rolling, the whole nation watched as the President, Vice-President, Gates and Crowley clicked glasses in what appeared to be an amiable toast. The principals agreed to meet again in the future, and with that, ostensibly, the matter was finished. The nation and the news media are back to business as usual—that is until the next sensational episode on race explodes, as most assuredly it will.

And therein lies the problem; America will revert to denial mode. Perhaps this is why Attorney General Eric Holder made the "controversial" remark that America is a "nation of cowards" when it comes to discussing race/racism. Of course, he was immediately lambasted by the rightwing attack machine while the rest of the commercialized/homogenized media chimed in uncritically. But truer words were never spoken. Many in White America are petrified by the thought of a real conversation about race. However, the "more perfect union" promised in the Declaration of Independence and Constitution will never fully be fulfilled until this nation confronts and deals with the issue of race in all of its dimensions.

The President termed the Gates arrest a "teachable moment" but rather than use it as an opportunity to initiate a process to educate on the issues of race, he settled for a "beer summit." Perhaps this is understandable given the huge number of complex issues his administration is working to address. There is no reason why he could not have instructed Attorney General Eric Holder to take some immediate steps to advance discussion and action on issues of race illuminated by Professor Gates' arrest. First, the Attorney General should have convened a national summit on police community relations to explore the wide range of grievances that exist between communities of color and police across the country. In some respects, the uproar over Professor Gates' arrest represents what Ellis Cose called the "rage of the privileged class," an unjust and embarrassing inconvenience. Professor Gates will soon return to a life of relative privilege as a member of the Black elite.

As Bob Herbert correctly notes in a recent *New York Times* article, the real issue is the hundreds of thousands of mostly poor and working-class Blacks who are routinely stopped, frisked or otherwise harassed by police on a daily basis. A national summit could have explored these issues and offered recommendations to remedy a potentially combustible situation. Second, the Obama administration could re-introduce a bill banning racial profiling, legislation long championed by the Rev. Al Sharpton and other civil rights/human leaders. These are some immediate steps that could have and should have been initiated as an outgrowth of the arrest of Professor Gates. But these actions would still fall short of the real conversation on race we need to engage.

Ultimately, a serious and substantive conversation on race as it relates to the experiences of Africans in America must begin with a thorough analysis of the original wound, enslavement and the institution of chattel slavery. As if there is no relationship between this "original sin" and the present, Black people are admonished to forget and move on as a precondition for acceptance. Pundits and politicians, especially conservatives, want to lecture Blacks for our failure to accept "personal responsibility" for the problems plaguing those at the bottom in Black America, without acknowledging the intergenerational impact of centuries of enslavement and de jure and de facto apartheid.

This is why I strongly favor the passage of HR-40, the "Commission to Study Reparations Proposals for African-Americans Act," which Congressman John Conyers, Jr. has introduced in Congress every year since 1989. In addition to acknowledging "the fundamental injustice, cruelty, brutality, and inhumanity of slavery in the United States and the 13 American colonies between 1619 and 1865," the bill would create a commission to study the impact of slavery and segregation on African Americans up to the present and recommend remedies to Congress to repair/heal damages where found.

I want to start the conversation at the most painful and controversial point, an exhaustive examination of what it was like to be reduced to property, a non-human in the United States. What were the consequences of being forbidden to practice one's religion, speak one's language or even play musical instruments integral to one's ethnic/national culture? What was the impact of being separated by ethnic group and the fracturing of families for commercial pursuit? What was the benefit to the nation and its citizens of centuries of free labor extracted from the subjects of the "peculiar institution?" What were the consequences of being "emancipated" without being granted land/property, resources or a stake in America's capitalist economy? What was the effect of being compelled to labor on plantations as sharecroppers and being leased out as convict labor from prisons? What was the effect of decades of racial violence directed at the formerly enslaved Africans, including thousands of lynchings? What were the lost opportunity costs to Blacks for being excluded from various occupations and/or being confined to the dirtiest, lowest paying jobs in various industries and occupations for generations?

These are the kinds of questions/issues that a Reparations Study Commission should address as part of a national conversation and education on race in America as it relates to the sons and daughters of Africa. And, the conversation must begin with the aggrieved, the victims, voicing their grievances and recounting the history of injustice heaped on them as they see it. Unfortunately, proponents of a national dialogue on race often act as if there is an experiential or moral equivalency between people of African descent (Blacks) and Euro-ethnics (Whites) in the conversation. This is a faulty premise. Whites were not enslaved or the subject of apartheid. Men can't command or demand a seat at the table as victims in a dialogue about gender equality! Women have to speak and men have to listen and respond. Similarly, the dialogue on race must necessarily begin with the evidence of Black oppression/victimization and Whites must listen and then respond.

The question is what do conservatives or White opponents of the Reparations Study Commission have to fear from a real conversation on race/racism? Perhaps it is that once the general public knows what really happened to people of African descent in history, using race/racism as a tool to divide and exploit will be neutralized. Equally important, with all the facts on the table, it is entirely possible that an educated public will view the Black experience in America with a more understanding and empathetic mind and embrace proposals to repair the damage and heal the wounds from this enormous blot on the American character. In so doing, all of us will move closer to "a more perfect union!"

The Case for Race-Based Remedies to Achieve Racial Justice

May, 2009

As I recounted in a previous article, progress for Blacks in general is fragile but especially perilous for the masses of working class and poor people in Black America. In my judgment, this is primarily because race-based remedies to overcome past and present affects of enslavement, segregation, discrimination and structural racism have virtually been eradicated. Though affirmative action was originally conceived as a remedy for past and present discrimination against Blacks, in the current climate of "race neutral" public policy and jurisprudence, it has largely been reduced to achieving "diversity" in the academy and workplace. Indeed, the "reverse discrimination" case filed by White firefighters in New Haven, Connecticut may spell the end of affirmative action as a race-based remedy. To add insult to injury, the Supreme Court is also scheduled to rule on whether Section Five of the Voting Rights Act should be terminated. This section provides that states with a history of exclusion or gerrymandering based on race must receive pre-clearance before making changes in voting procedures. Not surprisingly, the states of the old Confederacy are leading the charge to eliminate this provision.

Ironically, the election of America's first Black President may serve to impede efforts to come to grips with the persistent disparities and inequities which still have large numbers of Black people mired in poverty. There is a danger that many Americans will view improvements in "race relations" under a Black President as the culmination of the heroic struggle for freedom and equality by Africans in America. This is a perception that scholars, activists and organizers must resist at every turn, insisting that racial justice, achieving equity and parity in a just and humane society must be the ultimate goal of the Black freedom struggle. To this end, there must be a calculated and concerted effort to revive race-based remedies to achieve racial justice.

America's penchant for historical amnesia notwithstanding, the case for race-based remedies is deeply rooted in the nightmare of this nation's history of racial oppression and economic exploitation of Black people; oppression and exploitation that benefited/developed America and its Euro-ethnic/White residents while retarding/under developing the sons and daughters of Africa. As Dr. Claud Anderson details in *Black Labor, White Wealth*, a significant portion of the wealth of America is directly or indirectly attributable to the enormous super-profits derived from the trans-Atlantic slave trade and generations of free labor extracted from enslaved Africans who toiled from Wall Street, the plantations in the South to the nation's capital. Given the "acceleration principle" and "multiplier effect" as factors in economic growth/development, all Euro-ethnics benefited, though unevenly, from profits reaped from the "peculiar institution."

The institution of chattel slavery is the genesis of the persistent social/economic disparities between Africans and Europeans in this country; a state of chronic inequality which could only have been overcome by the vigorous application of race-specific remedies designed to fully incorporate formerly enslaved and quasi-free Africans as equal citizens in a land not of their choosing. Unfortunately, there has never been consistent political will to achieve this objective.

In his essay *The Constitutional Right of Negro Freedom*, noted

Constitutional scholar and people's attorney Arthur Kinoy persuasively argues that the 13th, 14th, and 15th Amendments to the Constitution, which abolished slavery, established citizenship and bestowed the right to vote on Blacks respectively, were specifically intended to fully incorporate formerly enslaved Africans into the nation as equals. Adopted in the decade immediately following the Civil War, these Reconstruction Amendments were the first race-based remedies. Setting aside the fact that a plebiscite was never conducted to ascertain whether the formerly enslaved Africans wished to become American citizens or not, these Amendments fell short of achieving the intended effect. By 1877 an explosive White backlash in the South resulted in a "compromise" that virtually nullified the rights and freedoms guaranteed by the Reconstruction Amendments. A rigid system of apartheid was instituted and violently enforced in the South. It would take nearly a century of struggle to regain the rights lost during the Post Reconstruction era.

Equally as telling, however, is the fact that the Reconstruction Amendments provided political/civil rights without accompanying social-economic rights. Impoverished formerly enslaved Africans were freed and made citizens of the United States, a capitalist society, without any compensation in the form of property and/or a permanent guarantee of entitlement to education, housing or healthcare. Having provided the free labor which generated wealth for a developing nation, no permanent programs were instituted to close the wealth gap between Blacks and Whites. Though Sherman's Field Order #15 allocated 40 acres and a mule for thousands of formerly enslaved Africans with land from South Carolina to Florida, the Order was revoked by President Andrew Johnson after the assassination of Abraham Lincoln. The Southern Homestead Act was also potentially a source of land/property for Blacks, but access to this program was fiercely resisted by Whites who systematically ensured that parcels of land went to their kith and kin; land which could be passed on to future generations to under gird their social-economic status. The Freedman's Bureau, which was established to provide healthcare, housing and educational opportunities for Black refugees from the Civil War, did offer useful services including establishing scores of educational institutions. Faced with Southern resistance, however, the Bureau was short-lived. With the advent of Post Reconstruction, Blacks faced the harsh reality that political rights had evaporated and no permanent programs had been instituted to ensure their social and economic development.

The case for race-based remedies does not end there, however. Much of American history can be described as a longstanding affirmative action program for Euro-ethnics which generated wealth and opportunity for Whites while stagnating and blunting the interests and aspirations of African Americans. We have already recounted how the Southern Homestead Act overwhelmingly benefited Whites rather that Blacks. Moreover, the southern apartheid system was designed to give privileges and opportunities to Whites over Blacks. Certain categories of jobs were "set aside" for "Whites only." In most instances where Blacks and Whites worked the same job, Whites were paid more for doing the same work. Blacks were locked in quasi-peonage in the South as sharecroppers, tenant farmers and agricultural laborers. There were few opportunities beyond these fields as Blacks were systematically excluded from skill crafts like carpentry and brick masons, occupations which they were well suited to pursue. In addition, in his essay *Demand for Black Labor*, Harold Barron points out that in the aftermath of rapid industrial growth in the North after the Civil War, more than 10 million immigrants were imported from Europe to fill relatively well paying jobs in the factories, foundries and mills; jobs which could have been filled by Black laborers from the South. These late arriving immigrants would eventually move up the ladder to achieve a more secure economic status than their Black counterparts.

Once the great migrations to the North by Blacks commenced, they found life better than the apartheid system in the South. But affirmative action for Whites was still the order of the day. Blacks were the "last hired and first fired" in most occupations. Certain occupations were off limits to Blacks even in the North, and in most occupations Blacks were confined to the most menial, dirty and low paying jobs. There was a color line blocking Blacks from reaching higher paying jobs. When the Hungarian Revolt against the Soviet Union erupted in 1956, thousands of Hungarian immigrants flocked to cities and towns in the U.S. like Youngstown, Ohio. I vividly recall Hungarian immigrants being immediately hired to jobs in the steel mill that my father was not allowed to work.

Agricultural extension agents in the South who systematically discriminated against Black farmers; a Federal Housing Administration (FHA) which assisted Whites to obtain home mortgages while denying Blacks; urban renewal programs which destroyed Black business districts and neighborhoods; red lining by banks that denied Blacks the capital to build businesses or develop their communities on an equal footing with Whites. American history, past and present, is replete with examples of affirmative action for Whites which produced benefits that could be transferred to the next generation. Because of structural racism, Blacks could only pass on deficits to the next generation.

In composite, this history of racial exclusion of Blacks and advantages, privileges and benefits accrued by Whites explains the persistent disparities in income, wealth and other social-economic indicators between the races. Comprehend these historical factors and you understand why ultimately race-based remedies are imperative if Africans in America are to achieve equity and parity with their White counterparts. This is the raw, naked truth which Americans must confront and address if racial justice and reconciliation are ever to become to part of "a more perfect union."

The Crisis of Youth Violence and the Demand for Reparations

October, 2009

T he crisis of youth violence and fratricide ripping at the sinews of the fabric of Black communities across this country should intensify the demand for reparations to repair the damage from enslavement and its aftermath. On the surface, one might question the relationship between the current crisis and slavery; after all, the enslavement of Africans ended in the 19th century with the Emancipation Proclamation and 14thAmendment. The answer lies in one of the most neglected aspects of the discussion on reparations, the intergenerational deficits and damage incurred by Africans in America as a consequence of the system of chattel slavery. I emphasis chattel slavery because only in the U.S. was a system of enslavement adopted which reduced human beings to property, to be owned like a "chicken, cow or a horse" as Malcolm put it. This dehumanization included cultural aggression, a concerted effort to take away the identity, institutions, language, music, religion, and wipe out the historical memory of enslaved Africans. A crucial element of the chattel slave system was the quest to de-Africanize the African as a mechanism to engender subservience and facilitate control.

Obviously the dehumanization and de-Africanization processes did not succeed. Our survival and development as Africans on these hostile shores is stark testimony to our resiliency and will as a people. In spite of the assault on our culture and humanity, our forebears forged a new African community in the U.S., built institutions and mustered the resolve to challenge a racist/exploitive system. However, the path from the auction block to the White House has been strewn with the "blood of the slaughtered." We have triumphed despite trials, tribulations and adversity, but it has not been without scars and damage.

One of the most insidious effects of enslavement was the unevenness of the survival and development process due in part to lapses in historical memory and the lack of consistency in what Dr. Maulana Karenga calls 'identity, purpose and direction." The continuity of culture and identity served as a foundation for social, economic and political advancement for other ethnic groups that migrated to this country. For African people, however, the assault on culture resulted in discontinuity, disorientation and became an obstacle to community development. Time and time again during the course of our evolution in America, we have had to rediscover our cultural roots and learn to re-identify ourselves as African people. This is

the problem Carter G. Woodson sought to address in his seminal work *The Mis-*

Education of the Negro. Whether it was in the early days of the Republic when leaders like Richard Allen and Absalom Jones created parallel institutions clearly identified as "African," the "search for a place" during the deliberations in the "Colored" People's Conventions in the pre-Civil War era, the intense debates on the direction of our people in the Post Reconstruction period, the Nationalism and Pan Africanism of Garvey and the explosion of "new Negro" creativity in the Harlem Renaissance to the era of Black Power and Black consciousness, previous generations have had to address the problem of identity, purpose and direction.

I contend that this disrupted path of survival and development is the direct consequence of the holocaust of enslavement and the destructive experience under the system of chattel slavery. The violence and fratricide afflicting our communities is in part attributable to historical amnesia or the loss of historical memory by significant numbers of Black youth and their parents in contemporary Black America. The social movements of the era of the 60s which strove to achieve freedom, justice and equality and an emphasis on pride in self and kind are largely absent from the minds and memories of this generation—let alone a knowledge/awareness of the centuries of struggle African sheroes and heroes waged for our survival and development.

Like my friend Dr. Ramona Edelin, I believe a "cultural offensive" with a focus on African-centered educational processes which reaffirm our identity as African people and challenge us individually and collectively to struggle to rescue and reconstruct our communities in the 21stcentury is imperative. It will take more than the standard educational, jobs, gang prevention and anti-violence programs to end the crisis of violence and fratricide in Black communities. We must restore historical memory and instill a new sense of identity, purpose and direction among this generation of young people. And, to overcome the recurring pattern of loss and rediscovery of historical memory we must put in place permanent structures, institutions and programs that continually transmit the culture and history of struggle which is responsible for our survival and development.

This is where the demand for reparations becomes crucial. The principal purpose of reparations is to repair the mental, cultural, spiritual and physical damages to a people. The assault on African culture under the system of chattel slavery is clearly a major cause of the recurring loss of memory that has plagued our community. That damage must be repaired. Reparations will enable Africans in America to institute the kind of permanent "cultural offensive" required to heal our communities so that epidemics of self-hating fratricide and violence are a phenomena of the past. Therefore, as we devise strategies to cope with the current crisis, the demand for reparations must be an indispensable part of the plan. America must pay for "taking away our names."

CARICOM Initiative Could Provide the Spark: Revitalizing the U.S. Reparations Movement

October, 2012

A few days before this year's Congressional Black Caucus Foundation, Inc. Annual Legislative Conference (CBCINC-ALC), I received a call to ask my opinion as to whether the Reparations Issues Forum should be on the agenda. The Forum has been standard fare every year as a way of promoting HR-40, the Reparation's Study bill, championed by Congressman John Conyers, Jr., and as a vehicle to discuss strategies for the coming year. The question was understandable given the relatively moribund state of the Reparations movement in the U.S.; a reality that is the consequence of the passing/transition of some of the key leaders of the movement, the decline of reparations advocacy organizations and the difficulty of gaining traction on the issue with the first African American President in the White House.

However, none of these factors negate the validity and relevance of the issue. Therefore, I answered in the affirmative but strongly suggested that the Forum highlight events or developments that might provide a new spark to the U.S. Reparations Movement. In the past, State Senator Bill Owens' proposal that the Massachusetts legislature pay reparations to African Americans in that state; Deadria Farmer-Paellmann's legal campaign against U.S. corporations that benefitted from slavery; the National Black United Front's "We Charge Genocide" Petition Campaign; December 12th Movement›s Millions Reparations March; Randall Robinson›s highly acclaimed book *The Debt*;

and, The National Coalition for Reparations for African Americans' (N'COBRA) Reparations Legal Team are examples of actions and events that breathed life into the movement and gave it momentum at particular moments. Unfortunately, in recent years there has been no significant action or event to keep reparations on the front burner of the discourse about Black interests and aspirations. Indeed, the election of the first African American President has likely had a chilling effect in terms of advancing the issue.

But, as I informed the conveners of the Forum, recent developments in the Caribbean have the potential for dramatically changing the tide in the U.S. and Pan African World. Spearheaded by Dr. Ralph Gonsalves, Prime Minister of St. Vincent and the Grenadines, in July the Caribbean Community (CARICOM) leaders "agreed to the formation of a region-wide Reparations Commission to seek compensation from Europe for native genocide and enslavement of Africans during colonisation." Subsequent to this historic resolution, PM Gonsalves convened a major Reparations Conference, September 15-17th in St. Vincent. The delegates agreed to form Reparation Commissions in each Caribbean nation. In addition, PM Gonsalves and several Caribbean leaders utilized the annual convening of the U.N. General Assembly as a platform to boldly incorporate the demand for reparations into their speeches. The CARICOM Reparations Initiative is a historic development, a potential game changer, not only in terms of the potential impact on the Reparations Movement in this country, but the prospect of a resurgent progressive Pan-Africanism, with a renewed focus on the root causes of the "underdevelopment" of people of African descent on the continent and in the Diaspora.

Another development which could spark a renewed interest in the U.S. Reparations Movement is the discovery of a little known speech by Dr. Martin Luther King, Jr. that addresses the issue. On the morning of the Reparations Issues Forum, I received an urgent email and voicemail message from SIRIUS/XM Radio Talk Show Host Mark Thompson, urging me to listen to an excerpt of a speech by Dr. King. Mark obviously felt it would be relevant to the subject. He was absolutely correct. In the space of two minutes, Dr. King recounts a range of benefits provided to European immigrants and White farmers like the Homestead Act that were systematically denied to the formerly enslaved Africans. In so doing, he emphatically lays out the equivalent of a rationale for reparations and concludes by proclaiming, when we come to Washington ...we're coming to get our check." When we played the clip the audience was stunned and exhilarated. Never before had the participants heard such a ringing rationale for reparations, coming from the lips of the world's most revered civil rights leader! Everyone instantly recognized that these words from Dr. King could be invaluable in providing legitimacy to the righteous demand for reparations.

I was delighted to moderate the Reparations Issues Forum this year because the developments above could well breathe new life into the quest for Africans in America to achieve a yet unfulfilled aspiration—reparations to repair the cultural, psychological, spiritual and physical damage to our people as a direct consequence of the holocaust of enslavement. Moreover, with the input of a Panel consisting of City Councilwoman JoAnn Watson of Detroit, Dr. Julianne Malveaux, Black America's leading political-economist and Attorney Nkechi Taifa, Senior Policy Analyst, Open Society Foundations, an action agenda to revitalize the U.S. Reparations Movement was devised.

The action agenda includes: the widespread circulation of Dr. King's speech, which provides a rationale for reparations; an Open Letter to President Barack Obama from Congressman John Conyers,

Jr. requesting that the President support HR-40, the Reparations Study Bill; a series of four community-based regional hearings on HR-40, chaired by Congressman Conyers with a stellar Panel of Resource People like Dr. Claud Anderson, Dr. Ray Winbush, Dr. Julianne Malveaux, Professor Charles Ogletree, Dr. Iva Carruthers, Attorney Nkechi Taifa and Councilwoman JoAnn Watson, to mention a few; utilizing Dr. King's assessment as a framework, the convening of a Special Hearing in Selma, Alabama with Black farmers, many of whom still feel aggrieved despite the settlement with the Department of Agriculture; an invitation extended by Congressman John Conyers, Jr. to Dr. Ralph Gonsalves to be a Special Guest and Keynote Speaker for the 2014 CBCINC-ALC Reparations Issues Forum; finally, the Institute of the Black World 21st Century (IBW) will contribute to the process by establishing a Reparations Resource Center on its website *www.ibw21.org* where interested parties can access important articles, documents, speeches and other relevant materials that might be useful for education, advocacy and organizing.

Inspired by the incredible developments noted above and armed with a feasible action agenda, we have an opportunity to revitalize the Reparations Movement in the U.S. In remembrance of our ancestors, a luta continua ... the struggle continues!

The National/International Summit: Seizing the Moment to Galvanize the U.S. and Global Reparations Movement

April, 2015

Queen Mother Audley Moore was an indefatigable teacher, advocate and organizer for Reparations, the fundamental idea that Africans in America are due compensation to repair the physical, cultural, spiritual and mental damages inflicted by the holocaust of enslavement. She called herself a "brain surgeon" dedicated to operating on the minds of constipated "Negroes" to create a consciousness of the urgent need for Reparations. I was a patient of this great "surgeon." Queen Mother Moore introduced me to the concept of Reparations and became my mentor on this issue. As the Institute of the Black World 21st Century (IBW) prepares to convene a potentially historic National/International Summit, April 9-12, in New York, I believe our "warrior woman" ancestor is looking down with pride and enthusiasm as reparations advocates from the U.S. and the Pan African world gather to galvanize and intensify the global Reparations Movement.

Reparations to repair the damages of enslavement has been a persistent demand within the multifaceted Black Freedom Struggle in the U.S. The movement ebbs and flows, being intense at certain moments in our history and subdued at others. Despite the fact that there is a "State of Emergency" in America's "dark ghettos," the pride associated with the election of the first African American President has not made this the most fertile period for the Reparations Movement. However, two events have potentially provided the impetus for a new moment of intense interest and advocacy for reparations in the months and years ahead.

First, as I have written recently, the courageous decision by the heads of state of nations in the Caribbean to demand reparations from the former European colonialists for Native Genocide and African enslavement and the formation of a CARICOM Reparations Commission has captured the imagination of reparations activists in the U.S. and the Pan African world. It is one thing for scholars and activists to advocate for reparations, it is quite another for the leaders of nations who are still in the neo-colonial clutches of the former colonial powers to make such a bold demand. By doing so, they risk economic and political retaliation. No doubt the dismal conditions of the masses of their people and the pressure from civil society organizations influenced their decision, but there is no belittling the fact that the demand for reparations was/is a gutsy decision!

Second, the brilliant essay "The Case for Reparations" by Ta-Nehisi Coates published in the *Atlantic* Magazine, has electrified a new generation of Black people who were largely unfamiliar with reparations or unconvinced of its validity and value as a goal. While a dedicated core of true believers has kept the issue of reparations alive, for the movement to grow it must be embraced by a new generation of potential advocates who, like Brother Coates, can be converted to the cause. Moreover, we need a moment when the movement can be broadened to form a critical mass, a formidable force to advance the demand for reparations. That moment may be at hand. Indeed, Queen Mother Moore would be excited to learn that a National African American Reparations Commission (NAARC) has been established in her memory! [visit the website www.ibw21.org for list of Members] Inspired by the CARICOM Reparations Commission and designed to function as a parallel body, NAARC's primary mission is to develop a preliminary Reparations Program/Agenda as part of an education and advocacy process to expand the Reparations Movement in the U.S. Ultimately, NAARC will develop a final Reparations Program/Agenda as an outgrowth of input from a series of regional community-based hearings and town hall meetings across the country.

This moment presents a major opportunity for discussions on how the Reparations Movement in the U.S. should proceed. The Coates article tapped into what appears to be growing sentiment that reparations are due Africans in America not only for enslavement, but the damages done to our people during the era of de jure and de facto segregation as well as post segregation. Coates' research on housing patterns in Chicago clearly demonstrates the intergenerational wealth deficit created by discriminatory housing policies and practices. Michelle Alexander has also added her voice to reparations advocates who believe compensation is due for the massive damages to Black families and communities as a direct result of the "New Jim Crow," mass incarceration. Damages from environmental racism are also a matter which some advocates contend should be on the table. These considerations expand the scope of the reparations demands.

There is also a need to discuss the collective versus individual payment of reparations. This often comes up as a question when arguing the case for reparations. While one could make an argument for both, I am hopeful that a consensus will emerge in favor of collective developmental assistance. The chronic wealth gap and state of emergency in America's dark ghettos are a direct consequence of generations of exploitation and oppression which should be addressed in terms of compensation that will be used to end the underdevelopment of the National Black Community. Individuals in the Black community would benefit from increased opportunities resulting from developmental assistance for the group/collective.

Consistent with the concept of collective developmental assistance, it would also be useful to develop a consensus for a Reparations Trust Fund or similar structure to administer the various types of compensation that might be received from the federal government, state and local governments, corporations/businesses and institutions like universities, implicated in enslavement or other damaging policies and practices inflicted in other eras. Such a Trust Fund would be governed by a Board comprised of a cross-section of credible Black leaders and organizations that would receive various forms of compensation and allocate resources in accordance with a strategic development plan. As an aside, I have a particular interest in demanding that federal lands be transferred to a Trust fund with the same kind of sovereignty and rights eventually granted Native Americans for the criminal dispossession of their lands.

As the case for reparations for Africans in America is advanced, we need a much more coherent message about key issues and questions that are often raised by our people like the ones cited above. Hopefully, as NAARC engages in its deliberations, it can be helpful in formulating and advancing recommendations on these vital issues and questions. I continue to believe that HR-40, the Reparations Study Bill, introduced by Congressman John Conyers, Jr. every year since 1989, can be a valuable organizing tool to generate discussion and action on this vital issue.

The National/International Reparations Summit will not only be a moment to galvanize the U.S. Reparations Movement, it will serve to galvanize an emerging global Reparations Movement. A key goal of the Summit is to explore avenues for systematic information-sharing and mutual support as a means of strengthening the global Reparations Movement. As such, it will provide an opportunity for a dialogue/interface between NAARC and the CARICOM Reparations Commission (CRC) and advocates from the Caribbean, Central and South America, Canada and Europe (21 countries as of this writing). Without question, the CRC will be most closely examined as the model which has given a major boost to the U.S. and global Reparations Movements. At the end of the deliberations, a mechanism will be put in place to sustain the momentum of this incredible moment in history. Let the word go out across the Pan African World, the global Reparations Movement is on the rise and Queen Mother Moore is pleased!

SECTION V

The Quest
Pan Africanism

The State of African Liberation and Development

June, 2010

May 25th is the date that Africans on the continent and the Diaspora commemorate African Liberation Day. I generally try to make a few observations around that time, but this year my preoccupation with the critical crisis in Haiti and decision to write a piece encouraging President Obama to offer more effective leadership around the disastrous oil spill prevented me from doing so. However, a recent article in the *New York Times*, "African States Weigh 50 Bittersweet Years of Independence," prompted me to offer a few thoughts on the state of African liberation and development. The *Times* article referenced the France-Africa Summit which was held at a plush resort on the French Riviera. Ostensibly the Summit is organized to celebrate the granting of independence by France to its African colonies. Equally important, the article noted that 17 African nations gained their independence in 1960. The underlying question posed by the article is how much progress has Africa made toward creating a better life for the masses of the people in the past 50 years.

As a committed Pan Africanist of longstanding, this is certainly a question worth pondering. As a young political activist, I was among a small group of newly converted Pan Africanists who met at Malcolm X Liberation University in Greensboro, NC in 1971 to embrace African Liberation Day as a focal point for mobilizing Africans in America and the Diaspora to support the liberation movements in South Africa, Mozambique, Zimbabwe (Rhodesia), Namibia

(Southwest Africa), Angola and Guinea-Bissau—the last remaining colonies on the continent. May 25, 1972, in one of the most memorable moments of my life, the African Liberation Day Support Committee turned out some 35,000 marchers/demonstrators in Washington, D.C., another 10,000 in the Bay Area of California and hundreds more in Toronto, Canada and Grenada in the Caribbean. These were the largest demonstrations in support of freedom/self-determination for Africa since the heyday of UNIA-ACL under the leadership of the Honorable Marcus Mosiah Garvey.

Inspired by our reading of DuBois, Garvey, Padmore, CLR James, Fanon, Nkrumah, Sekou Toure, Cabral, Malcolm X and other leading Pan Africanists, as young visionaries we had great hopes that a fully liberated and united African homeland would become the base for global Black Power. Considering the enormous wealth/riches Africa possesses, we believed that with the right leadership, the misery and poverty of the African masses would be eradicated, and Africa would become the anchor for cultural, political and economic/commercial ties for the entire Black world.

We were of course not naïve about the difficulties/challenges facing newly independent African nations. Fanon had cautioned that National Liberation, the seizure of power from the colonizer was simply the first step in what he called National Reconstruction, the total decolonization of the political, social and economic structures of oppression. Cabral articulated a similar formulation. And, of course, Nkrumah emphatically warned that "neo-colonialism," the indirect control of the economic resources by the former colonial masters, would be the "last stage of imperialism." The key ingredients for confronting and overcoming these challenges were progressive/visionary leadership and conscious, mobilized/organized constituencies among the people that would be dedicated to achieving National

Reconstruction.

As the article in the *New York Times* suggests, however, by and large, "independence" has not fulfilled the dream of real self-determination and the promise of a better life for the masses of African people. Far too much of the vast wealth of Africa is still controlled by former colonial rulers or new foreign forces who are currently gobbling up Africa's resources, in most instances, with the consent of the governing elites. "Flag independence" and the neo-colonial corrupt, ineffective, foreign aid dependent governments and self-aggrandizing, autocratic "presidents for life" are too prevalent in Africa. For example, the *Times* article points out that foreign aid accounts for anywhere from 25% to more than half of the budgets of a number of the former French colonies present at the France-Africa Summit. This is obviously not without cost in terms of access to the dependent nation's resources. In addition, nations like China, South Korea and India are being granted huge tracts of land to grow food for their home populations and/or concessions to extract mineral wealth to fuel their expanding economies. This, while many African rulers live lavish lifestyles, stash away fortunes skimmed from deals with foreign nations and companies and otherwise strut around with pomp and circumstance.

Needless to say, this is not what the young Pan African activists who organized African Liberation Day in 1972 envisioned. Fortunately, there are voices and forces on the continent and in the Diaspora who are disappointed with the course of Africa's development as well. Therefore, despite a relatively bleak picture, all is not lost. What is required is a grassroots Pan African movement—individuals, organizations and constituencies linked by a common vision and dedicated to the proposition that National Reconstruction is the imperative of the day. Somehow we must find a way to galvanize and connect the discontent across the continent into a coherent movement for the transformation of the motherland.

Toward that end, the Pan African Unity Dialogue, convened by the Institute of the Black World 21stCentury in the greater New York area, is developing a Declaration of Principles for Foreign Investment in Africa. The goal is to have civil rights/human rights, faith, labor, civic and political leaders in the Diaspora sign the Declaration and send it to the African Union for consideration. Far more important than how the Declaration is received by the AU is the mass distribution of the document via the Internet and social networks. The real goal is to spark a broad-based demand that African governments stop giving away the vast wealth/resources of the continent for a mere pittance. The Declaration may be a modest example of the kind of initiative that could ignite a multifaceted, grassroots movement for real change on the continent.

The bottom line is that as we reflect on the state of African liberation, we must not despair in the face of seemingly intractable problems and major challenges. As Pan Africanists, we must remain true to the vision of our great mentors and leaders and advance the process of National Reconstruction by whatever means possible!

In Memory of Marcus Garvey: The Challenge of Pan Africanism in Our Time

August, 2009

I always enjoy writing at this time of the year because it gives me an opportunity to pay tribute to the Honorable Marcus Mosiah Garvey, arguably the greatest mass organizer people of African descent have produced. Born August 17, 1887 in St. Ann's Bay, Jamaica, Garvey was the founder and President-General of the Universal Negro Improvement Association and African Communities League (UNIA-ACL). Without question, he was one of the most effective theoreticians and practitioners of Pan Africanism the world has ever seen. Not only was he a fervent devotee of the idea that people of African descent should unite, he believed that the African homeland must be liberated from European colonial rule and become the base for global Black Power. In one of his more notable declarations he said, "Europe for the Europeans, Asia for the Asians and Africa for the Africans at home and abroad." Beyond the theory of that bold proposition, more than any proponent of Pan Africanism of his time or since, Garvey built a mass based organization which resembled a nation and government in waiting.

Inspired by his message of African redemption, hundreds of thousands of Black people flocked to the UNIA-ACL to establish hundreds of chapters throughout the U.S., Canada, the Caribbean, Central and South America and Europe. As a universal symbol of African unity, Garvey developed the Red, Black and Green Flag which remains a part of his legacy today. Indeed, for several years, I have advocated that August 17th be recognized as Universal African Flag Day, an occasion where people of African descent all over the world should display the Red, Black and Green in some form.

I recently had the opportunity to discuss the state of Pan Africanism at the World African Diaspora Union (WADU) Summit in Atlanta. I took the opportunity to suggest that Pan Africanism, the principled unity of people of African descent around the world, is imperative if we are to realize Garvey's vision of Black power. A cursory survey of the world scene clearly indicates that despite ethnic and cultural differences, Europeans have managed to form the European Union and various regional grouping are in formation in Asia. With the creation of the African Union and the existence of regional organizations like the Southern African Development Community (SADC) in East and West Africa there is some progress towards building functional/operational unity on the continent. However, the state of Pan Africanism is a far cry from what is required if the resources of the richest continent on the face of the earth are to be utilized for the development and empowerment of African people on the continent and in the Diaspora.

The problem is that the implementation of Pan Africanism faces a number of obstacles, not the least of which is neo-colonialism, the lack of visionary leadership and ethnic strife. With rare exception, the economies of African nations are still in the stranglehold of the former colonial powers. They have "flag" independence, meaning that the government controls the political sphere but has little control over the most vital aspect of national development—the economy. Kwame Nkrumah, another legendary Pan Africanist and a student of Garvey, warned that neocolonialism would be the "last stage of imperialism."

Unfortunately, the debilitating process of neo-colonialism is often aided by self-aggrandizing leaders who are simply content to hold political office for the purpose of lining their pockets at the expense of the masses of the people. Lacking a vision beyond "national liberation," ending the direct rule of the colonizer, these leaders have not moved their nation to the stage of "national reconstruction" as revolutionaries like Franz Fanon, Amilcar Cabral, Julius K. Nyerere, Ahmed Sekou Toure and Kwame Nkrumah envisioned it. National reconstruction is the total "decolonization" of the structures of governance, economy and social systems such that the masses of the people become the beneficiaries of the resources of the nation. For example, it makes no sense for people to be living in unspeakable poverty and misery in the Delta region of Nigeria in the shadow of oil rigs and refineries which fill the coffers of foreign corporations and the bank accounts of corrupt government officials with incredible riches/wealth. We see this sad saga of poverty in the face of abundant natural resources/wealth being played out across the continent.

Dr. Leonard Jeffries reminds us that the process of decolonization must also include the African mind, the creation of an African-centered consciousness so that the interests and aspirations of African people are the foremost concern of the leaders of African nations. The lack of African- centered vision contributes to the perpetuation of neo-colonialism and renders nations vulnerable to ethnic tensions/strife. Foreign powers are obviously eager to fuel ethnic strife as a means of advancing their political and economic interests. The tragedy is that African leaders are sometimes willing to employ the same scheme in collaboration with foreign powers, or on their own, for personal gain. Greed and the thirst for power foster the "leader for life" syndrome, where presidents and heads of state are willing to do virtually anything to cling to power, irrespective of the welfare of the people and the nation. Leaders so infected are not likely to want to implement the kind of Pan Africanism that will require yielding a degree of power to a larger body like the African Union to promote the common good of the continent, including holding leaders of member nations accountable.

Marcus Garvey would not likely be pleased with this picture. But just as the Diaspora in his day played a leading role in defining the vision and mission of Pan Africanism, today I believe Garvey would be encouraging the Diaspora, the Sixth Region as designated by the African Union, to lead the way in rearticulating the moral and ethical imperatives of African leadership in the 21st Century. It is the Diaspora which will have to build relations with people based institutions and organizations on the ground throughout the continent as the foundation for compelling leaders to engage the process of "national reconstruction" as the order of the day.

This is an appropriate role for WADU under the wise leadership of veteran Pan Africanist and former Foreign Minister of Jamaica, the venerable Dudley Thompson. We in the Diaspora must once again take the lead in imagining the possibilities of Pan Africanism and connect with our sisters and brothers on the continent in mobilizing/organizing to push African leaders and the African Union to tap the collective potential of African people to achieve Black Power! In the spirit of Marcus Garvey, let our watch words continue to be: "Up you mighty race, you can accomplish what you will!"

The Passing of Mandela and the Unfinished Freedom Struggle in South Africa

December, 2013

As Chairman of Freedom, Inc. in Youngstown, Ohio, a community-based, Pan Africanist organization, I was privileged to be among a small group of activists/organizers who launched the mobilization to hold the first African Liberation Day (ALD) in the U.S. in 1972. The focus of ALD was to mobilize political and material support for the liberation movements fighting to achieve independence in the last remaining European colonial regimes in Africa—Cape Verde and Guinea-Bissau, Angola, Southwest Africa (Namibia), Rhodesia/Southern Rhodesia (Zimbabwe), Mozambique and of course South Africa. Of all these brutal regimes, the vicious apartheid regime in South Africa seemed to be the most impregnable. An entrenched and determined White minority ruthlessly controlled more than 85% of the land and resources and compelled the vast Black majority to live like sub-humans in wretched conditions under a system of rigid separation of the races.

Time and time again, the White supremacist regime demonstrated its willingness to use the state-controlled mechanisms of force/violence to crush protests, rallies and demonstrations as evidenced by the Sharpsville massacre in 1960, merciless suppression of the Soweto uprising in 1976 and countless overt efforts by the Black majority and its allies to shatter the shackles of apartheid. But, the thirst for freedom and will to resist oppression could not be extinguished in large measure because of the man who came to encapsulate and symbolize the aspirations of the people, Madiba, Nelson Mandela.

Mandela was the "tallest tree" in a forest that included many movements and stellar leaders, e.g., the Pan African Congress, Black Consciousness Movement, Mass Democratic Movement, Steve Biko, Bishop Desmond Tutu, Allan Boesak, Cyril Ramaphosa, Albertina and Walter Sisulu and Oliver Tambo, to mention a few. This is an important note because there is a tendency to cast successful movements as the result of the acts of a solitary heroic figure. As is the case in many reform and revolutionary struggles, in South Africa there was a multifaceted movement fighting to bring down the walls of apartheid. Nelson Mandela was part of the largest and most widely accepted organization within that movement, the African National Congress (ANC).

Mandela emerged as the face of struggle in South Africa and abroad because of his vision, courage and commitment as a leader and his willingness, if necessary to die for the cause—an expression of courage and commitment which he unapologetically stated at his trial before being sentenced to prison. His willingness to face death and suffer a long imprisonment while never surrendering or giving up on the dream of a multiracial, democratic South Africa is the stuff that made him the symbol and face of the movement, an icon and legend even before the apartheid regime was forced to release him.

"Free Mandela" became the battle cry of the freedom struggle in South Africa and the world. This was certainly the case in the U.S., most notably among the forces within the Black liberation movement. While sympathetic to various organizations in South Africa, most groups and leaders in the South Africa support movement embraced Mandela and ANC as the leader and organization with the broadest support and greatest potential to effectively dismantle apartheid.

Mandela's and ANC's pledge to "nationalize" the major means of production to ensure an improvement in the quality of life for the Black majority was also persuasive. At the human, visceral level, however, it was the story of Mandela's courageous commitment, sacrifice and suffering that made him the symbol of the South Africa support movement. "Free Mandela" signs and chants were standard fare at marches, rallies and demonstrations in the U.S. With his wife, the courageous, militant Winnie Mandela, consistently voicing the aspirations of the South African masses and keeping the memory of her husband alive, freeing Nelson Mandela to lead the people to the "promised land" of Black majority rule became a major goal of the evolving Free South Africa Movement in the U.S.

What an amazing era this was. In 1972, some 25,000 people marched/rallied in Washington, D.C. for the first African Liberation Day, another 10,000 in the San Francisco Bay Area and 10,000 in Toronto, Canada. Under the leadership of Maurice Bishop, the New Jewel Movement in Grenada also mobilized a solidarity rally. Though ALD 1972 was organized in support of liberation movements in all of the non-liberated territories, the struggle in South Africa had a prominent place on the agenda and chants of "Free Mandela" reverberated throughout the rallies.

An incredible movement was exploding across the country. Over the objection of the U.S. government, students organized campaigns to demand that colleges/universities divest or withdraw investments from South Africa. City councils around the nation followed suit. There was an aggressive effort to use economic sanctions/boycotts to force U.S. corporations doing business in South Africa to divest as well. South African lobster tails, Budweiser beer and Coca Cola Company come to mind as some of the targets. Indeed *"Coke Sweetens Apartheid"* was one of the more popular slogans of the time. The

Congressional Black Caucus mounted a vigorous campaign to impose economic sanctions on South Africa to break the back of apartheid. With the mass movement intensifying, Congress overrode the veto of President Ronald Reagan to impose sanctions and finally place the U.S. government on the right side of the heroic freedom struggle in South Africa. Hundreds of leaders, activists and organizers also converged on the South African Embassy on a regular basis for sit-in demonstrations to demand freedom, democracy and Black majority rule in South Africa.

In the face of fierce and unrelenting resistance inside the country and internationally, after 27 years, February 11, 1990, the illicit regime in South Africa was compelled to free Madiba, Nelson Mandela, the courageous leader and symbol of the movement for freedom, democracy and economic elevation of the masses of South Africans! What a memorable day. It seemed that the whole world watched as Mandela strode, tall, proud and confident out of the gates of imprisonment with Winnie Mandela at his side. I shall never forget Mandela's first speech after his release. Despite his iconic status, he made it clear that he was first and foremost a servant of the people, grounded in and accountable to the organization that had played a leading role in his emancipation, the ANC. He also struck a tone of reconciliation to unite all South Africans to create a new nation.

At last the slogan/chant "Free Mandela" had been realized and with it the hopes and dreams of a long suffering people seemed closer to fruition. Now Mandela and the ANC were faced with the daunting task of transforming a resistance movement into a governing Party and to navigate a risky path of negotiating an agreement with the National Party that represented the White minority. While the ANC had a military wing that had engaged in armed struggle, its forces were far too weak to seriously threaten the vastly superior might of the South Africa security forces, whose ultimate mission was to protect the economic interests of the elite. Under these circumstances, Mandela led the way in encouraging a "truth and reconciliation" process which essentially allowed those who had committed crimes against humanity to confess their transgressions in exchange for immunity from prosecution (persons with the resistance forces were also requested to confess their transgressions). The National Party was also provided certain constitutional guarantees to protect the political interests of the White minority.

Finally, Mandela persuaded the ANC to abandon the goal of nationalizing the major means of production, thereby assuring that the same individuals, families and companies that dominated the economy during the era of apartheid would be safely in control in the new South Africa. This did not mean that ANC abandoned its pledge to improve the quality of life for the Black majority, but the negotiated settlement meant that these promises would largely have to be met through policies enacted by the government. The hard fought victory to end apartheid meant that those who had been locked out of the political process could voice their aspirations at the ballot box. They could elect a President and government that could open opportunities for education, housing, jobs, healthcare and other benefits through public policies designed to achieve these objectives. However, the cold reality was/is that the Black majority held the keys to political power while the White minority held on to the keys to the means of production and control of the economy.

Now that our beloved Madiba, this giant of a man who inspired generations to engage the struggle for a free, non-racial, democratic South Africa has joined the ancestors, it marks the passing of an era. Perhaps his passing is an appropriate time not only to reflect on his heroic legacy but to assess the results of the negotiated settlement that has produced the "new South Africa." Perhaps it is time to examine the unfinished freedom struggle in South Africa.

Promoting and Practicing Pan Africanism in the Diaspora

August, 2009

I recently wrote an article in memory of the Honorable Marcus Mosiah Garvey in which I discussed the challenges of implementing the concept of Pan Africanism in the global context, particularly as it relates to the unification and development of Africa. I suggested that it may be the African Diaspora that will once more play a major role in articulating a progressive vision and program for Pan Africanism in the 21st century. In that regard, it is useful to recall that Pan Africanism, the concept that people of African descent wherever they are should unite to promote racial progress, was initially conceived and nurtured among Africans displaced/dispersed by the holocaust of enslavement. It was African leaders and thinkers like Martin R. Delaney, Bishop Henry McNeal Turner, Edward Wilmot Blyden, Henry Sylvester Williams, W.E.B. DuBois, Marcus Garvey, George Padmore and C.L.R. James who helped define and promulgate the concept of Pan Africanism.

Out of the bosom of sons and daughters of Africa, whom the slave master strove to strip of identity and culture, was born the yearning to unite with each other and their ancestral homeland to better the race. These thinkers would have an enormous impact on the emerging leadership of the anti-colonial struggles in Africa, most notably Kwame Nkrumah and Jomo Kenyatta (they would also have a powerful influence on the anti-colonial struggles in the Caribbean). After the historic Manchester Pan African Congress in 1945, African leaders, with the fervent support of leading Pan Africanists from the Diaspora, left for home irreversibly committed to the total liberation of Africa from European colonialists. A little more than a decade later, Ghana would win independence from Great Britain. Eventually, the entire continent would break the yoke of colonialism. The African Diaspora played a significant role in this process!

As Kwame Nkrumah warned, however, the end of colonialism, the direct control of Africa, would not be the end of external domination. Now Africa faces the challenges of neocolonialism, the indirect control of its resources and economies by Europe, the U.S. and increasingly nations like China and Korea. This fundamental contradiction is exacerbated by an overabundance of inept, incompetent and corrupt leaders, most of whom are too self-absorbed to envision the kind of Pan African unity required to free their nations from the clutches of neocolonialism. Some force must emerge to issue a clarion call for an end to neo-colonialism and the rape of Africa by external powers and corrupt leaders. In my judgment, that force must be the African Diaspora.

In the U.S., however, the African Diaspora cannot effectively play that role without simultaneously addressing the need to promote and practice Pan Africanism inside this country. The 2010 Census, if the count is accurate, will reveal that continental and Caribbean Africans now number in the millions in the U.S. There was a time when you would mostly find Caribbean and continental Africans in New York and Washington, D.C. Today you can find Africans from the continent and the Caribbean in virtually every region of the country from Atlanta to Jackson, Mississippi, New Orleans to Los Angeles, Chicago, Detroit, Columbus, Ohio, Memphis, Tennessee, Selma, Alabama ... everywhere! This dramatic influx of new African immigrants is changing the face of the African community in the U.S., potentially adding to the power of the Diaspora to impact U.S. policy toward Africa and to influence Africa's people and leaders. But, if the African Diaspora in the U.S. is to be in the forefront of promoting Pan Africanism in the 21st century, the first question that must be answered is "can we all get along"—can we practice Pan Africanism among the disparate ethnicities/nationalities and cultures in the African community in the U.S.?

By and large, various African nationalities/ethnicities co-exist within the Black community without meaningful communication, dialogue or relationships with each other. Indeed, sometimes there is competition, division and tension between the various groups. There are questions about what it means to be "African American" or whether that designation should be limited to a certain category of Africans in America. Some groups are vigorously pushing to be counted in the 2010 Census by their specific continental or regional identity, e.g., African or Caribbean as opposed to being counted as African American within the broader Black community. There is even a debate about what constitutes the African Diaspora, the sum total of all people of African descent in the U.S., or the more recent immigrants from Africa exclusively.

We cannot effectively achieve our full potential to promote Pan Africanist goals abroad unless we achieve better unity and cooperation among African groups in this country. When the New York Police Department tortured Abner Louima, an African from Haiti, gunned down Amadou Diallo, an African from the Guinea, and killed Sean Bell an African born in the U.S., they did not make a distinction based on their nationality or ethnicity. They were seen as suspicious/dangerous Black men in a nation where racism is still alive and well. Faced with this reality, as Marcus Garvey taught, we must instill the notion that we are one people with a common aim and destiny irrespective of our particular nationality or ethnicity.

As President of the Institute of the Black World 21st Century, I have been urging leaders from the various African nationalities/ethnicities to initiate dialogues to exchange information about the issues affecting our respective communities, to bridge divisions and promote cooperation, collaboration and joint action to advance the interests and aspirations of African people in our totality. This Pan African cooperation should focus on fully mobilizing/organizing the total African community to address issues of concern to Black people at the local, state and national levels. Equally important, the African community should be continually educated and mobilized to promote and defend the interests of Africa. This not only includes engaging in the policy formulation process but becoming the voice and force, relentlessly calling on our sisters and brothers in Africa to shed the shackles of neo-colonialism, embrace moral and ethical leadership and adopt people-oriented practices of governance and economy.

To move beyond theory to practice, IBW has convened Pan African Unity Dialogues in the greater New York area for the past two years. It is our hope that this effort will become a model for creating similar processes around the country. The ultimate goal is for a unified Diaspora to become a formidable force for liberation "at home and abroad." The key to "African redemption" in the 21st century may well depend on the degree to which we as Africans in the U.S. can effectively reclaim our role as the leading proponents of Pan Africanism in the Black World!

End the Sanctions Now: Time for a New Beginning in Zimbabwe

October 1, 2018

O n August 3rd the Zimbabwe Electoral Commission announced that Emmerson Mnangagwa of the ruling Zimbabwe African Union-Patriotic Front (ZANU-PF) had narrowly defeated Nelson Chamisa of the opposition Movement for Democratic Change (MDC) 50.8% to 44.3%. Mr. Mnangagwa's margin of victory was just enough to avoid a run-off. Though MDC initially protested the results, the Constitutional Court overruled the opposition's claims of substantial fraud and vote rigging. While international monitors acknowledged that there were some irregularities, the election was almost universally hailed as the most violence-free and transparent in decades.

The election of President Mnangagwa could potentially mark a new beginning for Zimbabwe after decades of iron-fisted autocratic rule by Robert Mugabe, a hero of the war for liberation, whose regime became increasingly authoritarian after early signs of great promise. Cronyism, corruption and violent suppression of the opposition became the order of the day as Mugabe resolved to cling to power at any cost. The problem is that President Mnangagwa was a fierce lieutenant of Mugabe who earned the name the "crocodile" for his willingness to ruthlessly carry out the will of his protégé.

But, Mnangagwa turned on his erstwhile leader after an internal power struggle in which he apparently fell out of favor with Mugabe. There was restlessness among the leadership of ZANU-PF that, after

37 years, the 94-year old Mugabe seemed determined to be "President for Life" with his wife Grace functioning as the defacto Co-President. Mnangagwa gained the upper hand in the power struggle when forces loyal to him within ZANU-PF staged a coup in which Mugabe was placed under house arrest. Faced with a motion for impeachment, Mugabe agreed to resign. Mnangagwa, the new man in charge, promised that there would be democratic elections to establish a new government, and though the process was not perfect, he kept his promise.

This context is important because Mnangagwa's election as President could simply represent a shuffling of the deck within a ruling party which has long since lost its way, or the dawning of a new day in Zimbabwe. As veteran pan-Africanist, I certainly hope it will be the latter. I have fond memories of playing a leading role in the African Liberation Support Movement in this country that enthusiastically embraced and supported Robert Mugabe and ZANU-PF. As the Chairman of Freedom, Inc. in Youngstown, Ohio, I can remember warmly receiving Tapson Mwere, ZANU-PF's U.S. representative for the African Cultural Weekend we sponsored annually. We had great hopes that the triumphant anti-colonial struggles in Zimbabwe and throughout Southern Africa would result in progressive governments that would be devoted to improving the quality of life for the masses of the people.

As noted earlier President Mugabe and ZANU-PF got off to a promising start as Zimbabwe's economy was ranked as one of the most prosperous in Africa. However, this prosperity was grossly uneven because the vast majority of the land remained in the hands of a small minority of White farmers and landlords who disproportionately benefited from the countries growing economy. Large numbers of Zimbabwe's peasants, including veterans of the war of liberation, were landless despite the Manchester House Agreement where Great

Britain pledged to provide resources to finance the acquisition of land from wealthy White landowners. Great Britain blatantly defaulted on the Manchester Agreement. In a defiant and correct act, that burnished his revolutionary credentials at home and abroad, Mugabe moved to seize land from the White landowners, ostensibly for the purpose of redistributing it to landless peasants.

This was all good, but there were already signs that the "revolution" was veering off course in a manner that would entrench and enrich Mugabe and his ZANU-PF cohorts. From 1983 to 1987 thousands of men, women and children from the Ndebele ethnic group were killed in the Gukurahundi massacres. This multi-year slaughter is widely believed to have been directly ordered by Mugabe and executed by his then loyal Lieutenant, the "Crocodile," to cleanse the country of potentially disloyal or oppositional groups. These massacres have left a deep wound in the nation; one that signaled Mugabe's determination to establish one-party rule and stamp out any opposition to his regime despite the human carnage. To that end, land and other patronage was largely dispensed to loyalists to bolster his rule. In addition, in a series of elections, Mugabe unleashed his forces to brutally suppress the opposition MDC under the leadership of his long-time rival Morgan Tsvangirai.

Needless to say, this is not what I had in mind when we supported Mugabe and ZANU-PF. These acts were tantamount to a betrayal of revolution rather than a continuation of it. Therefore, I am skeptical that someone like President Mnangagwa, who was actively complicit in the betrayal, can restore the vision of the revolution. My skepticism notwithstanding, I am willing to give him a chance to redeem himself. After all, neither he nor any of his allies need more wealth, they have already acquired more than enough to provide lavishly for their families and their children's children for generations to come. So, perhaps, just perhaps, the new President will have a flashback and remember the original goal of the anti-colonial struggle and re-commit himself to a revival of the revolution. But, in order for him to succeed in this pursuit, sanctions must be lifted immediately. The most recent election is an initial show of good faith on his part.

There are other steps which President Mnangagwa can also take to reignite the fervor of the revolution. He needs to take serious steps to heal the wounds of the Gukurahundi massacres. He should also reach out to the opposition MDC to explore a government of inclusion, where power and resources will be shared in a manner that defuses ethnic tensions. The President already has some experience in this regard as he was the central figure that negotiated a power sharing agreement with the MDC after the 2008 General Election. He should devise a Pan African development plan and strategy based on the regional, continent-wide and global utilization of African human and material resources to consolidate and expand Zimbabwe's economy. Finally, he should make a vigorous effort to engage the Diaspora in the social and economic development of the country.

We in the Diaspora can support the prospects for a new day in Zimbabwe by demanding the end of sanctions. We must reject the "reform first, removal of sanctions later" position of the U.S. Government. Moreover, we must support the call for Great Britain and multilateral agencies to implement the Manchester House Agreement. Finally, we can support the prospects of a new day in Zimbabwe by making it clear to President Emmerson Mnangagwa that our support is "critical support," that we expect adherence to principles of democratic governance and human rights and the creation of a people-based economy, targeted to benefit the masses of the people. That was what the "revolution" was supposed to be about. A luta Continua, the struggle continues!

Building a Constituency
for Haiti in the U.S.

February, 2009

Black History Month should never pass without people of African descent remembering the amazing Haitian Revolution which produced the first Black Republic in the world. While historians herald the contributions to humanity of the American and French Revolutions, I believe the Haitian Revolution was at least as significant in terms of advancing the concepts of human rights and equality. We must never forget that this improbable Revolution was consummated at a time when the holocaust of enslavement was wreaking havoc on Africa. Though the trans-Atlantic slave trade was initiated as an economic enterprise, it would not be long before the horrors of this genocidal undertaking would be rationalized by theories of "race" that designated Africans inferior beings. Pseudo-scientific theories gave birth to the myth of white supremacy.

But, the Haitian revolutionaries, inspired and led by Boukman, Alexander Petion, Henri Christophe, Jean Jacques Dessalines and the incomparable Toussaint Louverture were unwilling to validate this perverted theory of race. Over a tumultuous period from 1791 to 1803, Haitian freedom fighters defeated the armies of England, Spain and France—in the latter instance humiliating the vaunted forces of Emperor Napoleon Bonaparte. An army of "enslaved Africans" took destiny into their own hands and shattered the myth of white supremacy! January 1, 1804, Jean Jacques Dessalines declared Haiti the first Black Republic in the world. It was a declaration which reverberated around the world, especially among enslaved Africans in the U.S. and the Caribbean.

Despite the righteous platitudes of the American and French Revolutions, the idea of an independent Black Republic created through force of arms did not sit well with the powers that be in the Capitols of Europe and America. There was virtually universal agreement among the European/White leaders of the time, including President Thomas Jefferson, that the example of Haiti was a threat to their national interests—profiting from the slave trade and/or colonialism in Africa, the Caribbean, Central and South America. Therefore, it was imperative that Haiti be isolated, marginalized and rendered weak as a "Black nation." Under threat of a new invasion, Haiti succumbed to demands from France to pay millions of dollars in reparations for the loss of property (enslaved Africans and the plantations) incurred during the Revolution. The burden of this debt would cripple Haiti's struggle for development well into the 20th century. In 1915, the U.S. invaded and occupied Haiti until 1934, and has treated Haiti as a neo-colony ever sense.

It is my contention that people of African descent everywhere owe a special debt to Haiti for giving us back our dignity when we were on our knees. With the onslaught of the slave trade, colonialism and segregation/apartheid, the Haitian Revolution and the Black Republic it produced were beacons of inspiration, hope and promise for the entire Black World. Accordingly, raising Haiti to its rightful place in the sun must be a collective   Pan African priority in the 21st Century. As long as the first Black Republic is ridiculed as the "poorest nation in the western hemisphere," people of African descent everywhere are diminished. By uplifting Haiti and assisting the Haitian people to achieve genuine self-determination and an improved standard of living, Africans everywhere are elevated.

To that end, the Haiti Support Project (HSP) of the Institute of the Black World 21st Century has been working to build a formidable constituency for Haiti in the U.S. Our mission is to impact U.S. policy towards Haiti and to mobilize humanitarian and developmental assistance to support people based projects, programs and initiatives on the ground. As it relates to U.S. policy, an immediate goal is to rescind the long standing discriminatory policy of routinely incarcerating and returning Haitian refugees to Haiti without proper hearings. In fact, according to a recent Associated Press report, some 30,000 Haitian refugees are currently facing deportation in the near future. By contrast, Cuban refugees who manage to arrive on U.S. shores are immediately taken in and put on a fast track to receive Green Cards and eventually citizenship. While this racist policy is under review, Haitian refugees should be granted Temporary Protective Status (TPS). In the broader strategic sense, the U.S. should be constructively engaged in a long term and sustained effort to strengthen democracy and development in Haiti through assistance that will enhance the Government's capacity to build a sound and growing economy, generate jobs, and deliver vital services like education and health care.

In terms of private sector assistance, HSP is committed to educating and engaging the African American community to join with our Haitian American sisters and brothers to partner in the process of strengthening democracy and development in Haiti. Working together, this partnership can mobilize substantial humanitarian assistance to benefit schools, health care clinics and other critical projects. Equally important, we can take advantage of Haiti's incredible assets as the first Black Republic by encouraging cultural and historical tourism and investment in related economic development/business enterprises. In recent years, HSP has organized annual Pilgrimages to the magnificent Citadel and Sans Souci Palace in the northern part of the country near Milot as part of the Model City Initiative (for information visit www.ibw21.org). Our goal is to mobilize maximum resources to transform the town of Milot into a Mecca for cultural-historical tourism as an engine for people-based economic development. Other organizations or Churches may choose to adopt a town, school, healthcare center, orphanage or invest in an economic development project.

The bottom line is that we owe an enormous debt to Haiti and we must meet that obligation by building a powerful constituency that can assist our sisters and brothers in Haiti to resurrect the first Black Republic as a beacon of pride and hope for people of African descent everywhere. Long live the spirit of the Haitian Revolution!

Finishing the Unfinished Revolution: Strengthening Democracy and Development in Haiti

March, 2009

In my most recent article, I argued that the Haitian Revolution, which produced the first Black Republic in the world, was one of the most important revolutions in history. Never before had humankind witnessed an enslaved people rising up to defeat the super-powers of the day to achieve self-determination and nationhood. But as we discussed, the Haitian people have never really been permitted to fully realize the potential of this improbable triumph because the western slave masters were determined that these "uppity" Africans would be punished for shattering the myth of white supremacy. So, Haiti's path to democracy and development has been thwarted by denigration, isolation, marginalization and the chronic intervention into its affairs by foreign powers.

Haiti has also had its internal contradictions, not the least of which has been a small mulatto elite who owns the vast majority of the land, resources and wealth and has callously neglected or ruthlessly crushed the aspirations of the Haitian masses. This has often occurred in collaboration with and at the behest of foreign powers. This was certainly the case during the "Cold War" when the U.S. backed the draconian dictatorship of the Duvaliers with no regard for the regime's brutal suppression of democracy and human rights. Indeed, the competition within the elite to gain power for self-aggrandize-ment and the perennial tension/conflict between the "masses and the classes" have retarded the process of developing a sustained culture of democracy and people oriented development in Haiti. Chronic politi-cal instability and economic underdevelopment have been the order of the day. In a real sense, the Haitian Revolution is an unfinished revolution; a Black Republic that has been reduced to being "the poor-est nation in the western hemisphere."

Therefore, the critical imperative of the 21st century for Haiti and its allies/friends abroad is to finish the unfinished Revolution. And, this process must begin with a change in behavior by the U.S. and the western powers that have consistently trampled on the aspira-tions of the Haitian masses. In this regard, the U.S. government must take the lead by nurturing and supporting rather than interfering with and disrupting the fragile process of democratization in Hai-ti—including events of the most recent past. Secondly, the U.S. must demonstrate its respect for Haiti and the Haitian people by ending the racist, discriminatory and insulting policy towards Haitian refugees. Haitian refugees to this country should be treated the same as Cuban refugees; granted expedited hearings, Green Cards where appropri-ate, and a path to citizenship.

As this article goes to press, Trans Africa Forum has issued an urgent alert appealing to friends of Haiti to mobilize to block the de-portation of some 30,000 Haitians who have been held in U.S. deten-tion facilities. These refugees should be granted Temporary Protective Status (TPS) immediately. It is also important to halt these deporta-tions because included in the mix are Haitians with criminal records who are being sent back because of immigration violations. Without a process for re-education, reorientation and orderly re-entry into Haitian society, these deportees are prone to associate with or create criminal enterprises that can pose a threat to Haiti's security/stability. The U.S. Government must adopt a policy and process for the orderly re-entry of deportees that have run afoul of the law in this country.

In addition to major reforms in policy towards Haitian refugees and deportees with criminal records, the U.S. government can take several steps to significantly enhance and accelerate the process of democracy and development in Haiti.

Under the Jubilee Initiative, the U.S. should forgive hundreds of millions of dollars of debt, much of which was incurred during the regime of the Duvaliers. Ridding Haiti of this burden would be an enormous boost to the economy. In addition, working in a co-ordinating manner with Haitian authorities, the U.S. should devote significant resources to drug interdiction. Currently Haiti is a trans-shipment point for drugs between Columbia and markets in the U.S. In a desperately poor nation, the lure of profits from such a lucrative enterprise can engender pervasive corruption and degeneration of institutions of government, including the police and the courts. The U.S. must spare no effort to prevent Haiti from becoming a narco-state. Closely tied to this critical initiative is the urgent need to assist Haiti to build a viable, effective, politically neutral National Police Force and an efficiently functioning, impartial judiciary. Police and judges must be reasonably compensated to avoid the corrosive seduction of the drug traffic.

In terms of economic assistance, the U.S. must take the lead within the international community by sending aid for health, education, housing, infrastructure and other essential social programs directly to the Government as opposed to funneling it through Non-governmental Agencies (NGOs). Because of political instability, corruption, the lack of transparency and occasionally to punish particular Governments, the U.S. and the international community have directed aid via NGOs. This has had the effect of seriously undermining the capacity of the Government to meet some of the most vital needs of the country, thereby rendering it impotent and irrelevant in the eyes of the people. With successful efforts to improve systems of transparency and accountability under the current Government, this debilitating practice must end.

Finally, there are two additional public policy proposals which the Haiti Support Project (HSP) of the Institute of the Black World 21st Century (IBW) feels are of paramount importance. Massive unemployment/joblessness poses the greatest threat to stability and security in Haiti. While the passage of the HOPE Act to provide incentives for the manufacturing sector in Haiti was an important step, in essence it is a "trickle down" initiative which will take time to have maximum effect. In the meantime, millions of Haitians languish in poverty without jobs or the prospect of attaining employment in the near future. A huge number of the jobless are also young people who absent productive alternatives can become easy prey to the illicit economy.

Faced with this potentially combustible situation, HSP has strongly recommended that the U.S. and the international community collaborate with the Government of Haiti to create a massive New Deal, Works Progress Administration (WPA), Civilian Conservation Corp (CCC) type public works program that would put a minimum of 300,000—500,000 Haitians to work building, repairing and maintaining highways and bridges, building schools, hospitals and health care clinics, restoring historical sites, cleaning up the environment and undertaking massive reforestation projects. Taking a page from countries like Brazil, Haiti should also engage workers in projects that lay the foundation for a green economy. Education and vocational training should be an integral part of such a program in order to prepare the participants in the program for gainful employment in permanent careers as Haiti's economy expands.

In addition to a WPA, CCC type public works program, Haiti needs to create a National Strategic Highway Authority. One of the most frustrating and economically crippling realities in Haiti is the seemingly inability to build and maintain a system of roads and highways. It is absolutely axiomatic that business/commerce in Haiti will not thrive, including the crucial cultural-historical tourism sector, until the most vital highways can be paved and maintained on an on-going basis. Accordingly, the Government should identify the highways which are most crucial to Haiti's business/commercial development and designate them Strategic Highways. Rather than rely on the existing process of bidding out the construction and maintenance of these highways to the private sector, for a definable period, the Government would create a public authority charged with building and maintaining the nation's Strategic Highways. In so doing the life sustaining arteries of the economy will always be open for business!

While these policy prescriptions are not exhaustive, if adopted, they would go some distance in this crucial period in propelling Haiti along the path of sustained development. But, these proposals will count for little unless Haiti addresses some of its internal political contradictions. Chronic political instability must give way to a vibrant, resilient and sustained democracy.

From its inception, the tension/conflict between the wealthy elite and the impoverished masses has been a dominant theme in Haitian history. Moreover, while the passion for freedom and fierce fighting spirit to achieve it were characteristics which enabled the Haitian freedom fighters to defeat Napoleon, that same passion too often has manifested itself internally in political factionalism, zero sum politics and a winner take all attitude. Put another way, Haitians find it difficult to compromise and reconcile with each other when it comes to issues of politics, power and governance. This condition has been exacerbated by the intrusion of outside forces in nation's affairs, including the most recent disruption of Haiti's nascent democracy.

The corrective is to develop and nurture a culture of democracy which creates an agreed upon framework for promoting national goals and working out differences. Though the nation's constitution is helpful in this regard, ultimately enhancing the culture of democracy requires a systematic and sustained period of national reflection and dialogue among the political class and the masses of the Haitian people to constructively examine its political culture, the successes and failures of past regimes and foster justice and reconciliation. There must emerge a critical mass from all strata within society dedicated to bridging the political divides that have historically hampered Haiti's capacity to achieve a stable and enduring democracy. In this endeavor, the U.S. and the international community must be committed to nourishing this process as opposed to opportunistically operating to undermine and destroy it.

People of African descent, America and the world owe a debt of gratitude to Haiti for being at the forefront of the struggle for freedom and human rights through the Haitian Revolution and the declaration of the first Black Republic in the world. Now it is time to collectively pay that debt by rolling up our sleeves and respectfully aiding the Haitian people to finish the unfinished Haitian Revolution!

The Citadel: A Symbol of Freedom and Hope in Haiti

October, 2009

The Haiti Support Project of the Institute of the Black World 21st Century has just completed its Third Pilgrimage to Haiti to visit the Citadel and other important cultural/historical sites. The vision/mission of these Pilgrimages is to transform the town of Milot, which is strategically situated at the foot of the Citadel, into a Mecca for cultural/historical tourism as the engine for people based economic development in the area/region. In a broader sense, however, the Pilgrimages are intended to introduce people of African descent to the Haitian Revolution, which produced the first Black Republic in this hemisphere—one of the most incredible feats in human history. The magnificent Citadel, which sits atop a mountain 3,000 feet in the sky, is a powerful symbol of freedom and hope.

It was my seventh trek up the mountain to tour the Citadel ... and it never gets old. Every time I take the Pilgrimage, images and echoes of the heroic struggle of African people, who refused to submit to enslavement, flash through my mind's eye. Of the three great Revolutions, which occurred during the latter part of the 18th century, only the Haitian Revolution was waged by enslaved human beings who defeated the armies of Spain, England and the formidable forces of France under the leadership of Napoleon Bonaparte. At the height of the Trans-Atlantic slave trade and the propagation of racist theories of White superiority and Black inferiority, an improbable legion of Pan African freedom fighters decimated the armies of the greatest military powers in the world. The Haitian Revolution shattered the myth of white supremacy. The leaders of the Revolution declared the first Black Republic in this hemisphere as a living testimony to the triumph of the Haitian people in their determination to breathe free!

To defend the new African nation, Jean Jacques Dessalines (Toussaint Louverture died in a French prison before the Revolution was consummated) ordered an elaborate system of forts be constructed throughout the country, particularly the northern region where the decisive battles of the Revolution were fought. The goal was to ensure that the French or any other aggressor would never invade Haiti again. Conceived by Black minds and built by thousands of Black hands, the Citadel is the largest fortress in the western hemisphere. It is an architectural, engineering and military marvel, which was declared a World Heritage monument by UNESCO in 1982. Built by King Henri Christophe, this massive fortress was designed to protect the routes from the port city of Cap Haitien that lead into the interior of the Republic. Equipped with more than 300 of the finest artillery pieces in the world, the Citadel was constructed to house up to 20,000 military and support personnel.

As you make your way up the five miles of winding road and paths to the pinnacle of the mountain where the Citadel is perched, inevitably the question arises as to how it was possible for the Haitians to accomplish this incredible feat! Then one is compelled to remember the legacy of Imhotep, the world's first multi-genius, who pioneered the techniques used to build the great Pyramids in Kemet/ Egypt. The same blood that flows in the veins of those who built the Pyramids flows in the veins of the freedom fighters who conceived and constructed the Citadel.

The leaders of the Revolution proclaimed that whoever set foot on Haiti's soil would be free. Moreover, they made a commitment to assist any and all colonized people to overthrow their oppressors, provided slavery would be abolished once victory was won. Simon Bolivar was among the freedom fighters who accepted the offer. Winding up the path to the Citadel, I can hear voices of Denmark Vesey and his co-conspirators in Charleston, South Carolina as they plot an elaborate revolt to free thousands of enslaved Africans. Their ultimate destination was Haiti. Word of the Haitian Revolution reverberated throughout the slave quarters in North America and found its way into the proceedings of Colored Peoples Conventions where the likes of Frederick Douglass, David Walter and Martin R. Delaney debated strategies for liberating the race. The first Black Republic was a symbol of freedom and a beacon of hope for the enslaved and quasi-free Africans in the U.S. Most assuredly, word of the gallant deeds of the Haitian Revolutionaries was known throughout the Caribbean, Central and South America and on the African continent and served as a source of inspiration for anti-colonial struggles for liberation.

People of African descent and freedom loving people everywhere are indebted to Haiti for uplifting the banner of liberation and human rights in the face of white supremacist ideology and the ruthless exploitation, enslavement and colonialization of Africans and people of color. Unfortunately, Haiti has been scorned and punished for achieving that which was said to be impossible. The first Black Republic has been reduced to being "the poorest nation in the western hemisphere." Given what Haiti has bequeathed to people of African descent and the world, our task is to repay the debt by doing everything within our power to uplift the first Black Republic and assist the Haitian people to achieve their rightful place in the sun again.

The Citadel encapsulates the vision, courage and will of the Haitian people to be free and to share that freedom with enslaved and oppressed people of all races and nationalities. It is one of the world's foremost symbols of freedom and hope. Therefore, every person of African descent and friend of Haiti should strive to make the Pilgrimage to the Citadel at least once in a lifetime. By so doing, you will not only fulfill a sacred duty, you will nourish cultural/historical tourism as the vital lifeblood for economic development for the Haitian people.

In that spirit, as an outgrowth of Haiti Pilgrimage III, HSP is exploring the feasibility of a *Caribbean African Heritage Cruise* in August of 2010. With the active support of Radio Talk Show Host Warren Ballentine, *"The Number One Truth Fighter in America,"* Richard Muhammad, George Fraser, Joseph Beasley, Kangol Kid (our Special Guests for Haiti Pilgrimage III), and allies in the media, we hope to register 300-500 people to visit the Citadel. This will be the largest organized group of people of African descent and friends of Haiti ever to visit the Citadel. It's time to pay the debt and enjoy a transformative experience in the process. We hope you'll join us for this extraordinary journey. Boukman, Toussaint Louverture, Jean Jacques Dessalines, Henri Christophe and the legions of Haitian freedom fighters whose names are unknown are waiting to receive us!

African Americans as the Vital Third Leg in Haiti's Development

October, 2012

Since the inception of the Haiti Support Project in 1995, the concept of "socially responsible" economic business investment and development has been a central part of our mission. I recently wrote an article entitled Implanting a "Black Footprint" on an Economic Renaissance for Haiti in which I provided the historical context and cultural framework for people of African descent being engaged in the reconstruction and resurrection of Haiti after the devastating earthquake. As I prepare to leave for the *16th Annual New York Carib News Multinational Business Conference* in Jamaica, where Haiti's recovery post-earthquake will be a major focus, I thought it would be important to elaborate on the vital role African Americans can play in building a brighter future for the first Black Republic.

I contend that African Americans and other people of African descent in the U.S. should be the vital "third leg" in Haiti's development. Obviously the first responsibility for any nation's development is its own people. Therefore, the people of Haiti must always be in the forefront, the "first leg," of shaping the development and destiny of their country. The "second leg" is Haiti's vast and incredibly talented, experienced and relatively prosperous Diaspora, a resource which contributes nearly $2 billion in remittances annually and is energetically engaged in a multitude of humanitarian and development projects in Haiti. But, there is potentially a "third leg," African

Americans who should be cultivated as a major partner in Haiti's development. This is the niche the Haiti Support Project (HSP) has vigorously sought to fill over the past 16 years, as a troubadour relentlessly touting Haiti's history, culture, the necessity for a relationship with African Americans and the need for African Americans to become a vital partner in enriching the process of democracy and development.

As an independent Black nation, Haiti was the bright beacon of hope and promise for Africans in America struggling to break the yoke of generations of enslavement, southern apartheid and de facto segregation. Because Haiti was so important as a symbol of possibilities for Black people everyone, leaders of the NAACP and other civil rights organizations vigorously protested the U.S. occupation of Haiti (from 1915—1934) and consistently advocated for constructive engagement to develop the nation. For decades African American churches and civic associations have contributed to humanitarian assistance and sponsored charitable projects in Haiti. And, for a time the first Black Republic was a favorite destination of African American tourists. However, largely due to negative images of Haiti, African American tourism has dwindled to a trickle. This is a trend which can and must be reversed.

George Fraser, President/CEO of FraserNet, the largest network of Black professionals in the world, continually reminds us that despite stubborn vestiges of racism and discrimination, African Americans earn enough aggregate income to be considered the richest Black nation in the world. The civil rights movement has produced a thriving middle class with millions of Black professionals, hundreds of high profile and well paid artists, athletes and entertainers and a small but growing sector of Black millionaires and billionaires! African Americans spend hundreds of millions of dollars annually on tourism, much of it to travel to the sunny shores of the Caribbean. Given these assets, the historical affinity and relationship between African Americans and Haitians should be the basis for attracting thousands upon thousands of African Americans to Haiti as tourists. In addition, African Americans should also see Haiti as a prime market for economic development/business investment. Indeed, through the Model City Initiative in Milot in the north near the magnificent Citadel, HSP is actively working with local officials and the Local Development Committee to encourage cultural-historical tourism as the foundation for people based economic/business development. We say that every person of African descent should visit the Citadel at least once in a lifetime.

To fulfill this vision/mission, HSP conducts annual Pilgrimages to the Citadel and other important cultural/historical sites so that African Americans can be inspired by an immersion with the Haitian people and see a side of Haiti seldom portrayed in the news media. Over the past few years, HSP has exposed hundreds of African Americans to Haiti, including prominent leaders and personalities like Congressman Gregory Meeks (the first member of the Congressional Black Caucus to visit the Citadel); Oklahoma State Senator Constance Johnson; former Massachusetts State Representative Marie St. Fleur; George Curry, former Editor of *Emerge Magazine*; Bev Smith, American Urban Radio Networks; Gary Flowers, Executive Director, Black Leadership Forum; George Fraser, President/CEO, FraserNet; Warren Ballentine, RadioOne and SIRIUS/XM Radio; Hazel Trice-Edney, former Editor-in-Chief, National Newspaper Publishers Association; Omarosa, actress humanitarian; Joe Madison, "The Black Eagle," Radio-One and SIRIUS/XM; Richard Muhammad, Editor-in-Chief, *Final Call* newspaper; Herb Boyd, Staff Writer, *Amsterdam News,* Reporter, Free Speech T.V.; Edward Harris, award-winning Filmmaker;

and Kangol Kid, the first Haitian American Hip Hop Artist. Once Pilgrimage participants have experienced the first Black Republic, they return to the U.S. as "Ambassadors of Hope for Haiti!"

The African American market is a gold mine waiting to be tapped. First, it is important for African Americans to get beyond the myths and stereotypes propagated about Haiti to be willing to visit and invest. HSP is focused on attracting visitors to the Citadel to nourish the economy of the Milot/Cap Haitien Region and to identify individuals, organizations and corporations interested in investing in tourism-related enterprises. In that regard, we are preparing to launch a Haiti Investment Fund as a vehicle to attract and leverage investment dollars for business ventures in Milot as part of the Model City Initiative. We are also prepared to function as a facilitator for African Americans interested in investing in other regions and sectors of the Haitian economy. There are enormous opportunities waiting for investors to step up to the plate. Why not African Americans?

In order to maximize the potential of African Americans at the vital third leg in Haiti's development, however, the Government of Haiti and the private sector must prioritize and take special steps to encourage investment from Black America. HSP has stressed the need for the President, Prime Minister, Ministers of Government and key leaders from the private sector to take advantage of the Black Press in the U.S. to clearly express interest in African Americans visiting and investing in Haiti. HSP has had some success in arranging interviews for Haitian leaders on Black Talk Radio, but much more needs to be done. The Government and the private sector should actually devise a strategy for cultivating African American tourism and investment. HSP has recommended that such a strategy include an African American Advisory Commission for Tourism and Investment. Thus far, this recommendation has fallen on deaf ears. Hopefully, this will change under the Martelly Government. Moreover, agencies within the U.S. Government like USAID and international bodies such as the Inter-American Development Bank should also focus on devising strategies to encourage African American tourism and investment in Haiti. Finally, the Clinton Foundation and Clinton-Bush Initiative should be exploring ways to engage African Americans as major partners in Haiti's development post-earthquake.

At this juncture, the fact that African Americans could be an incredible source of tourism and investment does not appear to be on anyone's radar screen except the Haiti Support Project. Unless this changes, Haiti will miss a golden opportunity to utilize the ties that bind people of African descent in the U.S. to Haiti as a bond that could yield substantial dividends. HSP is determined that this opportunity not be lost. January 17-21, 2012, we will lead yet another Pilgrimage Delegation to Haiti to underline the importance of cultural historical tourism and socially responsible investment. And, the Pilgrimage of Hope

The Experience of a Life Time: Reflections on Cruising into History 2004

August, 2009

Five years ago, August 14-21, more than 500 African Americans, Haitian Americans and Friends of Haiti set sail from the Port of Miami on Royal Caribbean Cruise Line's Navigator of the Seas for an extraordinary journey—Cruising into History, a Caribbean Pilgrimage to commemorate the 200th Anniversary of the Haitian Revolution, which produced the first Black Republic in this hemisphere. The vision and mission of this remarkable Pilgrimage was to lift the veil of ignorance and misconceptions surrounding Haiti by exposing the participants to the rich history, culture and heritage of a much-maligned people and nation. In that vein, a major goal of Cruising into History (CIH) was to promote cultural/historical tourism as a vehicle for economic development for Haiti. As a veteran social/political activist and organizer, CIH was one of the most challenging and rewarding experiences of my life.

I have a deep and abiding passion for Haiti because of the phenomenal achievement of the Haitian revolutionaries in creating the first Black Republic in this hemisphere—the first time an enslaved people achieved such a feat in the history of the world. This improbable Revolution was consummated at the height of the holocaust of enslavement and the trans-Atlantic slave trade. It also coincided with the propagation of the myth of white supremacy. Time and time again, I have stated that Haiti was stigmatized, isolated, marginalized, subjugated, impoverished—punished for shattering the myth of white supremacy. It is my conviction that people of African descent and people of conscience/goodwill everywhere owe a special debt to Haiti.

Using CIH as a vehicle/hook, the commemoration of the Bicentennial of the Haitian Revolution offered an excellent opportunity to conduct a massive campaign to educate people about Haiti's incredible history and contributions to the world. Being an ambitious thinker, the original goal was to mobilize thousands of people to travel to Haiti to visit the Citadel, the magnificent mountaintop fortress built by King Henri Christophe after the Revolution to deter or defeat future invasions of Haiti. The Citadel is located in the northern part of the country in Milot near Cap Haitien. The problem was the lack of enough quality hotel rooms in the region to accommodate a large number of visitors. As a cruise lover, it occurred to me that the solution was to make a cruise ship the hotel! Hence was born the idea of Cruising into History!

Since Royal Caribbean International (RCI) is the only cruise line that travels to Haiti, HSP entered into discussions with them to provide a ship for the Pilgrimage. We were in the process of developing a positive working relationship with RCI, however, initially top brass from the company had great skepticism about the feasibility of CIH. Indeed, in my first conversation with their designated representative, she must have thought I was insane as I glibly articulated my dream of chartering two cruise ships to take upwards of 6,000 people to Haiti to visit the Citadel [in retrospect the idea was a bit delusional]. But once RCI was convinced that CIH was a worthy project, whatever the size, they made every effort to ensure its success. Ultimately we agreed that a half ship or 1,500 people was a more reasonable and attainable goal.

Given the negative images people have about Haiti, even

recruiting that number was no small undertaking. To educate the public about the history and culture of Haiti and recruit participants for CIH, HSP launched a multi-pronged public relations campaign. Marc Morial the outgoing Mayor of New Orleans, who is of Haitian descent, agreed to be Honorary Chairman of CIH. Danny Glover graciously accepted the position of Ambassador-at-Large. Bev Smith came on board as the official voice for the Pilgrimage via the American Urban Radio Networks. In short order a number of high-profile leaders and personalities signed on as Special Guests—Susan Taylor, Sonia Sanchez, Haki Madhubuti, George Fraser, Congress Members, John Conyers, Sheila Jackson-Lee and Maxine Waters and the legendary Katherine Dunham, to mention a few. RCI hosted receptions on its ships in Miami, New Orleans and New York to promote CIH. Special events were held in numerous cities across the country culminated with a seven-city tour by Dr. Ron Daniels and Leslie Voltaire, Minister for Haitians Living Abroad, with stops in New York, Boston, Pittsburgh, Detroit, Chicago, Atlanta and Fort Lauderdale. Even if the Cruise had never happened, millions of African Americans and other people of African descent learned more about Haiti than ever before as a result of the public relations campaign.

CIH almost didn't happen. January 1, 2004, I had the privilege of attending Haiti's Bicentennial Celebration at the National Palace in Port Au Prince along with Danny Glover and Herb Boyd. Tensions and conflicts inside the country were very much in evidence on this memorable occasion. In late February, after months of internal strife, Haiti was in turmoil after the U.S. orchestrated ouster of President Jean Bertrand Aristide. It was simply not safe to travel to any part of Haiti. In addition, there was the political question as to whether CIH might be viewed as an endorsement of the U.S. and U.N. installed Interim Government. Unfortunately, contracts with the cruise line had already been signed and more than 500 people had paid for their reservation. No doubt hundreds more would have signed on but were frightened away by the insurrection. Danny Glover and Sonia Sanchez withdrew from participating in CIH out of concern that the Pilgrimage would be viewed as condoning the Interim Government and by extension the ouster of President Aristide.

It was a painful moment of crisis, personally and institutionally. To address the concerns, a compromise was reached where it was agreed that the visit to Haiti would not include entering the country to visit the Citadel. Instead, CIH would be welcomed at Labadee by the Local Development Committee of Milot, our partners on the ground in Haiti, and local artists and musicians with no role or support from the Interim Government. After the U.S. sent troops to re-establish order, the situation calmed down sufficiently for CIH to continue.

Under these conditions, CIH set forth on what would still be a once in a life time experience.

The itinerary included stops in Nassau, Bahamas, St. Thomas, U.S. Virgin Islands, San Juan, Puerto Rico and the climatic stopover at Labadee in Haiti. At every port, we were welcomed by officials of Government and leaders from the community. In a very moving gesture, Danny Glover met the group in Nassau to state his emphatic opposition to the ouster of President Aristide and share his decision to withdraw from participating in CIH. Congresswoman Donna Christian Christiansen welcomed us in St. Thomas and local musicians treated us to a superb cultural performance. In San Juan, members of the group participated in an African Heritage Tour. As we moved from port to port, onboard the ship there was an incredible series of educational seminars, cultural performances and films as the group bonded in preparation for touching the soil of Haiti.

When we landed at Labadee, we were greeted by the Local

Development Committee of Milot. The compromise was extremely disappointing to the Committee and the residents of the region
who had been preparing for months to greet their Haitian American and African American sisters and brothers. Scores of vendors
had purchased wares anticipating an opportunity to do a banner day
of business. From our perspective, the compromise was the best we
could make of a bad situation. After some heartfelt explanations, the
Welcome Ceremony complete with Haitian drummers and dancers
proceeded. We pledged to repay the losses incurred by the vendors
who had invested their precious monies (many bought wares with
their children's tuition for school). Equally important, HSP pledged
to focus its humanitarian and developmental support efforts on Milot
and to assist the population to transform the town into a Mecca for
cultural/historical tourism and people-based economic development
for the area/region. As evidence of our commitment, HSP promised
to lead a Pilgrimage to the Citadel in 2006, the 200th Anniversary of
the construction of this spectacular fortress. It was at the moment on
the beach in Labadee that HSP's Model City Initiative for Milot was
born.

Back on the ship, participants made generous contributions to
assist HSP to repay the vendors and begin the process of creating an
infrastructure for economic development in Milot. In 2006, HSP kept
its promise by sponsoring the first annual Pilgrimage to the Citadel.
This was followed by another Pilgrimage in 2007. As we prepare for
the Third Annual Pilgrimage to the Citadel, October 8-12 of this year,
it is useful to remember that the incredible education and organizing
around CIH in 2004, with all its challenges, has born tremendous
fruit. The once relatively obscure town of Milot is now a focal point of
national and international attention as the Citadel is rapidly emerging
as the face of cultural/historical tourism for the first Black

Republic in this hemisphere. I would like to believe that Cruising into History and HSP's Pilgrimages to the Citadel have made a modest contribution to the new promise on the horizon for the first Black Republic in this hemisphere!

The Haitian Masses Deserve Free, Fair and Transparent Elections

February 8, 2016

I recently penned an article in which I encouraged President Obama to visit Haiti before the end of his term, to pay tribute to the unique history/heritage of the first Black Republic in the world and as an expression of gratitude to the Haitian people for their contribution towards building the United States of America. However, the political turmoil on the ground at the moment suggests that an Obama visit is far from what's needed. The best thing President Obama can do is to put the full weight of the prestige, resources and political will of the U.S. behind ensuring free, fair and transparent elections in Haiti. There is a potentially disastrous political crisis in Haiti because of massive opposition to the first round of the recent presidential election that was widely perceived by observers inside and outside the country as flawed and fraudulent.

The tragedy is that even in the face of mounting opposition to the first round, the U.S. and the international community stubbornly insisted that the second round, the run-off, proceed anyway. Frankly, it was insulting and disgusting. It was like saying to the Haitian masses, that any election no matter how flawed or fraught with fraud will do, that the aspirations of the Haitian masses for an election and democracy they can believe in does not matter to the United States and the international community. The long suffering Haitian masses deserve better than that.

I stress "Haitian masses" because their hopes/dreams for a better way of life and brighter future have been continually denied by a powerful, parasitical elite, a largely self-centered and self-aggrandizing political class and the machinations, meddling and interference in Haiti's affairs by the U.S. and other foreign powers. Shakespeare once said, "the fault... is not in our stars but in ourselves, that we are underlings." In the Haitian political context, the fault is not with the Haitian masses of the poor, peasants, and the miniscule, struggling middle class, but with the elite, the political class and the interference of foreign powers that Haiti has failed to reach its full potential as the world's first Black Republic! The courageous, resilient, energetic, creative, hardworking and long suffering Haitian masses deserve better, and those who love Haiti and its people must stand with them in the fight for a brighter future. And, President Obama can make a difference by helping the Haitian masses achieve this righteous cause.

The Haiti Support Project of the Institute of the Black World 21st Century unites with organizations in the Haitian Diaspora and in Haiti in the call for free, fair and transparent elections. Fortunately, the Electoral Commission has postponed the second-round of the presidential elections until April (this may be too soon). This is an important first step in what must be a conscientious effort to produce elections that the Haitian masses can embrace. Therefore, the elections should not be rushed. "Haste makes waste." All stakeholders concerned should take sufficient time to get the elections right this time. In that same vein, it was critically important that President Martelly, as a partisan with a stake in the outcome, step down at the end of his term. His exit from office as required by the Constitution should help the process.

An "inclusive" Interim or Transitional Government must now be constituted with a mandate to manage the country in the short-term and to oversee the organization of transparent legislative and presidential elections. Given the travesty of recent elections, a complete do over is in order to inspire confidence in the process. The key to a transparent process is the creation of an independent/non-partisan, inclusive Electoral Commission. In the past there has been the perception that the Electoral Commission was simply an arm of whatever government was in power. This perception must end if the vast majority of the Haitian people are to have confidence in the fairness and transparency of the process.

I stress "inclusive" because it is important that the "winner take all" tendency within Haiti's embryonic democracy be countered by cultivating a sense of unity of purpose, of "Haiti first," to achieve social, economic and political progress. Hence, the Haitian masses of all political persuasions should see an Interim or Transitional Government and Electoral Commission which is broadly inclusive/representative of the political spectrum in the country. And, no matter which party ultimately wins the presidential election, friends and supporters of Haiti would do well to encourage the new President to form an inclusive government, one which is tantamount to a Government of National Unity; a Government that includes representatives of various political parties and constituencies; a Government committed to putting Haiti and the interests and aspirations of the Haitian masses above the narrow interests of the elite and the political class. Indeed, there is an argument to be made that when the lives of the Haitian masses are improved, the prospects for prosperity for everyone, including the political class, will improve because of the political stability and social/economic growth that will occur.

I still want President Obama to visit Haiti, but I want him to lay the ground work for an historic journey by showing respect for the wishes of the Haitian masses for free, fair and transparent elections.

As President of the United States, he should expend whatever resources necessary to achieve this end. Then, he can arrive in Haiti having truly earned the admiration and respect of the Haitian people!

SECTION VI

Africans in America: Engaging the U.S. Political System

Blacks and the Republican Party: Rational Choice or Complicity with Reactionaries

May, 2010

A recent article in the *New York Times* reported that 32 African Americans are running for Congress as Republicans in this year's mid-term elections, the largest number since the era of Reconstruction. The article attributed the "surge" in Black Republican candidates to the election of Barack Obama as the first African American President of the United States. At first glance this would seem to be a positive development. It seems logical that Blacks would want to be represented in both major political parties as a means of ensuring that our interests are being advanced and that we are not taken for granted by either party. For this reason, noted journalist and television talk show host Tony Brown was a strong proponent of Black engagement in the Republican Party for many years. Upon reflection, however, one might question whether the mainstream agenda of African Americans is compatible with the current politics and policies of the Republican Party. Put another way, though Blacks may have grievances with the Democrats, running for office as a Republican might be like jumping from the "frying pan into the fire."

African Americans are certainly no strangers to the Republican Party. For nearly a century Blacks were staunchly entrenched in the Republican Party. This was largely due to the fact that Abraham Lincoln issued the Emancipation Proclamation and "radical" Republicans like Charles Summer and Thaddeus Stevens led the charge to adopt the 13th, 14th and 15thAmendments to the Constitution. Republican-controlled Congresses also passed far-ranging civil rights acts from 1866-1876, the post Civil War period known as Reconstruction. These Amendments and civil rights statutes led to the largest group of Blacks being elected to public office until the present. Blacks held posts as city and county officials, Congressmen, Lieutenant Governor and Senator. Black political power was so dominant in the South that some called the era "Black Reconstruction." Virtually every one of these Black elected officials was a Republican. In the political competition between Democrats and Republicans in the South, newly enfranchised Blacks were a reliable base for the Republicans, a fact that not only had local implications, but ensured Republic political hegemony at the national level including the presidency.

Then came the infamous "betrayal of 1876," the Hayes-Tilden Compromise. In a presidential election so close that it was deadlocked in the Electoral College, the Republicans agreed to a deal to pull all federal troops out of the South and essentially leave the plight of Blacks to the States in exchange for gaining enough Democratic votes to make the Republican, Rutherford B. Hayes, President. The effect of this betrayal was swift and predictable. To regain and maintain political power, Democrats in the South disenfranchised Blacks and ultimately instituted a rigid system of segregation/separation of the races. Blacks were stripped of political power, reduced to quasi-peonage in the labor market and socially ostracized. For decades after the betrayal of 1876, the few Blacks who could vote in the South were between a "rock and a hard place." They were unwelcome in the Democratic Party and abandoned by the Republicans. Nonetheless, because of the legacy of Lincoln and the Emancipation Proclamation and achievements during Reconstruction, Blacks remained loyal to the Republicans. In the North, where there were very few Blacks prior to the great migrations, the antipathy of European immigrants who became Democrats for the most part as well as the legacy of Lincoln persuaded Blacks to remain Republicans.

A gradual political shift began with the great migrations to the North as Blacks increasingly became part of and identified with causes of labor/workers despite ongoing hostility and discrimination from White bosses and workers. The Great Depression and the rise to power of Franklin Delano Roosevelt was the other factor contributing to the shift of Blacks from the Republican to the Democratic Party. With large blocks of Blacks concentrated in urban-industrial centers, it now made sense for the Democratic Party to compete for Black votes. FDR's New Deal was also like a God send for Blacks, mired at the bottom of the economic ladder during the Depression. I can still hear my mother and father reverently describing what a life saver the New Deal was for Black families. This coupled with FDR's capitulation to A. Philip Randolph's demand for a federal Fair Employment Practices Act (Randolph threatened a March on Washington), which FDR enacted by Executive Order, cemented the growing shift to and allegiance by Blacks to the Democratic Party.

However, the decisive move to the Democratic Party did not occur until the historic election of John F. Kennedy in 1960. Black voters viewed their interests and allegiances to the two parties ideologically and pragmatically. Despite the promise of the New Deal, a significant number of Blacks remained Republicans until the 60's because there were moderates and liberals in the Republican Party— yes, moderates and liberals, who identified with and supported Black issues and concerns, particularly the demand for voting rights and an end to segregation. Indeed, even after Kennedy's victory in 1960, there were Republicans who supported civil rights. Senator Everett Dirkson of Illinois, Senators Jacob Javits and Kenneth Keating of

New York, Clifford Case of New Jersey, Governor William Scranton of Pennsylvania, Governor Nelson Rockefeller of New York and John Lindsey, Mayor of New York, come to mind as moderates and liberals who supported civil rights. No less a historical personage than Jackie Robinson was a staunch Republican and close friend of Nelson Rockefeller. Even Richard Nixon was not averse to supporting initiatives viewed as favorable to Black interests. It is useful to recall that it was Nixon who adopted the concept of affirmative action upon the recommendation of Art Fletcher, a prominent African American Republican. Edward Brooke, an African American, was elected to the Senate as a Republican from Massachusetts. What Jackie Robinson, Art Fletcher and Senator Brooke have in common is that they could play prominent roles in a Party that had a moderate and liberal wing committed to civil rights, labor and women's issues—there was political space to advance the mainstream Black agenda in the Republican Party.

Unfortunately, that is not the case today. These notable figures would feel unwelcome in a Republican Party where liberal is a dirty word and moderates are a rare species. With conservative ideological purists like Rush Limbaugh, Glenn Beck, Sean Hannity, former Vice-President Dick Cheney, Sarah Palin and the Tea Party Patriots holding disproportionate sway over the Party, to be a Republican today is tantamount to being a conservative—Republican equals conservative with all this entails in terms of an anti-affirmative action/ civil rights, anti-immigrant, anti-women's rights, anti-gay rights, anti-labor, anti-environment, anti-regulation, pro-big business, pro-gun, pro-war agenda! Today the most prominent Black Republicans are the likes of Armstrong Williams, Larry Elder, Ward Connerly, Allan Keyes, Ken Blackwell, Rev. Jesse Peterson and, of course, RNC Chairman Michael Steele. What they have in common is that they either embrace or have been whipped into line to extol the virtues of the reactionary conservative agenda referenced above, an agenda which is far removed from a mainstream Black agenda. Indeed, this is precisely why the Republican Party has made few gains in cutting into the Black vote as the most loyal constituency in the Democratic Party—the Republican agenda is repugnant and a turn-off to the vast majority of Black voters.

So, for aspiring Republican candidates the lesson and message should be clear: to be effective in promoting a mainstream Black agenda you must fight to create political space on unwelcome terrain. The problem is, I suspect, most of these candidates have already either passed the conservative litmus test or are willing to acquiesce to the conservative cause to advance their individual interest. In any event, unless they are willing to fight for Black interests and aspirations, they will be mere pawns in the Republican/Conservative Party and in complicity with reactionaries!

The Obama Presidency:
Will Progressives
Offer a Vision for a
More Perfect Union?

March, 2009

As it became increasingly clear that Barack Obama was poised to make history as the first African American President of the United States, it was also clear that this was potentially a big moment for the progressive movement—a time to articulate a vision for a new America and to organize to advance an agenda for reform and fundamental change. As the Obama presidency unfolds, the question is whether the progressive movement is prepared to seize the opportunity presented by this remarkable moment in   history.

In my view, the major theme of America's history is the perpetual struggle to define the ultimate nature of "a more perfect union." When George W. Bush proudly proclaimed himself a "strict constructionist" during his campaign for President in 2000, he was associating himself with a political tendency within the conservative movement that has sought to narrowly/literally interpret the Constitution in ways that would restrict democracy to White men with property, power and privilege. Indeed, the system which was birthed in 1787 was essentially "democracy for the few," with women, Blacks, Native Americans and White men without property excluded from the franchise. The fate of the infant nation was placed in the hands of White men with property.

The genius of the Constitution, however, is its "elasticity." Through social and political movements, it can be stretched or constricted to include or exclude constituencies and categories of rights based on how it is interpreted. Historically, arrayed against the strict constructionists has been liberal-left-progressive movements which have sought to stretch the Constitution to include those initially locked out and to expand civil liberties, civil and social rights in the quest to achieve a "more perfect union."

The Bill of Rights to the Constitution, the abolition of slavery, women's suffrage, antitrust laws and other statutes regulating business/corporations, labor rights, the reaffirmation of civil rights for Blacks and minorities, expansion of rights for women, consumer protection, environmental protection and recognition of rights of lesbian and gay people are a direct legacy of women and men, Democrats, Republicans, Socialists, Communists, independents, elected and non-elected leaders—the liberal-left progressive forces that have struggled to expand democracy. Taken together with the social safety network created during the New Deal and expanded by subsequent moderate-liberal administrations, a fragile "culture of rights" was emerging to protect workers, poor people and the middle class against the rapacious nature of unbridled Capitalism.

With the election of Ronald Reagan, a strict constructionist, we witnessed the opening salvo in the strategic effort by the conservatives to turn back the clock, to reverse the minimal gains achieved by liberal-left-progressive forces as a result of generations of hard fought, often bloody struggles. With the firing of members of the Professional Air Traffic Controllers Association (PATCO), Reagan declared outright war on labor while unabashedly advocating economic policies to benefit corporations and the wealthy. He launched a ferocious attack on affirmative action and race-based remedies and began the process of undermining the culture of rights by ripping huge holes in the social safety net.

Reagan gained substantial popular support for his anti-labor and pro-corporate policies by persuading a sizeable segment of the American electorate that social programs were a heavy burden on the backs of the people. Employing race as a tactic to divide and exploit, there was the suggestion that Blacks and minorities were the exclusive beneficiaries of social programs. The rise to hegemony of the right gained momentum in 1994 when Republicans took control of both Houses of Congress. The rightward tide was so strong that Bill Clinton governed as a centrist who embraced some of the Republicans' flagship initiatives, e.g., downsizing government, ending "welfare as we know it" and lobbying for the passage of the North American Free Trade Agreement (NAFTA). The march to rightwing supremacy was consummated with the seizure of power by George W. Bush in the flawed 2000 election—ushering in one of the most reckless, corrupt, greed driven and dangerous eras in American history.

Consequently, in my mind, there was no doubt that defeating the forces of the right was an absolute imperative in the 2008 election. The first order of business was to stop the damage and create space for progressives to maneuver. That an African American named Barack Obama was capturing the imagination of the nation and the world with his pledge to bring "Change," we could believe in was all the more promising. However, we should never have had any illusions that Obama was committed to or could by himself have the capacity to foster the kind of major reforms and fundamental change progressives would envision for a new America. This is not to say that what President Obama is doing is insignificant. The policy recommendations he is advancing mark a decided shift from the catastrophic policies of the Reagan-Bush era. But his incremental approach lacks an overarching vision and the bold policy prescriptions necessary to expand the culture of rights that has been severely constricted by the reign of the conservatives.

At a time when the Republicans, with their mascot "Joe the Plumber," are accusing

President Obama of leading the nation down the path to Socialism or the "Europeanization" of America, progressives should be seizing the opportunity created by the greatest crisis since the Great Depression to educate the American people about the urgent need for far-ranging and fundamental change. But, progressives seem locked in a mode of critiquing and refining Obama's incremental agenda. This may be due to the utter relief of being rid of the horrific years under George W. Bush. However, relief from Bush is not enough. Now is the time for the progressive movement to boldly articulate its vision and program for a more perfect union. If we fail to act, we may miss our moment!

In the Era of Obama, Is There a Need for a Black Agenda

April, 2009

O ur cities are crime-haunted dying grounds. Huge sectors of our youth...face permanent unemployment... Neither the courts nor the prisons contribute anything resembling justice or reformation. The schools are unable—or unwilling—to educate our children for the real world of our struggles. Meanwhile, the officially approved epidemic of drugs threatens to wipe out the minds and strengths of our best young warriors." When people ask me whether we need a Black Agenda in the era of Obama, I am reminded that much about this quotation, from the Preamble to the National Black Agenda adopted in Gary, Indiana in 1972, is the reality today for vast numbers of Blacks.

President Barack Obama speaks proudly of his days as an organizer on the South Side of Chicago where his wife Michelle was also raised in a working-class family. There are certainly sections of Chicago's south side that are still "crime-haunted dying grounds." In addition, when Mark Morial, President/CEO of the National Urban League, recently threw down the gauntlet after releasing the annual "State of Black America Report," which continues to show troubling disparities between Blacks and Whites in education, health care, income and wealth, he was implicitly making the case for the ongoing need for a Black Agenda.

The conditions prevalent in Black America 37 years after the Gary Convention, coupled with this year's "State of Black America

Report," tempt me to say, "The more things change, the more they stay the same." However, things have changed for Africans in America. Indeed, because of the Black Political Convention in 1972, we now have thousands of Black elected officials occupying positions as local school board representatives, sheriffs, mayors, congresspersons and of course, the President of the United States. We have a greatly expanded Black middle and upper class with an abundance of Black professionals, high- paid artists, athletes, entertainers and heads of Fortune 500 Corporations. No one can deny that the Black freedom struggle has produced significant gains for the sons and daughters of Africa in America.

Nevertheless, far too many Black people are mired in conditions similar to those we faced in the 60's. According to a study released by the *Community Service Society of New York* a couple of years ago, some 50% of Black and 40% of Latino youth are unemployed in this city when you include those who have dropped out of the labor market. Bronx County New York, with a predominately Black and Latino population, is the poorest urban county in America! Schools that fail to educate Black children are the prevailing reality in Black poor and working class neighborhoods, creating a pipeline to an exploding prison-jail industrial complex where the dominant complexion of the prisoners is black and brown. That these debilitating conditions persist for large numbers of Blacks in the 21st century clearly indicates that the "color line," institutional/structural racism remains a roadblock to "freedom" particularly for Black working class and poor people.

Here again, that faded document from the Gary Black Political Convention is still relevant and instructive: "The crises we face as Black people are the crises of the entire society. They go deep to the very bones and marrow, to the essential nature of America's economic, political and cultural systems. They are the natural end product of a society built on the twin foundation of white racism and white capitalism." It does not occur to me, a veteran social and political activist, with this analysis informing my assessment of the condition of Black working class and poor people that we are somehow in a "post-racist" society. The fact that America has progressed to the point that a Black family can occupy the White House has not eradicated the myriad maladies of race and class that continue to constrain the aspirations of millions of Black people in this nation. Therefore, the idea of a Black Agenda is not only relevant, it is imperative if Africans in America, as a group, are to enter the "promised land" that Martin Luther King envisioned from his view from the mountaintop in Memphis.

In the first instance, a Black Agenda is imperative because promoting and defending one's interest is fundamental to achieving your aspirations within a pluralistic, competitive process in this Capitalist political economy. The Hispanic leadership that recently met with President Obama was not there to show they have "access," to have tea and crumpets or to have a photo op; they were there to discuss how their 67% vote for the President must translate into tangible gains for Latinos. The Obama administration's refusal to participate in the forthcoming U.N. Conference on Racism, because of fears that Israel may be attacked for its human rights violations during the invasion of Gaza, is a direct reflection of the power of the Israeli lobby in the U.S.

It is foolhardy for any African American to think that by simply electing a Black President the intractable problems facing Black poor and working people will miraculously disappear. They will only be resolved under this President or any President if we identify those issues that are of critical interest to our people and demand that they be solved. That's why Marc Morial's action in demanding that President

Obama do something about the gross disparities between Blacks and Whites in education, health, income and wealth was courageous and exemplary. I am certain Mr. Morial admires our President, as I do, but in the world of politics, that is beside the point. We need symbols and substance not symbols without substance; otherwise, those "crime-haunted dying grounds" are where the dreams of many Black people will continue to be buried!

In Defense of
"Identity Politics"

(June, 2009)

The nomination of Judge Sotomayor for Justice on the Supreme Court has simply sent some conservatives into a tizzy, searching for anything that might derail her historic quest to be the first Latina to occupy a seat on this august body. One of the allegations that has surfaced is that she is a proponent of "identity politics," the appeal to solidarity within a racial, ethnic or issue constituency to advance the interest/agenda of a particular group. Conservatives have widely disparaged such efforts as separatist, divisive and corrosive of the idea of assimilating into the American culture. Critics point to Judge Sotomayor's statement that a "wise Latina" might bring a better perspective on some issues than a White man and description of herself as an "affirmative action baby" as evidence that she is a captive of identity politics. In a recent column in the *New York Times*, conservative columnist David Brooks, who actually had some favorable things to say about Judge Sotomayor, suggested that she attended Princeton University when "the whole race, class and gender academic-industrial complex seemed fresh, exciting and just." He goes on to say that "there is no way she was going to get out of that unscarred." Brooks obviously subscribes to the notion that identity politics is damaging to the American way.

In my view conservatives who espouse this view are either naïve, ignorant of American history or posturing for political advantage (it could be all of the above). Identity politics is not contrary to the

American way; it is the American way! With few exceptions the initial wave of intruders who sailed to these shores and dispossessed the indigenous people were White Anglo-Saxon Protestants (WASP). It is this body of Euro-ethnics along with their Scandinavian and Germanic kith and kin who established the foundations for the American culture and "identity." WASPS also captured the vital levers of power and privilege in the emerging new nation.

America was largely a WASP nation until the great migrations which occurred in response to the industrial revolution after the Civil War. Now mixed in with the Anglo-Germanic and Scandinavian people arriving on these shores were the Catholic (including Irish) and darker-skinned Euro-ethnics from Southern and Eastern Europe, Italians, Greeks, Poles and other Slavic immigrants. All of these non-WASP Euro-ethnics were treated as foreigners and viewed as a threat to "American culture." They were also locked out of the centers of economic and political power. As marginalized groups, non-WASP ethnics were compelled to look inward, to use their ethnic identity, culture and religion as sources of strength in a hostile land. Their solidarity served as the foundation for internal socio-economic development and entry into the electoral political arena.

As the major political parties competed for power in local, state and national elections, organized blocs of self-identified new immigrants who were once reviled and marginalized became more attractive as potential allies to achieve electoral victories. Indeed, some marginalized ethnic groups, most notably the Irish, became so adept at welding power that they became the dominant force in some of the most powerful political machines in this country, e.g., Boss Tweed in Boston, the Daley machine in Chicago and the O'Connell Machine in Albany. Marginalized groups used "identity politics" to break down the walls of social, economic and political exclusion.

For decades in most of the urban centers in the country, with the exception of the South, political parties used "ticket balancing" to make certain that every ethnic identity group was represented on their slates of candidates to improve prospects for electoral success/victory. Over time other constituent groups like labor began to flex their muscles and therefore had to be considered as part of the electoral political equation. It is this mix of ethnic groups and issue-related interest groups that the venerable Political Scientist V.O. Keys discusses in his classic work, *Politics, Parties and Pressure Groups*. Identity politics is as "American as apple pie."

If White, non-WASP Euro-ethnics were forced to utilize identity politics to achieve more just and equitable treatment in their new homeland, it has been imperative that people of African descent and other people of color do likewise. Deep-seated racism/white supremacy in America has been a formidable barrier to access to first class citizenship, equity and parity for Blacks and people of color. While it may have been difficult to distinguish between various Euro-ethnic groups because of their "whiteness," there was no hiding place for Blacks and people of color. Indeed, antagonism toward people of color has often been a source of unity among Whites despite their inter-ethnic rivalries. Consequently, racial/ethnic/cultural solidarity has been an essential element in the struggle to eradicate discrimination, segregation and exclusion from economic and political power for people of color in this country. Like their White counterparts, people of color have been compelled to utilize identity politics to demand respect, dignity, equal opportunity and democratic rights.

Based on their historical experiences as marginalized, however, Blacks and people of color are expanding the definition of the "American way" to be a more inclusive, multi-ethnic, multi-cultural, multi-religious, "empathetic," just and humane society. In this quest, they are joined by other "identity" groups like proponents of women's rights and lesbian and gay advocates. This is the real problem conservatives have with identity politics. They fear the possibility that a "Rainbow Coalition" of identity groups will pose a fundamental threat to "our cherished American way of life." And, they have every right to be fearful because "wise" representatives of Rainbow identity groups are likely to see and wish for a far different world then White men and women who are apostles of a restrictive and homogenized American identity and way of life.

No More Lectures:
What President Obama
Can Do for Black America

June, 2013

When I was at Lafayette Park (across from the White House) recently checking the logistics/arrangements for IBW's June 17th Day of Direct Action to pressure President Obama to end the War on Drugs and invest in inner-city Black communities, I confess to having been filled with pride thinking about the reality of a Black Family occupying the White House! But, I pinched myself to get past the fact that Barack Obama is the first African American President of the USA. I had to quickly remind myself that electoral politics is about who gets what, how much and when. At least that's what our beloved Dr. Ronald Walters spent much of his life striving to teach us. It doesn't matter the color, race, ethnicity or even political persuasion of the resident in the White House, Presidents should respond to the crises of people/groups because they are part of the body politic of this nation. If a constituency/group is a key part of the President's political support base, there is an even more compelling reason to attend to their needs. Unfortunately, as it relates to Blacks, these basic expectations of electoral politics seem not to apply. For decades Presidents have failed to respond to the crises in Black America in proportion to our needs or political support—particularly the Democratic Party.

Thus far, this is certainly the case with President Obama. Despite the "State of Emergency" in America's "dark ghettos," he refuses to directly respond to the urgent needs of Blacks who marched on ballot boxes in record numbers to ensure his election and re-election. Instead of policies and programs specifically designed/targeted to ameliorating and ultimately transforming the conditions in distressed urban communities, Black America is treated to symbolism, access and lectures about personal responsibility. Many Blacks seem to be content with President Obama's approach, choosing to give him a pass because he is a "brother." On the other hand, there are growing numbers of Blacks from all walks of life who are simply getting tired, frustrated and angry at the President's reluctance to openly address what can only be considered a moral and political crisis in terms of depression levels of joblessness, horrific gun violence, fratricide and mass incarceration in urban inner-city Black communities. For some, Obama is like a Black Nero fiddling while Black communities are imploding!

No doubt, deep down inside this President may want to identify with the needs of Black people, but apparently he is afraid of a "White backlash" if he shows his true colors. So, in lieu of programs and policies directed/targeted to relieve distressed Black communities, we get symbolism—the President and First Lady delivering commencement addresses at historically Black colleges and universities or visiting inner-city schools. Certainly there is no harm in symbolism except when it's a substitute for the kind of substantive policies which would alleviate the pain and suffering of people who not only need a kind word, but jobs, economic development and relief from violence and fratricide. The same applies for "access" to the White House.

Never in my life have I witnessed Blacks having so much access to the White House via conference calls, Black talk radio interviews, briefings and celebratory gatherings/parties (folks brag about jamming at the White House with the First Lady and the Prez). And, of course, the Congressional Black Caucus, National Urban League, NAACP and National Action Network have been favored with appearances at their conventions by the most powerful leader in the world—who happens to be a Black man! The problem is that the President seldom, if ever, speaks directly to the most urgent concerns of Black America at these auspicious gatherings—the State of Emergency in America's dark ghettos. Can you imagine President Obama speaking to a Latino convention and not addressing the issue of immigration policy reform or talking to a lesbian and gay organization without discussing marriage equality and LBGT rights? He wouldn't dare insult these groups by not directly addressing their priority agendas.

Finally, and perhaps the most egregious act of all, is President Obama's persistent lecturing to Black audiences/Black people about personal responsibility. The most recent instance was his pep talk to the highly-accomplished graduates of Morehouse College—who hardly needed a lecture on altering their behavior to be more responsible young men. President Obama has also used Father's Day to become "daddy-in-chief," exhorting us to just behave better, and more responsibly. There is nothing inherently wrong with encouraging people to do better but it would have much more credibility and impact if the lecture was accompanied by a call on the nation and its political and economic institutions to invest in revitalizing communities ravished by disinvestment, deindustrialization, the war on drugs and mass incarceration. Otherwise, these patronizing lectures are an insult to Black people!

As we gear up for the June 17th Day of Direct Action, what President Obama can do for Black America is not radical and should not be racially divisive. Instead of another demeaning Father's Day lecture, he should declare joblessness in the inner-cities a national crisis and propose a massive jobs/economic investment program with a priority on training and hiring formerly incarcerated persons. Though they are not likely to join our *Drum Majors for Justice* at the gates of the White House, virtually every civil rights leader from Rev. Al Sharpton, National Action Network, to Marc Morial, National Urban League, Melanie Campbell, National Coalition for Black Civic Participation, to Benjamin Jealous, NAACP, and the Congressional Black Caucus agree that something similar to a targeted jobs/economic program is a top priority to revitalize distressed Black communities. I think they would also agree that what Black America does not need is another lecture!

The State of the Union:
President Obama Ignores Crises
in America's "Dark Ghettos"

February, 2013

Last week, once again President Barack Hussein Obama mounted the podium at the Capitol to deliver the State of the Union Address to a Joint Session of Congress, the nation and the world. By all reasonable measures the address was an impressive center-left, moderate-liberal agenda on domestic issues like jobs, the minimum wage, infra-structure repair, energy, early childhood education, tax reform, deficit reduction, gender equity, marriage equality, immigration and gun security—a policy prescriptions vastly superior to the dangerous/extremist positions of the radical conservatives and Tea Party obstructionists. President Obama's Inaugural and State of the Union messages vindicated the massive march on ballot boxes by people of African descent and a Rainbow Coalition of constituencies and interest groups to repel the repugnant assault of the right-wing Neanderthals. As I wrote in the weeks preceding the 2012 election, President Obama was clearly the "better choice."

But, there is a major problem. Once again the myriad crises, the State of Emergency in America›s «dark ghettos» was missing from the agenda! While he has taken great care to directly address issues of vital concerns to Latinos, women, lesbian and gay people and youth/students, time and time again, President Obama has refused to directly address the devastation and disaster in urban inner-city neighborhoods—intolerable conditions of depression level joblessness, inferior education, crime, violence, fratricide and mass incarceration. Time and time again defenders of the administration quietly pass the word to justifiably disgruntled Black supporters that our community is indirectly benefiting from policies like the Affordable Health Care Act. And, this is absolutely true. The problem is that the State of Emergency in America's dark ghettos is so immense, so intractable, that it requires the conviction and courage of a President who is willing to speak the truth to the American people—50 years after the March on Washington, millions of Africans in America are "still far from the Dream."

Instead, Obama behaves as if issues of structural/institutional racism are a thing of the past. Therefore, no racial remedies are required to address the pain, suffering, imprisoned and murdered aspirations of the sons and daughters of Africa in America's dark ghettos. In his Inaugural address, the President eloquently referenced Seneca Falls, the site of the launch of the first wave of the women's rights movement;, Stonewall, the event which sparked the lesbian and gay rights movement; and, Selma, a high water mark of the Black Freedom Struggle. During his tenure in office, the President has consistently and correctly pushed policies to eradicate gender inequality and discrimination against lesbian and gay people as part of his quest to finish an unfinished civil rights/human rights agenda in this country. But, when it comes to Black people, it is as if Selma represents the pinnacle of the movement, after which no meaningful direct action is required. We are reduced to commemorating the past with no explicit recognition of our present pain and suffering. It is as if we are "invisible."

To be fair, President Obama did not create the crises afflicting America's dark ghettos. For decades, urban inner-city areas have been victimized by massive disinvestment as a result of the "white backlash" against the "gains" of the Civil Rights Movement and dein-dustrialization occasioned by globalization. Blatant neglect has been the order of the day as politicians at all levels have essentially substituted "get tough on crime" policies, paramilitary policing strategies, tougher sentencing, jails and mass incarceration for social, economic and racial justice. Rather than continuing the War Poverty, Black people have been victimized by a "War on Drugs" that is a "war on us." Ever since the era of Ronald Reagan, urban inner-city areas have been treated like dangerous, crime-infested wastelands that must be controlled/occupied.

So, President Obama did not create the crises, he inherited it. The problem is that like previous Presidents, he is guilty of ignoring the crises or failing to explicitly address it. As an African American who experienced living and organizing on the south side of Chicago and attended Trinity United Church of Christ, deep down inside, President Obama must know and feel the pain and suffering of Black people struggling to survive in urban-inner city America. His real perceptions and feelings notwithstanding, it is abundantly clear that he and his advisors have made a calculated decision to keep race out of the public discourse and racial remedies off the public policy table. Apparently, there is a fear that to mention race or address "racial grievances" would lead to charges that he is partial to Black people or that it would fuel racial resentment. While the White House ponders and pontificates on how to develop "stealth" or "trickle down" strategies to address the State of Emergency in America's dark ghettos, millions of Black people are suffering. This is a big problem and it cannot be allowed to stand!

Mr. President, it's time for a wake-up call. The agenda you have put forth is commendable, but it simply does not go far enough to combat the crises in urban inner-city neighborhoods. We respect you, but just as Martin Luther King and other civil rights leaders were compelled to confront John F. Kennedy and Lyndon B. Johnson (Presidents who they respected) to demand government action to end southern apartheid, we today must raise our voices to demand social and economic justice for distressed Black communities. Race based remedies must be resurrected as part of the discourse on public policy. There is growing consensus among civil rights/human rights and political leaders in Black America that you must call for and educate the America people on the urgent need for social and economic policies and programs targeted directly to ending the State of Emergency in America's dark ghettos.

Based on the Declaration of Intent to Heal Black Families and communities, the Action Agenda of State of the Black World Conference III, IBW has already expressed our determination to use direct action, if necessary, to vigorously press for an end to the "War on Drugs;" jobs and economic development programs for distressed Black communities; and just and equitable immigration reform that protects the interests of people of African descent. Mr. President, race still matters in America. It's time to face this reality and act with vision, courage and conviction to end the state of emergency in distressed/marginalized Black communities. Be forewarned, we are not and will not be invisible!

Where There Is No Vision the People Perish: Why Bernie Sanders' Campaign Matters

February, 2016

In 1988 Rev. Jesse L. Jackson galvanized the progressive movement and much of the Democratic Party as he campaigned for President on the slogan: "Bold Leadership and a New Direction." The 1988 campaign was the sequel to the electrifying campaign of 1984 in which he popularized the notion of a Rainbow Coalition as a multiracial, multi-constituency force to advance a progressive agenda. Rev. Jackson challenged the Democratic Party to hold true to and fight for its principles by unapologetically articulating a vision to improve the quality of life for the majority of Blacks, people of color, the poor, working people and the struggling middle class. His slogan and platform was proclaiming that vision matters! As a result, millions of people flocked to the Jackson campaign, large numbers of whom were young people who had never voted or participated in electoral politics before.

I believe it is "the vision thing" that is producing stunning results as surprising numbers of people, particularly young people, are enthusiastically joining a movement fueled by their feel of and affection for the "Bern." Let me be clear, Hillary Clinton is a far better choice for President than any of the extremist candidates from a Republican Party whose views on some issues border on atavistic. Bernie Sanders made it clear in his victory speech in New Hampshire that it is absolutely imperative that these rightwing, retrograde forces be stopped. However, having said that, for decades there has been a pent-up yearning for a truly progressive candidate like Bernie Sanders who could stretch the imagination to envision and articulate what should be rather than what's "practical."

Under fierce assault from reactionary forces on the right, for decades the Democratic Party has retreated from the hard-fought gains secured over generations of struggle, a culture of rights for poor and working people, much of which is reflected in Roosevelt's New Deal. At the heart of this culture of rights is the notion that the "public space," public education, housing, health care, transportation, jobs and other government provided services and opportunities function as an "equalizer" to ameliorate the harsh edges, the negative outcomes for ordinary people in a Capitalist political-economy. For decades, the "public space" has been withering away as Democrats have largely capitulated to the conservative onslaught, demanding smaller government, privatization of public services, elimination or drastic reductions in social programs, tax cuts for the wealthy and reduced regulations to ensure unfettered, free markets—free rein for corporations and financial interests, "freedom" for Wall Street!

A good case can be made that this capitulation was aided and abetted by the Democratic Leadership Conference (DLC), an organization within the Democratic Party led by former President William Jefferson Clinton. The DLC never claimed to be "progressive." It was a self-avowed moderate/centrist organization whose claim to fame was its opposition to the liberal-progressive wing of the Party. The DLC's formula for success was to achieve electoral victories, including winning the White House, by minimizing discussion of the traditional values and policies of the Democratic Party. The DLC advocated co-opting aspects of the Republic Party's platform and message on policies like defense, the size of government, welfare, social programs and trade. They essentially favored an incremental, pro-business, "Republican light," pragmatic agenda!

The consequences of the DLC led capitulation has been disastrous, particularly in terms of dramatically increased inequality, the downward spiral or stagnation of wages/incomes for working people and marginalization of the poor. Indeed, the working class and the poor became virtually invisible in the public discourse on public policy as Democrats, no doubt influenced by the "consultant class," increasingly focused on the "middle class."

There is also a State of Emergency in America's "dark ghettos," Black communities/neighborhoods in cities like Ferguson and Baltimore which is the product of decades of disinvestment, deindustrialization and blatant neglect. Clinton abandoned urban policy and responded to the crises in Black communities by proposing the Omnibus Crime Bill of 1994 which opened the flood gates to staggering levels of incarceration of Black people. The Clintons are not progressives; they consciously/deliberately, calculatingly chose to be moderate/centrists.

The Sanders' Campaign matters because he is audaciously declaring that workers, the poor and people on the margins and the struggling middle class, the vast majority of people in this nation, matter. His relentless popular education of the electorate about the utter unfairness and injustice of the insatiable greed and obscene accumulation of wealth on Wall Street, as brilliantly exposed by the Occupy Wall Street Movement, is resoundingly resonating on Main Street. Sanders is not only excoriating the greed of the 1%, he is exposing and condemning the corrosive effect of the death grip of "billionaire classes'" on the electoral political process through lobbyists and super pacs.

One year before his death, Dr. Martin Luther King mounted the podium at Riverside Church and proclaimed: "True compassion is more than flinging a coin to a beggar; it comes to see that the edifice that produces beggars needs restructuring." Dr. King also called for a "radical revolution of values," stating that "when machines, computers, profit motives, and property rights are considered more important than people, the giant triplets of racism, materialism and militarism are incapable of being conquered." In that spirit, Bernie Sanders, in a manner reminiscent of Dr. King's call for an Economic Bill of Rights, is calling for a "revolution" to loosen the grip of Wall Street, the billionaire class, on the political system in this country by articulating a vision of what should be rather than drowning hope, dwelling on what is and what's practical/realistic. As Dr. Maulana Karenga, the creator of Kwanzaa, once said, "we are realistic, but as for reality, we have come to change it!"

Why should the richest and most technologically endowed nation on the face of the earth accept the fact that 25 million human beings in this society suffer without health insurance while millions more are under-insured? This, despite the passage of the Affordable Care Act which was/is an important incremental victory. Why is it that every western industrialized nation in the world has universal health care "except" the United States? This is not the kind of "exceptionalism" Americans should be proud of or have to endure. Bernie Sanders would have us envision a society where health care is a basic human right, not a privilege. Therefore, he advocates a Medicare-for-all, Single Payer health care system that would cover every American and drastically reduce costs; a system based on health care for people not profits for the giant insurance and pharmaceutical companies.

Why should the poor, working class and struggling middle class families and their children be burdened with enormous debt to secure an education in America? Bernie Sanders asks us to dream of a nation which provides free, "public" education for the daughters and sons of ordinary people. He also calls upon us to dream of a society which provides a decent standard of living for all its people by establishing a national living wage of at least $15.00 an hour; offering paid sick leave and pregnancy leave for mothers and fathers; fighting for passage of the Equal Rights Amendment to guarantee women equal pay for equal work; ensuring that our seniors will live in dignity by expanding, not reducing, Social Security benefits; and promoting a green, sustainable, well-paying, job generating economy. And, Bernie Sanders is urging us to join the fight to end the scourge of mass incarceration brought on by an ill-conceived War on Drugs that has devastated Black and Brown communities across this nation.

Bernie Sanders is articulating a bold vision of what should and can be achieved if millions believe and join the "revolution" by educating, mobilizing and marching on ballot boxes to chasten the billionaire class, the oligarchy, to transform the face of this nation. A parasitical billionaire class, Wall Street, must be compelled to pay the price for a more just and humane America. Millions of people are "sick and tired of being sick and tired" of pedestrian politics and business as usual. Vision matters, and it is Bernie Sanders' vision and the meaning of the message that is motivating millions to join the "revolution and march on ballot boxes to embrace a truly progressive policy agenda.

However, it is important to caution that the progressive "revolution," which Sanders is inspiring, will fall short of its potential if it does not clearly recognize and emphatically assert that "race matters" in this country; that because of structural racism, the ravishes of inequality and the exploitation and neglect of poor and working people disproportionately afflict Blacks and people of color. In a recent appearance on the *Melissa Harris Perry Show* on MSNBC, Dr. Khalil

G. Muhammad, the brilliant Director of the Schomburg Center in New York, was correct to point out that, in the past, progressives have often de-emphasized or ignored racial issues while emphasizing issues of class. Put another way, White progressive reformers have too often minimized racial concerns and remedies for fear of alienating Whites.

Black lives matter. Bernie Sanders would do well to address the issue of structural racism and its effects on Blacks and people of color head-on. Indeed, it would be useful if he took time to deliver a major address on race in American society and outline a comprehensive policy agenda for addressing racial issues, particularly as they effect Black and Brown people. And, on the question of his position on Reparations for Blacks for slavery and ongoing discrimination, Sanders should at least support HR-40, Congressman John Conyers bill that would authorize a Commission to study slavery and its aftermath and determine whether reparations are warranted. These steps would be major strides towards constructively bridging the race-class divide in order to advance an inclusive, unified revolution!

Will the Sanders' inspired "revolution" dismantle America's Capitalist political-economy? No, it will not. But, it will be a significant interim or transitional step forward advancing a politics of social transformation in this country. The "Bern" is encouraging millions of people to envision, to dream of a nation that is more humane than the indignities and injustices they suffer with the status-quo. In that regard, the Sanders' campaign is already victorious! Millions of people are awake, seizing the moment to take matters into their own hands to contest the oligarchs, to battle Wall Street, proclaiming we are human beings, and we deserve to live with dignity and decency in this nation!

This remarkable, improbable revolution may well propel Bernie

Sanders into the White House and other progressives into elected offices across the country. But, winning an election should not be the sole objective. Win or lose the election, the movement, the revolution must continue. One of the worst things that could happen is for Sanders to win and the movement is disbanded. Or for Sanders to fall short and fail to strenuously work to make the movement, the revolution, a permanent new force in American politics broadly defined. Some years ago, Danny Glover and veteran labor and social justice activist Bill Fletcher proposed the creation of a new Rainbow Coalition (I was honored to serve as an Executive Director of the Rainbow Coalition). Perhaps, the time is ripe for Bernie Sanders to revisit that idea. What the success of his campaign suggests is that millions of people are ready to be part of a new progressive force in American politics. That's why Bernie Sanders' Campaign matters. Let the "revolution" continue!

Elections Matter: Trump Will Be Reagan on Steroids

The first of Three Essays on the Impact and Consequences
of the 2016 Presidential Election
December, 2016

During the months leading up to the 2016 presidential election I was totally immersed in an all-out effort to ensure the success of the historic State of the Black World Conference IV in Newark. Therefore, I had precious little time to pen my views on the election or its aftermath. With the Conference behind me, this is my first opportunity to offer my assessment of one of the most bizarre and consequential elections in American history; an election which resulted in Donald Trump ascending to the office of President of the United States; a dire outcome which will produce a regime that will be like Reagan on steroids.

I recently had occasion to be Panelist for *The People's Democracy Conference,* organized at the National Press Club by Atty. Barbara Arnwine's Transformative Justice Coalition. The focus of the Conference was the numerous voter suppression schemes employed by the Republicans that helped deliver the election to Trump. While providing testimony on voting suppression tactics in North Carolina, Brenda Harding, Chairperson of the Board of The Transformative Justice Coalition, also pointedly reminded the audience that "elections matter." She was suggesting that in addition to voter suppression, far too many potential voters sat out the election for various reasons, apparently oblivious to the potential consequences of a Trump presidency or for that matter the concrete ways in which the policy outcomes of any election affect the lives of people.

The words "elections matter" certainly struck a chord with me because it echoed the constant warnings I expressed on my radio show on WBAI, the Pacifica Network affiliate in New York, my weekly segment on *Make It Plain* with Mark Thompson on SIRIUSXM and interviews on other media. Yes, elections matter, and I am shocked that some who did not take this reality seriously were shocked, dismayed, depressed and traumatized by the outcome of the November 8th election. There were far too many potential voters who failed to cast ballots because of apathy or indifference (some of which is understandable); others who felt that both candidates were flawed, identical or simply representative of different manifestations of "evil" within the Capitalist "empire;" or as it relates to Hillary Clinton, there was the oft repeated refrain, "I just don't trust her."

Frankly, I understand and am sympathetic to these misgivings, but tried mightily to persuade well-meaning skeptics to consider the Ron Daniels axiom: *The differences between the Democrats and the Republicans are not fundamental, they are incremental but not inconsequential in terms of policy outcomes on the lives of people.* I devised this axiom as a way of encouraging liberals, progressives and revolutionaries to consider the notion that, by definition, neither Establishment Party is committed to transforming the Capitalist political-economy, but that it is important to make critical tactical choices within the electoral process as we pursue the strategic goal of radical, fundamental transformation—the creating a new society.

Simply put, we must creatively exploit the differences between the Establishment Parties and factions within the ruling elite in a manner that builds mass based/popular support for a politics of social transformation. This means always considering how our decisions will impact the lives of the people we hope to enlist in the quest for a new society. The rhetoric of revolution, progressive sloganeering and mechanical ideological formations are easy to advance and may play well among the true-believers, but will be irrelevant if they do not deal in a meaningful way with the reality of the day to day lives of oppressed Black people, other people of color, women, workers, the poor and the struggling middle class. It's the difference between simplicity and complicity. In the real world, we who claim to be progressives and revolutionaries must face the need to make complex decisions. The presidential election of 2016 was certainly such a moment.

The Trump administration will be like Reagan on steroids. Reagan rode a racially inspired "white backlash" into office, pledging to undue the "reverse racism" of affirmative action and social programs perceived to be of benefit to Blacks. Hence, his appointment of William French as Attorney General was calculated not to enforce Civil Rights statutes and regulations but to undermine them. Reagan also vowed to undo, reverse or dismantle programs he claimed were advantaging Blacks to the disadvantage of Whites. He was also determined to wage war on organized labor. It's hard to imagine an administration that did more damage to Civil Rights, social programs and labor than Ronald Reagan, but that regime is about to occupy the White House.

Almost immediately, President Trump will revoke Obama's Executive Order which provides temporary legal status for Dreamers and other categories of undocumented immigrants to remain in the country without fear of deportation; cancel the Executive Order extending the right to overtime pay to some four million workers; and, issue Executive Orders loosening regulations on corporations and financial institutions. These are "modest" reversals compared to the damage Trump's Cabinet appointees will inflict. Consider the following:

Scott Pruitt, Oklahoma Attorney General, is an outright climate change denier who will rip up environmental regulations in order to give the fossil fuel industry a free pass to maximize profits.

He will have a willing co-partner in former Texas Governor Rick Perry, who as a presidential candidate, vowed to eliminate the Department of Energy as a presidential candidate to free the fossil fuel industry of the proverbial onerous regulations. He will now head the Department he once promised to kill—a double death blow to rational efforts to save the environment and the planet.

Congressman Tom Price of Georgia, who is a medical doctor, is the perfect choice as Secretary of Health and Human Services to lead the charge to "end Obamacare," rollback Medicaid expansion and take aim at privatizing Medicare and aspects of Social Security. In his view the "free market" will solve all ills.

Andrew Pudzer, CEO of CKE Restaurants, is a fierce opponent of Labor who will serve as the new Secretary of Labor. He is vehemently opposed to the minimum wage, period, let along an increase in the paltry $7.25 an hour. Pudzer also opposes extending overtime benefits and paid pregnancy and sick leave. He views all of these benefits as impediments to job creation in the free-market.

Senator Jeff Sessions, Senator from Alabama who has expressed racist sentiments in the past, will block any attempt to strengthen the voting rights act, weaken civil rights enforcement at every turn and attempt to undo the significant criminal justice reforms implemented under President Obama. He will be the anti-justice head of the Department of Justice.

Then there is Stephen K. Bannon, the white nationalist Director of the ultra, ultra, rightwing *Breitbart News*, who will be securely positioned in the White House as President Trump's Chief Strategist.

To top it off, President Trump will nominate ultra-conservative judges to the Supreme Court in the mold of the late Antonin Scalia that will provide judicial sanction to this radical rightwing retrenchment. The Trump Supreme Court will be in position to inflict damage for decades.

Now liberals, progressives and revolutionaries who couldn't stomach Hillary Clinton should answer a simple question, would she have appointed these kinds of people to her Cabinet or to the Supreme Court? The honest answer is no! We would have justifiably complained that some of Hillary Clinton's picks were too cozy with Wall Street, others too interventionist for our taste and that most of her appointments were not progressive enough. But, that's a far cry from a Cabinet filled with billionaires in lock step with Wall Street and agency heads bent on turning the clock back on the hard-fought gains of civil rights, women's rights, health care, labor, the environment and consumer protection.

To the millions of immigrants who will now face deportation; the millions of workers who will lose the right to file for overtime, and others who can no longer look forward to an increase in the minimum wage; millions who will lose help health care benefits and have their lives shortened as a result; Black and Brown communities that will have less protection against environmental racism; untold thousands, if not millions, of women who may be forced again to endure unsafe abortions; and, millions of potential voters who will continue to be disenfranchised because of voter suppression policies, practices and laws that will be upheld by a rightwing Supreme Court, the differences between Donald Trump and Hillary Clinton were not fundamental, they were largely incremental but they were absolutely not inconsequential! Trump is Reagan on steroids, and millions of people will suffer the consequences. Elections matter!

There are certainly lessons to be learned from this bizarre and frightening election and it should not have taken hindsight to see them. For liberals, progressives and revolutionaries, Hillary Clinton was not the "lesser evil." Tactically, she was clearly the "better choice" given a serious analysis of the "clear and present danger" posed by Trumpism. This is why progressives like Angela Davis and Danny Glover could make a somber decision to support Clinton despite her flaws—because her flaws paled in comparison to Trump's.

Another lesson to be learned is the way Conservatives and Republicans of all stripes united around Trump, despite the ugliness of his rhetoric, his loose-lipped shoot from the hip style and differences with him on policy positions. The majority of Republican leaders kept their eyes on the prize—securing national electoral power by winning the White House/presidency! While there were a few "never Trump" Republicans, Paul Ryan, Mitch McConnell, Marco Rubio, Ted Cruz, Rick Perry and the majority of Republicans closed ranks behind Trump. Even if they had to hold their noses, they adopted a *win first argue over differences later approach*, realizing that winning the presidency would dramatically improve the likelihood of imposing their agenda on this country. They understood that elections matter and did everything possible to win. Now you are seeing them argue over some policy positions, though they seem in synch on much of the big picture agenda.

On the liberal, progressive side, the reluctance to enter the electoral arena by some, distaste for Hillary Clinton by many, or righteous desire to support a third-party candidate by others prevented us from forging a united front to turn back the virulent tide of Trumpism. Now we must deal with the consequences.

And, here's the real danger: Over the next four years if Trump is able to distribute enough largess to individuals and sectors of the

African American and Latino communities such that he can win just 15% of the African American and 25% of the Latino vote and maintain or broaden the support of his White base, he will flip the script and by entrenching a rightwing, reactionary Rainbow Coalition— the ultimate counter-revolution/post-reconstruction scenario! That's frightening.

But, all is not lost. We must constantly remind ourselves and the American electorate that this is a "minority regime" that did not win the majority of those who voted. Trump and Trumpism lost the popular vote by nearly three million ballots and more than that when you add in the votes of third party candidates. So, having learned the painful lessons and consequences of this election, it's time for a season of resiliency and resistance; a time to gather the progressive forces to devise strategies and actions to reverse the temporary triumph of Trumpism, fully confident that "the arc of the universe bends toward justice" when the forces of righteousness unite and engage the struggle to make it so!

An Inside Outside Strategy: Toward A Third Force in American Politics

The final Essay in a Series of Three on the Impact and Consequences of the 2016 Presidential Election
February, 2017

The season of resistance to "eradicate the virus of Trumpism" is unfolding with a fury. The Women's March on Washington may well be remembered as one of the great moments of resistance and calls for transformation in American history. And, Trump's ill-conceived and awkwardly rolled-out, Islamophobic ban on Muslims was met with massive demonstrations at airports and seats of government across the country and the world. Protesters have also filled the halls of Congress, disrupting hearings of the likes of Jeff Sessions, the "anti-justice" nominee for Attorney General, in hopes of stiffening the backbone of Democratic Senators to righteously obstruct the confirmation of rightwing extremists and the confirmation of Judge Neil Gorsuch, the Scalia clone Trump has nominated to the Supreme Court. Given the fact that Republicans refused to even give Judge Merrick Garland, President Obama's nominee, a hearing and the incredible stakes in terms of the ideological direction of the Court, Democrats have every right to block every nominee deemed unfit for the next four years.

It is absolutely essential that the protest component of the resistance continue in creative ways for the duration of Trump's term in office. Given his thin-skinned, egocentric, narcistic nature and erratic means of responding, there is a reasonable chance that the protests, demonstrations and disruption may drive Trump and his administration to implode. But, no matter the outcome of this critical dimension of the struggle, it is imperative that progressives find a way to harness the tremendous energy of the resistance to build a permanent/institutionalized formidable force for transformative change—an independent/third force in American politics. If we believe that the election of Trump by a minority of the popular vote represents the last desperate, dying gasp of the old order, then defeating Trump is not the end, it is a means to an end, the creation of the New America.

Therefore, an independent Third Force must be shaped with that future in mind. It cannot simply be a vehicle focused on electoral politics/elections; an independent Third Force must be multifaceted with the capacity to utilize community organizing, campaigns around issues, protests, marches, demonstrations, boycotts, elections and policy advocacy to advance a vision/mission and agenda for transformative change. It must devise mechanisms to endorse major or third party candidates or run candidates as independents. In this regard, it is in the best interest of a Third Force to advocate for local, state and national policies which make it easier for third party and independent candidates to secure ballot access and processes which not only eliminate barriers to registration and voting but encourage greater voter participation; voter participation policies and processes like same-day on-site registration, making voter registration permanent, election holidays, Ranked Choice/Instant Run-off Voting and public financing of elections.

And, of utmost importance, an independent Third Force must place a premium on participatory processes that build solid relationships with people through engagement with them on issues and struggles that affect their daily lives: conducting civic education forums and workshops; training community organizers and candidates for public office; engaging people and constituencies in community conventions and assemblies to establish political agendas. We must be ever mindful that "elections do not equal democracy, participation is the essence of democracy."

The progressive Third Force I envision must be "independent" of the Democratic Party but function decisively to influence the direction of the Party. Functionally, the Third Force should be on the left what the Tea Party became on the right, obviously with a different vision, values and objectives. The Tea Party was/is an independent structure that nonetheless strove to push the Republican Party to the right by articulating a clear message and endorsing, running and electing candidates to public office. Ultimately, the power of the Tea Party was manifest in the actual election of officials at the local, state and federal level. The Tea Party Caucus in the U.S. Congress was/is a powerful vehicle which dramatically pulled the Republican Party to the far right. Grassroots advocacy, protests and demonstrations helped to put the Tea Party on the map, but the translation of movement into electoral success is what made it such a potent force. The progressive movement needs a similar strategy. It is an integral component of an "inside/outside" strategy.

The Democratic Party must be reinvented and an Independent Third Force is the vehicle which should take on this task. First and foremost, a Third Force must articulate and work for the adoption of a popular/understandable progressive agenda within the Democratic Party, confident that the majority of Americans embrace liberal/progressive policy proposals on vital issues related to jobs, healthcare, education and social programs. For example, it is interesting to note that in the 2014 mid-term elections a state like Arkansas adopted an increase in the minimum wage despite being a "red state." This suggests potential to educate and organize middle, working class and poor people in red states with well thought-out and executed, culturally-sensitive strategies.

Equally important, progressives must push the Democratic Party to exemplify participatory democracy: a Party that prioritizes working with people and constituencies on issues of concern to them consistently. As previously stated, the tired method of gearing up to mobilize constituents prior to elections is doomed to fail. The Democratic Party, for that matter any Party which aspires to advance a progressive agenda, must build relationships with people, communities and constituencies to succeed. Civic education, involvement in social and community affairs, engagement around issues, creating community-based voter education and mobilizing structures will pave the way to increased voter registration and turn-out in elections. Building a new participatory Democratic Party requires confronting and overcoming old style political machines/organizations, bossism, attitudes and practices of "incumbency protection." Participatory values, processes and structures must be the order of the day. Absent this approach, it will be virtually impossible to organize the unorganized, the apathetic, alienated and indifferent who are essential to defeating the rightwing extremists who are currently ascendant.

Of necessity, this approach also requires abandoning a reliance on what has become the professional "consultant class" of campaign strategists, pollsters, managers and operatives who are hired from election to election. I have long felt that the focus of the consultant class on "probable voter" models is in direct contradiction to the urgent need for the Democratic party to mobilize/organize the unorganized, the "non-probable" voters. During his tenure on the Democratic National Committee, the late Maynard Jackson strongly urged the Party to invest more resources in expanding its efforts beyond

Blue and Battleground states to states like Georgia with large numbers of African Americans, a sizeable number of White liberal/progressives and a growing immigrant population.

Despite having a large Voting Aged Population (VAP), significant numbers of Blacks remain unregistered or fail to vote in states like Georgia. Maynard Jackson argued that investing more human and material resources and effort in educating and engaging "non-probable" voters would eventually bear fruit. Indeed, candidate Trump consistently defied the advice of the Republican "consultant class" by campaigning among non-probable voters in Battleground states. His instincts were rewarded with an Electoral College Map Victory.

If the Democrats persist in utilizing the same old tired methods, they do so at their own peril. A new Democratic Party must be born if it is to play a significant role in eradicating "Trumpisim" and emerging in the forefront of the transformative struggle for a new America. And, that means electing representatives to the Democratic National Committee (DNC) and a Chairperson who embody and are committed to the transformation of the Party. The creation of a new type of Party will also necessitate serious investment of resources in the participatory strategy, tactics, processes, advocacy campaigns, structures and systems outlined above—including heavy investment in Blacks, a bulwark of the Party that rightfully feels neglected and taken for granted. The Democratic Party must reinvent itself or become irrelevant to the struggle to create a New America.

To conclude, I would like to say a word about the particular role of White progressives and people of African descent in building an Independent Third Force. The demographic trends favor success for a Rainbow Coalition that can count on solid support among people of African descent/Blacks coupled with high percentages of Latinos,

Asians, other people of color and a minority of Whites from various strata. To ensure prospects for success, the first priority is to solidify the expanding people of color base of this Rainbow Coalition. However, it is also important to solidify and expand support among various strata and constituencies of Whites. I view achieving the latter task as the special role of White progressive strategists, organizers and advocates.

A majority of Whites have not voted for a Democratic candidate for President in decades. However, Trumpism attracted a sizeable segment of alienated and disaffected White voters, some of whom were motivated by racism, sexism, homophobia, anti-immigration fever and Islamophobia. Some were also angered by a sense of economic abandonment, a sentiment which also ran deep among Bernie Sanders supporters. I am not willing to attribute the disaffection of all the White voters who supported Trump to racism and bigotry. There is no doubt a substantial number of Whites will never be converted to support liberal/progressive proposals or formations as long as they perceive them as pandering to "identity politics." After all, racism has been one of the most effective "divide and exploit" strategies employed by adversaries of progressive change for generations.

I sense there are Whites in every region of the country, including rural areas and the South that can be reached by a persuasive, popular/understandable message and platform; one that connects them via economic common ground to their natural allies irrespective of race, ethnicity, gender, sexual orientation or religion. Gaining the support of these reachable/convertible Whites is important in principle, but as a practical matter will create a permanent majority for a progressive Rainbow Coalition dedicated to the creation of the New America. To reiterate, achieving this goal is the special task of White progressives. People of African descent and other people of color who have borne the brunt of racism and white supremacy should not bear the burden of converting and mobilizing/organizing Whites to enlist in the struggle for progressive change.

In this regards, I strongly disagree with those who believe that to attract greater support among Whites, the progressive movement and the Democratic Party must deemphasize targeted policy proposals or "identity politics." Blacks, in particular, have seen this movie before, the proverbial downplaying or sacrifice of issues/concerns/matters or race and racism on the altar of class or the interests of the working class as "the primary contradiction." Race, ethnicity, class, gender, sexual orientation and religion matter and the concerns that arise from them must be addressed in their particularity in any meaningful progressive program, platform and formation. Intersectionality and inclusiveness must be the order of the day in terms of forging and acting on a progressive agenda for transformative change.

At our best, African Americans have long served as a bastion of resistance to oppression and the conscience of this country in terms of advocating for transformative change, not only for Black people but all oppressed people. This vision/mission is captured in the Preamble of the Black Political Agenda adopted at the National Black Political Convention in Gary, Indiana in 1972. That document reads in part: "If we are serious, the Black politics of Gary must accept major responsibility for creating both the atmosphere and the program for fundamental, far-ranging change in America. Such a responsibility is ours because it is our people who are most deeply hurt and ravaged by the present systems of society... It is the challenge to consolidate and organize our own Black role as the vanguard in the struggle for a new society."

People of African descent/Black people in America must play a central role in the struggle for a new society. The issues, grievances and concerns of the oppressed, the most "affected" must be at the center of a progressive agenda for change. And, the most affected, particularly people of African descent and other people of color must be substantially in the leadership of the struggle for transformative change. The reality of ingrained, structural racism and the historical tendency of White progressives to minimize racial oppression to advance issues of class, demands that people of African descent and other people of color be in the forefront of movements, organizations, agencies and institutions engaged in the struggle for a new society.

People of African descent can also "lead" by devising models of participatory engagement that can be replicated throughout the progressive movement. For example, there is a critical need to reinstitute the principles and practice of convening broad-based district, city-wide and state Black Agenda Conferences to adopt Black Agendas as an outgrowth of the input of constituencies in communities. Ideally, Black Agenda Conferences would be organized and convened by Independent Political Organizations whose memberships are reflective/representative of the community. Black Agendas adopted by the people in Agenda Conferences should be the basis for running or endorsing candidates for public office. It is by embracing principles of participatory democracy, building Independent Political Organizations and convening Black Agenda Conferences that Malcolm X's exhortation that Black people "control the politics and politicians of our community" can be achieved.

As a new generation of Black leaders emerges, it is my hope that the Movement for Black Lives and similar formations will revisit the lessons of the Gary Black Political Convention and the teachings of Malcolm X and boldly push for a new politics in Black America; a politics grounded in movement and institution-building, participatory engagement in Black communities, the election of thousands of "servant leaders" to public office, and a Black politics dedicated to vigorously advancing the vision/mission of creating the New America which must become if there is ever to be a more perfect union on these shores. Heeding the charge in the Preamble of the Black Political Agenda from Gary, Black people must assume a leadership role in building a progressive, independent Third Force to undertake this vital mission.

While the struggle to create a new society is our ultimate goal, the immediate task for the progressive movement is to eradicate the virus of Trumpism. Creating an independent third force in American politics that can implement an inside/outside strategy is key to accomplishing this crucial short-term task. A progressive Third Force can be the engine pushing the Democratic Party to reinvent itself in ways I have suggested while simultaneously engaging with other progressive Parties and formations to galvanize and energize a permanent majority to seize the reins of electoral power at all levels. Indeed, one of the most encouraging outcomes of the Women's March on Washington was that hundreds of women have signed up to undergo training to run for public office. This is a good sign.

The alarming contradictions and crises precipitated by the election of Trump and the temporary ascendancy of Trumpism must be viewed as a major opportunity to engage the unengaged, organize the unorganized, give hope to those who have lost hope and build a powerful multifaceted movement that will ultimately create the New America. The question is, will progressives take advantage of this moment? The fate of the Union may rest on the answer!

Will Blacks Be Screwed by Immigration Policy Reform?

April, 2013

As the "Gang of Eight" Senators in the U.S. Congress prepare to outline their proposals for comprehensive immigration reform, there is alarm in some quarters of the Black Diaspora that the legislation they put forth may harm the interests of people of African descent. We cannot stand by and let this happen. In the Declaration of Intent to Heal Black Families and Communities, the Action Agenda for State of the Black World Conference III, we state: "IBW favors just and equitable immigration reforms which respect the interests of people of African descent. We do not view it as a 'Kum ba yah' exercise but a matter of critical importance to the interests and aspirations of people of African descent in a pluralistic society."

Because people of Latin/Hispanic origin constitute the overwhelming majority of the estimated 11 million undocumented residents in the U.S., immigration reform has largely been viewed as a "Latino issue." While African Americans and other people of African descent have always been in the forefront advocating for the civil and human rights of others, in this instance, it is crucial that all parties in the immigration policy reform effort recognize that the Black Diaspora has a major stake in this issue. Indeed, despite the solid support for immigration reform among Black leaders, there are misgivings on the ground in Black communities because of real or perceived concerns that the interests of people of African descent will be excluded from reform legislation. Simply stated, Black people want assurances

that undocumented people of African descent from Africa, the Caribbean, Central and South America will not be discriminated against
in the formulation of legislation. Programs to facilitate the incorpora-
tion of the undocumented into this country must be available to all,
irrespective of ethnicity or nationality. Equally important, there is
a concern that people of African descent have the same right to im-
migrate to the U.S. as other groups—that is say there should be no
favoritism granted to any group based on race, ethnicity or categories
tied to "education" and "skill."

To address these concerns, the Pan African Unity Dialogue
(PAUD) of New York, an umbrella group convened by the Institute of
the Black World 21st Century that promotes collaboration between
Caribbean Americans, Afro-Latinos, Continental Africans and African Americans, has thoroughly explored this issue and developed
an Immigration Reform Call to Action [see website www.ibw21.org].
Under the leadership of Dr. Waldaba Stewart, Chairman of the Board
of the Caribbean Research Center at Medgar Evers College, a number
of issues were flagged within various policy proposals which were
detrimental to Black interests. Accordingly, the PAUD document
identifies these issues and offers recommendations for resolving them
in a way that protects the interests of people of African descent as part
of the overall quest to achieve immigration policy reform—reform
that people of African descent can enthusiastically support because
our interests are included.

Representatives of the PAUD Immigration Task Force recently
traveled to Washington to conduct a Black press briefing and consult
with Congresswoman Yvette Clarke, Co-Chairperson of the Congressional Black Caucus Afri-Centric Task Force on Immigration,
and Hilary Shelton, Vice-President for Public Policy and Advocacy for the NAACP. During these meetings, we were informed that

Senator Charles Schumer of New York, a key player in the Gang of Eight, was prepared to yield to a demand from the Republicans to eliminate the Diversity Visa Program and replace it with a STEM Visa Program, ostensibly to incentivize the immigration of skilled workers and professionals to this country. The problem is that 48% of the 55,000 Diversity Visas granted annually are to people from nations in Africa and the Caribbean. Eliminating this Program would severely stem the flow of legal immigration to the U.S. by people of African descent. Congresswoman Clarke and Hilary Shelton indicated that this was totally unacceptable and would fight to see that this egregious act does not happen.

March 20th, under the leadership of Bishop Orlando Findlayter, hundreds of reform advocates from Churches United to Save and Heal (CUSH) and the Black Immigration Network (BIN) also traveled to Washington to call for just, equitable, inclusive and non-discriminatory immigration legislation. But, apparently the appeals of PAUD, CUSH and BIN have fallen on deaf ears in Washington. The word circulating as of this writing is that the Diversity Visa Program will be sacrificed in a compromise calculated to please the Republicans. Thus far some quiet protests may be occurring, but there appears to be no visible and vocal opposition by Black leadership. Perhaps, this is because of a reluctance to "rock the boat" in terms of relations with our Latino allies. "The road to hell is paved with good intentions." We cannot allow people of African descent to be screwed by "well meaning" immigration policy reform!

Coalitions and alliances are based on mutual interest and reciprocity. Therefore, people of African descent cannot allow their interests to be ignored in deference to anyone. Accordingly, it is imperative that Black political, faith, civil rights and human rights leaders mount a visible and vocal campaign to salvage the Diversity Visa Program.

Indeed, what is really required is for the Congressional Black Caucus to draft legislation that reflects and protects the interests of people of African descent and inject it into the legislative process as a bargaining tool. A clause indicating that the provisions of any legislation adopted will be equitable and non-discriminatory is essential to provide a basis for legal action once reforms are enacted. Far from antagonizing our friends/allies, respect for our interests dictates that Latinos, Asians and others join a righteous effort to preserve the Diversity Visa Program and similar measures that we declare to be vital to our interests as people of African descent.

The "Color" of Immigration Policy Reform

July, 2018

It is critically important that all people of conscience and goodwill continue to condemn the horrifying, uncivilized policy of separating children from parents from Mexico and Central America entering this country seeking asylum or a better life for their families. While some might debate the "legality" of people crossing the border without documents, absolutely nothing justifies treating human beings inhumanely. Therefore, African Americans and people of African descent must maintain a principled position of fighting against family separation and for humane treatment of all persons entering this country for whatever reason.

Justice demands that there also be a focus on the "color" of immigration policy reform. African Americans and people of African descent are increasingly taking note that there is virtually no attention paid to the fact that Haitians seeking entry into the U.S. are often sent to detention centers where they languish for months. And, when DACA is front and center in the policy debate between Trump and Congress, the face of the "Dreamers" is seen as Brown (Latino) not Black (people of African descent). This is despite the fact that there are untold thousands of Black Dreamers from Africa, the Caribbean, Central and South America in this country. The plight/condition of Black immigrants deserves attention, and it is fair to ask our allies to deliberately and intentionally make this point. To do otherwise risks breeding hostility and resentment among people of color nationalities/ethnicities who should be united in their quest for just immigration policy reform.

Finally, lost in the essential struggle to prevent separation of families is the fact that every major piece of legislation advanced by Trump and the Republicans to address the plight of the Dreamers and the need for comprehensive immigration reform eliminates the "Visa Lottery" Program—better known to African American advocates as the "Diversity Visa Program." For years this Program has been the primary gateway for immigrants from Africa and the Caribbean, people of African descent/ Black people, to gain entry to this country. Though the quotas have been relatively small, to sacrifice this Program is to eliminate a crucial pathway to entry and citizenship for Black immigrants.

It is not in the political and economic interest of African Americans to shut off this pathway. On the contrary it is in the best interest of African Americans that this pathway be open so that large numbers of Continental Africans and people of African descent from the Caribbean, Central and South America can become part of diverse and growing Black communities in the U.S. Immigrants of African descent are potentially new warriors in the struggle for righteous Black empowerment in the U.S. and the Pan African World. Therefore, the New York based Pan African Unity Dialogue has persistently advocated for a dramatic expansion of the Diversity Visa Program as a cornerstone of its demand for non-discriminatory, just, equitable and inclusive immigration reform, consistent with the legitimate interests and aspirations of people of African descent in this country! The "Color" of Immigration Policy Reform must include Black people!

The Parasitical System of Development/ Underdevelopment

July, 2018

Much of the immigration reform debate is understandably focused on the separation of children from their parents, the plight of the "Dreamers," the "Diversity Visa Program," a "Guest Worker Program" to feed the agricultural sector's appetite for cheap labor and border protection to block the "hordes" of undocumented "suspects" from illegally entering this country. While these are important issues for debate and resolution, from my vantage point, virtually no attention is being devoted to the big picture, the root causes of the often dangerous and desperate journey to the borders of U.S. by human beings from Mexico, Central and South America and regions of the Caribbean: The long history of ruthless exploitation of these regions by U.S. Corporations at the behest of or in complicity with the U.S. Government.

In his classic work *How Europe Underdeveloped Africa*, Walter Rodney documents the myriad ways that the nations of Europe benefitted enormously from the systematic trafficking of enslaved Africans. Whole cities and towns blossomed in Europe as a consequence of the trafficking in Black bodies. Major corporations like Lloyds of London and Barclays Bank were nourished by this parasitical enterprise. Rodney's seminal point is that while Europe developed, the ravishes of the slave trade wreaked havoc on the economies of kingdoms and nations in Africa. European nations became global economic and political powers; Africa was left weakened, underdeveloped and vulnerable to colonization and further exploitation.

The same can be said for the U.S. relationship with the nations in Central and South America and parts of the Caribbean. Under variations of the "Monroe Doctrine" Central and South America and the Caribbean were declared to be essentially the domain of the United States. The human and material resources of these regions were viewed as assets to be exploited to benefit the pecuniary interests of corporations and financial institutions in this country. The Caribbean was seen as America's "private lake" where nations were compelled to bow to U.S. corporate interests, enforced by "Gun Boat Diplomacy." Nations in Central and South America were reduced to "Banana Republics," forcibly subdued and subservient to the likes of the United Fruit Company. The human and material resources of these regions were systematically exploited to develop the American "empire." The "client states" of the region were left impoverished, underdeveloped and largely dependent on the largess of "Big Brother" to the North. The wealth and development of the U.S. was in no small measure further enriched, expanded and accelerated due to its parasitical relationship with the peoples and nations of Central and South America and the Caribbean; a legacy which continues to plague these regions today.

Now the proverbial "chickens have come home to roost" as the sons and daughters of those who have been dispossessed, disadvantaged and disinherited by generations of chronic underdevelopment are at the gates, the border, the "wall" of the architect, the perpetrator, the nation that has grown fat off the exploitation of their homelands. One might say, they are coming to reclaim some of that which is rightfully theirs! This is the big picture which progressives must incorporate into our analysis as a transformative agenda for immigration policy reform is formulated.

The principles of "reparative justice" demand that the U.S. invest massive resources in a "Marshall Plan" type Initiative to strengthen and develop the economies of underdeveloped nations in Central and South America and the Caribbean. No policy which does not include provisions to enable the nations of the regions to develop thriving, people-based economies will ultimately succeed in stemming the tide of the disinherited, rightfully hammering at and penetrating the "walls" of the parasites who pillaged their homelands. It goes without saying that what applies to this hemisphere also applies to the former slave trafficking, colonial and neo-colonial nations of Europe. They too cannot escape their sins. "…The moral arc of the universe is long, but it bends towards justice!"

Condemning the Message but Not the Messenger: Hypocrisy Taints Republican Reaction to Bigotry: A Recurring Theme in America's History

August, 2017

The vicious assault on counter-protesters in Charlottesville, Virginia by a volatile amalgam of Neo-Nazis, Ku Klux Klan, Alt Right and other white nationalist forces was one of the most horrific acts of domestic terrorism in American history. The day after a Klan-like torch light, racist and anti-Semitic show of force on the campus of University of Virginia, a White nationalist terrorist used his car as a weapon and ploughed through peaceful protesters killing Heather Heyer and seriously injuring several other people. The words of former Ku Klux Klan Imperial Wizard David Duke captured the motive and aspirations of the largest gathering of White Nationalists in recent history: "We are determined to take our country back....... We are going to fulfill the promises of Donald Trump." Much of America and the world was shocked by this vile and ugly show of force in the "land of the free and home of the brave."

Predictably, there was almost universal expression of outrage and condemnations of the hateful white nationalist army that perpetrated the deadly acts of violence in Charlottesville. Divisions between Democrats and Republicans were swept aside as political leaders of both parties came forward to vociferously denounce these acts of terrorism by white supremacists, that is except the President of the United States. Donald Trump initially condemned the hatred and violence on "all sides," thereby equating the righteous protests of the counter-demonstrators with the White supremacist terrorists; equating those who were standing for the vision of an inclusive multi-racial, multi-ethnic society with freedom and justice for all irrespective of race, ethnicity, nationality, culture, religion, gender or sexual orientation with those who wish to "Make America Great Again" by turning the clock back to the good old days of White male hegemony.

The condemnations of Trump were swift and furious. They came from every quarter, including leading Republicans. There was a strong push for Trump to use the moral authority of the Presidency to condemn the white supremacists by name. Political leaders, pundits and commentators suggested that he was missing his moment to pull the nation together and heal its racial divisions. When he eventually did speak-out, Republicans in particular breathed a sigh of relief that Trump had finally done that which was "politically correct." Now the Party and the country could return to business as usual.

But, oops, the sigh of relief was short-lived. Even as I was penning this article, in an impromptu press conference at Trump Tower in New York, Trump went off script and unleashed a tirade, angrily doubling down on his original contention that there was blame on both sides. He went even further by claiming that there were "alt left" demonstrators who charged and attacked a legitimate rally by Neo-Nazis, KKK activists and white nationalists. It was a moral abomination! This time the condemnations were also swift and even more furious as increasing numbers of Republicans tweeted their uncompromising condemnation of racism, anti-Semitism and bigotry.

On the surface this all sounds good, but from my vantage point the condemnation of Trump by the Republicans rings hollow and hypocritical. As Chris Cuomo correctly pointed out on CNN'S *New Day*, as of this writing, only Senator John McCain, Senator Jeff Flake, Senator Bob Corker and Senator Tim Scott have condemned the President by name. The rest have sanctimoniously taken to twitter to denounce the message without denouncing the messenger.

In fact, Republicans enabled Trump by refusing to repudiate him decisively during the campaign and after his election to the White House. My dear friend Mtumishi St. Julien from New Orleans has a line in a Sifa, African prayer he wrote, which says, "principle is more important than power." Despite a vile and vicious campaign, clearly Republicans made a calculated decision that power is more important than principle. They have stood with Trump despite his erratic and often hurtful behavior as President in hopes of implementing their rightwing, reactionary agenda.

They know who Trump is. He is the originator of the racist birther movement that relentlessly questioned whether President Barack Obama was born in the U.S. This is the Donald Trump who cemented his credibility with xenophobic, anti-immigrant adherents by blatantly labeling Mexican immigrants rapists and murderers; the same Donald Trump who castigated and insulted an American Judge of Mexican descent; the same Donald Trump who claimed he did not know who David Duke was and equivocated on condemning him; the same Donald Trump who brought an Alt-Right, White national-ist Steve Bannon into the White House as his "Chief Strategist!" The Republicans know who he is, but for the sake of advancing their reac-tionary agenda, they have embraced, enabled and empowered Donald Trump. Now their lack of principle and moral courage has exploded in their faces like a pus-infected wound.

From the campaign to his brief and horrifying tenure as

President, the Republican reactionaries' treatment of Trump represents the height of hypocrisy! If President Obama had committed any of Trump's transgressions, the Republican reactionaries would have condemned him unmercifully and called for him to resign. But, by and large they have refused to condemn and abandon Trump. They know him; they enabled him, and they own him and should suffer the consequences of their blatant hypocrisy!

Actually, hypocrisy runs deep in the "conservative" ranks of the Republican Party. While Richard Nixon was the first to unveil the "Southern Strategy," Lee Atwater employed it with devastating effectiveness as a strategist for Ronald Reagan's campaign for President. The strategy was designed to use code words to fuel and enflame anti-Black sentiment in the South and was used to appeal to the disgruntled supporters of Alabama Governor George Wallace. Who can forget that Ronald Reagan launched his first campaign in Philadelphia, Mississippi a few miles from the site where civil rights workers Schwerner, Goodman and Chaney were murdered. Though the insensitive selection of the site may have been coincidental, Reagan was clearly signaling to Wallace's supporters that he was on their side.

As President, Reagan did deliver a stinging denunciation of white supremacists, but this was after he played to their fears and aspirations (like Trump) to become President. Moreover, Reagan continued to feed the "white backlash" against the progress of the Civil Rights Movement by invoking terms like "Black racism" and "reverse discrimination." And, he appointed Attorney Generals whose mandate (like that of Jeff Sessions) was to minimize enforcement of civil rights laws and statutes. Hence, Reagan's perfunctory denunciations of white supremacists were as hypocritical as those of his conservative progeny today. The real deal is that the rightwing reactionaries have courted, appealed to and appeased white supremacist sentiments and forces for decades. The only difference is that Trump made the mistake of doing it openly. Trump brought the bigots and haters that conservative Republicans have been courting under the table, from the fringes, from the margins into the mainstream of American politics; from "the outhouse to the White House."

The one thing Trump was right about in his unscripted, heartfelt tirade was that George Washington and Thomas Jefferson were slave owners. Though it was not his intent, Trump pointed to America's "original sins" and original hypocrisy. First the Pilgrims, pioneers and colonizers ruthlessly seized this land from Native Americans. Then, to create this new nation, the founding fathers compromised on the vital question of how enslaved Africans would be included and treated. Despite the lofty rhetoric about the equality of all "men" and "inalienable rights" contained in the *Declaration of Independence*, enslaved Africans were enshrined in the Constitution as 3/5 human beings for the purposes of taxation and representation in the Congress of the United States. Native Americans were spared that indignity but denied citizenship in a nation created on their land.

In addition, shortly after the adoption of the Constitution, Congress passed the Naturalization Act of 1790 that essentially declared America a White man's land. These original sins, original hypocrisy and overt commitment to establish a privileged status for White men has plagued this nation right up to the present. The tragic events of Charlottesville are the latest manifestations of the failure of this nation to acknowledge, reckon with and resolve these contradictions. Hence, there is an ongoing struggle between those who would restrict America to being a nation of Eurocentric cultural dominance, patriarchy and White male privilege versus those who envision an expansive, inclusive multi-racial, multi-ethnic, multi-religious nation, free of discrimination or oppression on the basis of class, gender or sexual orientation.

Whether intended or not, the founding fathers crafted a Constitution which created space for the potential resolution of this hypocrisy and contradictions. The genius of the Constitution is its elasticity. Under its provisions, political and economic democracy can be stretched/expanded or constricted based on the impact of social movements. The elasticity of the Constitution may be the saving grace of this nation. Charlottesville may well represent the dying gasp of the hard core, reactionary, white supremacist adherents who are now a formidable force within the Republican Party. They must be confronted and defeated. But, they will not succumb willingly or easily. They are emboldened and energized by the blessing of Donald Trump and the complicity of the shriveling, equivocating hypocrites who have placed power over principle in their quest to impose their reactionary agenda.

In this crucial moment, those who stand for a progressive vision of America must build a powerful social movement utilizing protests, economic sanctions, civil disobedience and the ballot to righteously overwhelm the racist and reactionary forces. And, then we must compel this nation to confront its original sins and hypocrisy and repair the centuries of damages inflicted on Native peoples and people of African descent as the basis for creating a "more perfect union."

Author's Note: Steve Bannon has been removed from the White House, but his co-partners Stephen Miller and Sebastian Gorka remain. Irrespective of who is in or out of the White House the damage is already done and the hypocrisy continues.

Dedicated to the Memory of Dr. Martin Luther King, Jr.: Toward a Movement to Expand the Public Space and Culture of Rights in America

March 12, 2018

The headline in the February 13th edition of the *New York Times* front page was glaring: "Needs of Public A Low Priority in Rebuilding." The headline was in reference to President Trump's long awaited, so called infrastructure plan. The essence of this much ballyhooed "plan" is a dramatic shift in how the federal government has traditionally approached the construction of public highways, tunnels, bridges, harbors, railways, airports and other vital pieces of the nation's infrastructure. In the past, the federal government would bear about 80% of the cost for infrastructure projects with state and local governments pitching in 20%. But, Trump's has a new "market driven" formula that flips the script by proposing that the federal government allocate 20% while demanding that state and local governments allocate 80%. And, there is another fundamental shift in the way the federal government would do "business" with state and local governments. There is a proviso that projects that can attract "private" investment will have the highest priority for receiving the 20%.

Columbia University Professor Elliott Sclar gets at the destructive nature of Trump's approach in the *Times* article: "Instead of the public sector deciding on public needs and public priorities, the projects that are most attractive to private investment are the ones that will go to the head of the line…. Private investors will become the tail that wags the dog, because they'll want projects that will give returns." The *Times* article notes that this perversion overturns a tradition of federal investment to spur economic development for the public good that dates back to the "early 1800s." And, as if Trump's perverse infrastructure proposal is not alarming enough in terms of its assault on the concept of the "public good," his overall budget takes an axe to social programs of vital need to the nation's poor. In one of the worst examples of the attack on the idea of a basic "culture of rights" or safety net for all Americans, Trump is proposing to slash $21 billion from the Supplemental Nutrition and Assistance Program (SNAP) which currently serves more than 40 million people. Under his plan a "Harvest Box" of food products chosen by the government would be provided to a large number of SNAP recipients, thereby depriving them of the right to choose the foodstuffs they feel are most needed and beneficial!

Trump's perverse infrastructure proposal and onerous budget cuts targeting the poor illustrate the degree to which the radical right has succeeded in diminishing the obligation of government to serve the "public good" and undermining the concept of a safety net to assist the poor/needy in American society. Shrinking/starving government, privatization, reducing taxes on the wealthy and loosening the reins of regulation on business and commerce are part of the blueprint for unleashing the forces of the market, unbridled Capitalism to solve the needs of society based on the profit motive.

It is far past time for this draconian triumph of the radical right to be reversed. For years, I have been bemoaning the failure of liberals and progressives to rigorously and vigorously defend the "public space" as a modest equalizer within the American Capitalist political economy; the space that ameliorates the brutal edges of an amoral, profit-driven system for the middle and working classes and the poor by potentially providing a safety net of social and economic benefits, e.g., public education, housing, employment/jobs, hospitals, transportation, welfare. In the area of higher education, for example, the public space can ensure that the daughters and sons of the middle and working classes and the poor can secure a quality education which will allow them to compete with the daughters and sons of graduates of prestigious, private institutions like Harvard and Yale. The City University of New York, where I serve as a Distinguished Lecturer at York College, is an example of this opportunity and prospect.

The quest to have government create public spaces to serve the needs of working and middle-class people and the poor is one of the great advocations of the liberal, progressive, left movement, particularly socialists, in the history of this nation. Regulating corporations to protect the public from their avaricious behavior, the right to organize and maintain labor unions, Social Security and the New Deal Programs are a legacy of this advocacy; ingraining in the nation's consciousness a commitment to a basic "culture of rights" for all Americans irrespective of class. Lyndon Baines Johnson's Great Society was part of that lineage. The War on Poverty, Model Cities Program, Comprehensive Employment and Training Administration (CETA), Jobs Corps, Urban Development Block Grants, public housing via the Department of Housing and Urban Development (HUD,) federal public assistance to needy families through Welfare and affirmative action to address discrimination against Blacks and minorities are illustrative of this budding and expanding culture of rights, a safety-net via public spaces. This was/is a proud and defensible legacy of generations of successful struggle by liberal, progressive, left movements.

But things began to change dramatically with a furious on-slaught from conservatives, fueled by the suggestion that these "big government, tax and spend" programs were primarily benefiting Blacks, people of color and undeserving poor people. Ronald Reagan, the second-rate actor turned politician, was a master at persuading a critical mass of Americans that big government social programs were benefitting Blacks to the detriment of hardworking White tax-payers; that programs like affirmative action constituted "reverse" racism that was giving undue advantage to Blacks. Propagandizing with phrases like "welfare queens" and food "stamp chiselers" that evoked images of Black people, Reagan convinced large numbers of Whites that big government, "pro-Black" social programs were being forced on them by misguided, elitists, northeastern liberals who were in control of the Democratic Party. He promised to lift the "burden of government" off the backs of the people.

Sensing an opening to escalate the advance of a rightwing agen-da, in the public discourse, an increasingly conservative Republican Party enthusiastically embraced Reagan's mantra and began to re-lentlessly hammer Democrats as big government, tax and spend liber-als. Shredding the safety network of social programs, shrinking the size of government, reducing taxes on the wealthy and privatization of government services became the order of the day. A major goal of the conservatives was to discredit the term liberal and brand it as a dirty word in American politics!

The strategy worked as large numbers of liberal and progressive Democrats panicked and retreated in the face of the "White backlash," abandoning their lineage and legacy and moonwalking away from the term "liberal" faster than Michael Jackson! Rather than fiercely defending the legacy of struggle that produced a growing culture of rights that benefitted working and middle-class people, minorities and the poor, many Democrats succumbed to the centrist proposition that "coopting" elements of the Republican Party's agenda was a "winning" strategy, e.g., ending welfare, reducing the size of government, cracking down on crime, privatization of public programs. This "Republican lite" strategy was advanced by William Jefferson Clinton and the Democratic Leadership Conference (DLC) which emerged as the dominant force in the Democratic Party for decades. The conservative onslaught had successfully pulled the Democratic Party to the right by disconnecting it from its roots as the Party which had produced a legacy of creating public spaces to serve the needs of the masses of working and middle -class people, minorities and the poor.

The election of Donald Trump and the elaboration of "Trumpism" as reflected in the passage of the massive tax-cut for the wealthy, his Infrastructure Proposal and Budget represent the ultimate triumph of radical rightwing conservatism. A recent analysis in the *New York Times* by Eduardo Porter entitled *When the Next Recession Hits, Don't Count on the Safety Net*, drives home the point: " By slashing taxes while increasing spending, President Trump and his allies in Congress have boxed the economy into a corner, reducing the space for emergency government action were it to be needed….To top it off, a Republican president and a Republican Congress seem set on the longstanding Republican project to gut the safety net built by Presidents Franklin D. Roosevelt and Lyndon Baines Johnson."

The daunting obstacle of resisting and reversing the radical rightwing tide notwithstanding, I sense the season is ripe for a major counter-offensive to reclaim the liberal, progressive, left legacy and lineage of a culture of rights by boldly articulating the virtues of the public space as an equalizer in this nation's Capitalist political economy. Indeed, the moment may be at hand to advance a substantive policy-driven vision of social transformation!

It is a season in which Black Lives Matter and the Movement for Black Lives was born with uncompromising demands to eradicate structural/institutional racism and to repair the damages resulting for generations of destructive racially-biased government sponsored policies and practices; it is a season where women, especially Black women and women of color, are surging to the forefront determined to engage in politics in all of its manifestations (marches, protests, demonstrations, civil disobedience, elections) to fight for a more just and humane society; it is a season in which the #ME TOO Movement is confronting sexual violence, harassment and misconduct as protected practices within a patriarchal society and uncompromisingly demanding fundamental change; it is a season where activists and organizers are working inside and outside the Democratic Party to promote more participatory, democratic, community-based approaches to building a multifaceted movement to advance and politics of social transformation; it is a season where the National Urban League and Center for American Progress, Mayor Ras J. Baraka and the Institute of the Black World 21st Century have resurrected the call for a Domestic Marshall Plan to demand massive investment in urban and rural communities to overcome decades of benign and blatant neglect of distressed/marginalized communities; it is a season where the Rev. Dr. William Barber, leader of the Moral Monday Movement, has called for the launching of a new "Poor Peoples Campaign in the spirit of Rev. Dr. Martin Luther King, Jr.

Finally, it is the season of the 50th Memorial Commemoration of the assassination of our beloved Rev. Dr. Martin Luther King who proclaimed in his historic speech at the Riverside Church in 1967, "True compassion is more than flinging a coin to a beggar; it comes to see that the edifice which produces beggars needs restructuring." One year later as he journeyed to Memphis, Dr. King was in the midst of planning the Poor People's Campaign. But, what is often overlooked is that the ultimate objective of the Campaign was to present to the nation, the President and the Congress an Economic Bill of Rights which would provide a guaranteed annual income, quality housing, healthcare and education to every person in this nation as a basic human right! As he peered into the promised land from the mountaintop, he was determined to push the edifice that produces beggars to restructure.

I sense that it is the season to seize the moment to courageously re-embrace the legacy and lineage of struggle to create a culture of rights, public spaces that promote and protect the interests of the majority against the few; a season to be visionary and bold as we ultimately strive/struggle to create a "promised land" where there are no beggars!

The Orange Man's Approval Ratings: The Dangers of "Trumpism"

August, 2018

With all the vile acts that Donald Trump, "the orange man," has committed and the barrage of media coverage of his egomaniacal behavior, you would think that his approval rating would be tanking. But, that's not the case. A recent CNN Poll showed Trump's approval rating at 42%, up from 5-10% depending on which polls one chooses to cite. Now 42% is nothing to brag about, and he has never cracked 50%. Nonetheless, that 42% of the American people support the orange man is mystifying!

Trump's litany of foul acts is legion. He recently signed a Defense Authorization Bill named after ailing Senator John McCain, while he was still alive, and refused to utter his name. At a rally the same day, he disparaged McCain for casting the vote that derailed the Republican effort to kill Obamacare. Trump can't resist blurting out nasty comments about women. He recently called Rev. Omarosa Manigault-Newman, his former Communications Director turned vicious critic, a "dog." The Orange man never passes up an opportunity to make broad-brush generalizations about immigrants from Mexico and Central America, characterizing them as "rapists" and "murderers." He labeled Haiti and some African countries "s-hole" nations and continues to question the mental capacity of African Americans. And, there's more.

I can't imagine any other President's standing not being reduced to the point of resigning as a consequence of revelations from the likes of a Michael Cohen, Trump's personal attorney, the felony convictions against Paul Manafort, his Campaign Chairman and other notables who "flipped" last week to corroborate the corruption in the White House. His approval rating might slip some, but somewhere between 30%—35% of the electorate appear to be bedrock, even cult-like devotees of Trump. This many people embracing the madness emanating from the White House is astounding and dangerous!

It is dangerous because of the elements and constituencies that comprise Trump's "base;" a combustible caldron of Tea Party adherents, angry victims of economic dislocation, anti-immigrant xenophobia, racism, sexism, homophobia, islamophobia, white nationalism, opportunistic "conservatives" and ignorance. The orange man's base has essentially seized control of the Republican Party and the traditional leaderships is terrified. Accordingly, it is dangerous when leaders of the Republican Party refuse to standup to a demagogue either because they fear his base or more importantly because he has been the vehicle for promoting reactionary, right-wing policies; an agenda which is antithetical to the interests of Black and Brown people, women, LBTQ persons, labor, poor and working people. And, he seeks to seal the deal by appointing rightwing judges that will provide the judicial sanction for this retrograde agenda well into the future.

There is a method to the madness. It is this agenda which is the essence of "Trumpism." It is dangerous because, due to racism, rampant phobias and ignorance, a mindboggling 30%—35% of Americans have been mesmerized, persuaded to support policies and regulations that are clearly contrary to their interests. That such a large block of Americans openly support "Trumpism" is a "clear and present danger" to democracy and the quest to achieve a more perfect union in this country.

Herein lies the challenge to the liberal, left, progressive forces; we must mobilize in a life and death struggle for the soul of this nation. There is no time for apathy, inaction and destructive dissension in the face of this grave danger. We urgently need a united front to confront and eradicate Trumpism and advance a visionary agenda for transformative change. Protests, disruption, civil disobedience, economic sanctions/boycotts and marching on ballot boxes with a sense of urgency, any and all legitimate means necessary must be employed to snuff out the danger of Trumpism as a pre-condition for creating the new America which must be born!

Remember Dr. Christine Blasey Ford: Mobilize the "Mob" to March on Ballot Boxes: Eradicate Trumpism

October 8, 2018

We must never forget the humble, dignified and courageous testimony of a Dr. Christine Blasey Ford before the Senate Judiciary Committee. With no outside witnesses being called, the Hearing was deliberately rigged to be a "she said, he said" spectacle. We must never forget the bias treatment of Dr. Blasey Ford by the Committee's Chairman Charles Grassley, who complimented her for coming into the lion's den, and then attempted to discredit her in his opening statement. He also slammed Senator Diane Feinstein, Ranking Member of the Committee, another woman, for messing up the coronation of the "choir boy," Judge Brett Kavanaugh, by not violating Dr. Ford's explicit wish that her story be held confidential until she was prepared to make it public. Grassley and the Republicans were more concerned about the "process" than a credible allegation of sexual assault. To add insult to injury, the hearing proceeded with the cowardly, Republican White men hiding behind a hired hit woman, Rachel Mitchell, Esq., to do their dirty work.

Through it all Dr. Blasey Ford, who volunteered that she was "terrified," calmly and courageously told her story, emphatically asserting that she was "100% certain" that it was a youthful, drunken Brett Kavanaugh who viciously and violently assaulted her. The whole world witnessed her courage and determination to come forth under adverse circumstances, an unlevel playing field, to tell her story as a matter of non-partisan civic duty. She was believable and credible. She told the truth!

Then came the calculated, angry, defiant, belligerent, hyper-partisan testimony of the "choir boy," Judge Brett Kavanaugh, who proclaimed that he was "100% certain" that he did not assault Dr. Blasey Ford. The cowardly Republican Senators quickly pushed Rachel Mitchell aside, tripping over themselves for a turn to heap praise on Kavanaugh for his judicial record and life of public service. They expressed sorrow and outrage over the shameful way he was treated in having to face a decades old accusation based on "no corroborating evidence." Suddenly, the alleged perpetrator of the sexual assault against Dr. Blasey Ford was being treated as if he were the victim!

When the Democratic Members sought to question Kavanaugh, he arrogantly tried to turn the tables by refusing to answer or posing questions back to the Senators. When Mr. "choir boy" was asked about reports by high school and college classmates that he drank heavily, he cavalierly dismissed the inquiries and even insulted Senator Amy Klobuchar, another woman, by asking her if she had ever drank too much! The sense of privilege and entitlement oozed out of every pore in his body. Judge Kavanaugh lied about his habitual drunkenness and if he lied about that, he most certainly lied about assaulting Dr. Christine Blasey Ford. The image of this angry, defiant, bellicose, arrogant, truth-denying man interrogating the Members of the Judiciary Committee is a spectacle that should forever be seared into our consciousness.

We must never forget the legions of women and men who courageously organized protest rallies and demonstrations in support of Dr. Ford and marched into the halls of Congress to challenge Senators to believe Dr. Ford's truth. For a brief moment a memorable encounter in an elevator, with wavering, retiring Senator Jeff Flake of Arizona, gave rise to hope that an FBI investigation would reveal the lies of the choir boy and validate Dr. Ford's truth. But, the White House deliberately limited the scope of the investigation in a manner that rendered it a charade. Neither Dr. Blasey Ford, Kavanaugh or scores of witnesses to the choir boy's drunkenness and out of control behavior were interviewed. It was sham foisted on the American people under the guise of conducting a thorough investigation. The White men, who controlled the process, were not interested in justice, they had a political agenda; the decisive control of the Supreme Court to sanction their retrograde policies for decades to come.

Finally, against the backdrop of the choir boy's belligerent behavior during the fake Hearing, we must never forget the "orange man's" despicable, repeated mocking of Dr. Christine Blasey Ford at a campaign rally and his subsequent characterization of the women and men who marched, rallied and protested to support her as a "mob;" a label that was subsequently echoed by Chairman Charles Grassley, Senate Majority Leader Mitch McConnell and Senator Lindsey Graham to feed "red meat" to the Republican base and fire them up for the Mid-Term elections. These White men readily put power over principle and their political agenda over the truth of a victim of sexual assault; they spat in the face of the untold thousands, if not millions of victims of sexual assault, by insulting demonstrators, many of whom were women by branding them a "mob."

But, "truth crushed to earth will rise again." The "mob" of righteous, indignant people, some of whom have never voted before, must be mobilized to rise up and defiantly march on ballot boxes with the words "we remember Dr. Christine Blasey Ford" reverberating through-out the land. Lest the nation forget, the images of the "orange man" mocking Dr. Ford should be replayed repeatedly on social media platforms and in campaign commercials. The vile ugliness of Trumpism and all that it represents must be eradicated and the cleansing must begin with the massive, irresistible mobilization of the "mob" to march on ballot boxes November 6th in the critical mid-term elections. We remember Dr. Christine Blasey Ford!

"Trumpism":
The Hate That Produces Hate

October, 2018

With the attempted assassination of a series of Democratic leaders and the savage murder of 11 worshipers in the Tree of Life Synagogue in Pittsburgh in the past week, the American people are witnessing one of the most horrific seasons of hate and terror in recent memory. And, while there is debate about the link between rhetoric and the actions of individuals, it is absolutely clear that President Trump, "the Orange man," has deliberately stoked the flames of fear, intolerance, bigotry, racism, anti-Semitism and neo-fascism. Viruses which have long festered beneath the surface have burst into the open with a vengeance with the tacit or explicit encouragement of the "President" of the United States. He has engaged in this un-ethical and immoral behavior as a means of "firing-up" the base in order to retain the Republican's hold on the House of Representatives and Senate. Trump's goal, and that of the cabal that tolerates him, is cementing a reactionary agenda into law, sanctioned by the Supreme Court.

By appointing Steve Bannon, the Alt-Right White Nationalist, to the position of Chief Political Strategist, the Orange man signaled from the outset that he was comfortable with the support of the hate-filled forces on the right. This posture was reaffirmed when he refused to unequivocally condemn the Neo-Nazis who rallied/marched in Charlottesville, brazenly chanting anti-Semitic slogans and violently charging into the ranks of peaceful counter-demonstrators. Trump's infamous response to this hate-filled behavior was that there were troublemakers on "both sides!"

In his tweets and performances at rallies, he has relentlessly attacked immigrants as criminals, gang members, murderers and rapists; demeaned a Judge of Mexican heritage; disparaged NFL players who protested during the National Anthem, most of whom were Black; openly intimated that beating up opponents at his rallies was okay and praised a Republican elected official for "body slamming" a reporter, etc., etc., etc., etc. His assault on the "fake news media" has also been vicious and relentless, causing fear among reporters that they might be assaulted at his rallies.

This is the hate that inspired Cesar Sayoc, Jr., an angry, frustrated, deranged "Make America Great Again" supporter of the "Orangeman," to send mail bombs to a number of prominent Democrats and Trump critics—President Obama, Hillary Clinton, Congresswoman Maxine Waters, Senator Kamala Harris, George Soros and Robert DeNiro among them. Bombs were also sent to CNN. It is not an accident that each of these persons and CNN have been the frequent targets of the Orangeman's venom! Sayoc's social media posts also revealed a deep hatred for Jews, Blacks, immigrants and LGBTQ folks.

This is the hate that produced a frenetic, fear-infused atmosphere that made it conducive for Robert Bowers, an angry, hate-filled, Neo-Nazi sympathizer to come out of the shadows and murder 11 Jews as they worshipped in the quietude of their Synagogue. He is an anti-Semite who was also furious about the "Caravan" moving towards the U.S. border with people the Orange man has falsely branded dangerous criminals trying to "invade" our country. He targeted the Tree of Life Synagogue because members of the congregation had traveled to the boarder to provide comfort and sanctuary for the "invaders." Both of these unhinged individuals viewed their hate-filled assaults as heroic, patriotic acts to preserve the purity and greatness of America!

The tragedy is that the Orange man shows no sign of changing his tone or poisonous rhetoric. He refused to mention any of the targets of Sayoc's mail bombs by name or to place a call to even President Obama as a gesture of reassurance. When asked by a reporter whether he intended to talk to any of the intended targets, he responded, "I think I'll pass on that." To "appear" civil or "act" presidential, as he occasionally does when he is on script, would risk disappointing his base and thereby the prospects that they will not turn out to vote in the massive numbers needed to hang onto the House and the Senate. It's beneath his dignity, because he has no dignity; he knows no shame when it comes to promoting himself and the Republican's retrograde agenda. Even as I am penning this article, in an interview on Fox News, Trump called Andrew Gillum, the African American Mayor of Tallahassee, Florida and candidate for Governor, "a stone-cold thief," a racist dog whistle calculated to fire-up the base in an unexpectedly close race.

The tragedy is that the vast majority of Republican elected officials refuse to denounce the Orange man's hateful behavior, either because they fear his base will turn on and de-elect them or because they are willing to be silent because he is pushing through their reactionary agenda. Trump also enjoys a very high approval rating among the base because they are willing to overlook his ugly, unethical and immoral behavior as long as he is "getting things done" on issues like "the wall," ending Obamacare, loosening regulations on business, relaxing environmental regulations, eroding a woman's right to choose, opposing LGBTQ rights. For the Republican establishment and the Orange man's base of supporters, the means justify the end. After all, at least the "trains will run on time" if Trump and his cohorts can cling to power.

The vile means of Trump will never justify the end. Indeed, his reckless and dangerous behavior precludes any reasonable obligation to respect him as the occupant of the office of President of the United States. The person and the office have merged to become an abomination of epic proportions; an abomination which must be swept from power by righteous non-violent action.

My sense is that millions of people are angry, frustrated, disgusted and turned-off by the behavior of the "President" and his opportunist cabal. But, anger and disgust are not enough to rid this nation of the scourge of Trumpism. Anger and disgust must be the impetus for mobilizing a massive Rainbow Wave of righteous warriors for justice, determined to use their ballots on November 6th, election day, to begin the process of washing away, cleansing this nation of "Trumpism." November 6, 2018 must mark the day that a Rainbow Wave or righteous warriors made major strides toward advancing a politics of dignity, freedom, justice, equality and opportunity for all in this nation; strides toward a politics of social transformation!

The Unfulfilled Power
of the Black Vote

September 18, 2018

For decades I have been hammering home the point that in a low voter participation environment, the group that effectively educates, mobilizes and organizes its voters to turn-out on election day will wield power disproportionate to its numbers in the overall electorate. Put another way, a relatively small group that registers and turns out a high percentage of its potential voters will exercise greater influence than a much larger group that fails to register and turn-out a high percentage of its potential voters. This is a Daniels political axiom. And, as Frank Watkins, Advisor to Rev. Jesse Jackson puts it, "an organized minority is a political majority."

The United States has the lowest voter participation rate of any of the western democracies. I have suggested somewhat facetiously that the biggest political party in the U.S. is not the Democrats or Republicans but non-voters. A voter turn-out in this country in the range of 50-55% of the eligible electorate is hailed by political commentators as spectacular. This is absolutely abysmal when compared to western democracies where voter turn-out is routinely 80% or better. But, the reality of this low voter participation environment creates a major opportunity for Black voters to exercise power disproportionate to our numbers in the electorate. We may be out-numbered by Whites, but a large percentage of Whites don't bother to vote. It is not by accident that Republicans are openly implementing polices to suppress or disenfranchise Black voters. They fear the Black vote. The forces of reaction realize that if Blacks maximize voter registration and mobilize/organize large voter turn-outs, it is a threat to their retrograde agenda.

Rev. Jesse L. Jackson has relentlessly urged Black folks to register and vote in massive numbers to maximize our political power. At a session during the recent Congressional Black Caucus Foundation's Annual Legislative Conference, he shared data that illuminates the unfulfilled power of the Black vote. He noted that there are still 8 million Blacks who are not registered to vote, 4 million in the South. In 2016 some 2.5 million Blacks, who were registered, failed to vote in an election which was determined by less than 100,000 votes total in key battleground states with a large concentration of Black voters! Rev. Jackson's point is that a potent key to political resistance and transformation is in Black hands, the ballot. The challenge is to organize/mobilize and turn-out the unorganized, Black people who, for whatever reason, do not believe that voting matters as a means of changing their lives.

There is increasing evidence that a new generation of Black leaders, particularly women and young people, understand the potential of the Black vote as foundational to coalitions that can beat back the conservative tide of Trumpism by advancing people-centered, progressive policies. Stacey Abrams has an excellent chance to become the first Black Governor of Georgia by educating and inspiring hundreds of thousands of unregistered, "improbable" Black voters to register and turn-out in massive numbers on election day. Ben Jealous has launched a grassroots campaign to employ the same formula in Maryland. The polls in Boston showed Ayanna Pressley trailing long term Congressman Michael Capuano by 10 points among "probable" voters in the Democratic Primary. She won by more than 10 points because she organized/mobilized the unorganized; the improbable voters showed up in massive numbers as the anchor of her progressive coalition.

Rev. Jackson points out that in Florida Andrew Gillum, who shocked the pundits by winning the Democratic primary for Governor, can win because there are more than 1.8 million Blacks who are eligible to register in that state coupled with more than 300,000 recently arrived Puerto Ricans who fled the Island in the wake of Hurricane Maria. When the improbable voters from these constituencies are energized to march on the ballot box, there is a very high probability that Gillum will become the first African American Governor of Florida.

It is important to note that in the instances cited above, only 15%—20% of forward-thinking White voters are needed to achieve victory. The Daniels' Axiom applies: In a low voter participation environment, where large numbers of Whites will remain unregistered or will not vote, all that is required is for the unorganized, the improbable voters in the Black community and our allies to mobilize/organize and turn-out in massive numbers to achieve victory! So, the mandate is clear; Black leaders must devise strategies to educate, motivate, inspire and energize millions of unregistered, improbable Black voters to burst into the arena to become the cornerstone of progressive coalitions. These coalitions of the improbable have the potential to fundamentally alter the political landscape in the U.S. by ushering in an era of resistance to Trumpism and more importantly advancing progressive policies which can create a new America!

Can the Working Families Party Emerge as the Progressive Third Force in American Politics?

November, 2018

For much of my life's work as a social and political activist, I have been a proponent of independent Black politics and the creation of a progressive, independent, third force in American politics as a vehicle to advance a visionary politics of social transformation; a politics which will not emerge from the dominant, mainstream political Parties. Back in the day, progressive activists hoped that Rev. Jesse Jackson's historic, electrifying and progressive Presidential campaigns in 1984 and 1988 and his Rainbow Coalition would evolve into a third force; a formation which could undertake an inside/outside strategy by supporting acceptable Democratic candidates as well as endorsing or running independent candidates to advance a progressive agenda. But, for reasons too numerous to recount, this was not to be. Indeed, the Ron Daniels Independent Campaign for President in 1992 and subsequent formation of the Campaign for a New Tomorrow (CNT) was in part a response to the fact that the National Rainbow Coalition did not become an independent, mass-based, progressive, third force in American Politics.

For decades various leaders and organizations have issued calls for either the revival of the Rainbow Coalition or a similar formation to establish a viable alternative to the mainstream political Parties;

Over the years what has been missing is a vehicle, a structure or mechanism to achieve this objective. Bernie Sanders' presidential bid was arguably the most powerful effort since Rev. Jackson's presidential campaigns in the 1980's, but in the end, no permanent structure was created to harness the energy, enthusiasm and talent of the campaign. Now that a new generation of social and political activists have boldly burst onto the stage of history to achieve a major victory in the 2018 mid-term elections, the moment may have arrived for the creation of the long-awaited but elusive third force. And, the vehicle to advance this cause may be the Working Families Party.

Under the dedicated leadership of Dan Cantor, who served as Labor Coordinator for Rev. Jesse Jackson's 1988 campaign for President (where I also served as Deputy Campaign Manager), the Working Families Party has quietly and methodically spread from its original base in New York State and has established chartered chapters in 13 states, and there are plans to develop chapters in a number of additional States. Because of Cantor's strong relationships with unions, WFP also has solid roots in the labor movement. Equally important, in a major cross-generational transfer of leadership, Maurice Mitchell, a brilliant, courageous and visionary African American activist/organizer, who rose to prominence with the Movement for Black Lives after demonstrating his extraordinary skills in Ferguson, has been selected as the new National Director of the Working Families Party. His acceptance of this position occurs at an opportune moment in this crucial period.

"There is a time for all things in season," and the season is ripe for a third force in American politics. The emergence of Black Lives Matter (BLM) and the broader Movement for Black Lives (M4BL) may well have marked a turning point in the history of social movements in this country, not only because of their uncompromising demand for police reform/accountability/restructuring, but the insistence that "all Black lives matter," including the voices of LGBTQ persons. This principled stance helped pave the way for an incredible array of leaders with amazing experience, talent, skill and commitment to come out of the shadows to assume their rightful place in the forefront of movements for social justice and transformative change.

The time is ripe because the Women's March on Washington, with the equitable inclusion and leadership of women of color, unleashed a wave of activism among women unprecedented in recent history. The time is ripe because it has become abundantly clear to the vast majority in the progressive movement that "Trumpism" is a malignant abomination which must be purged from the American body politic as a moral and political imperative in the struggle to advance a politics of social transformation.

These factors and forces generated the energy and enthusiasm that produced major victories for progressives all across the country in the much-anticipated mid-term elections of 2018. Some skeptical pundits proclaimed that candidates like Stacey Abrams in Georgia, Andrew Gillum in Florida and Beto O'Rourke in Texas, who ran on unapologetically progressive platforms had failed, but they missed the point: few would have imagined that an African American woman would come within a whisker of becoming Governor of the State of Georgia; that an African American man would do likewise in Florida; or that a White progressive man would come close to unseating Ted Cruz in ruby red Texas. And, though O'Rourke did not take the top prize, progressive Democrats made major gains down ballot in state and local races. Even more amazing, who would have imagined that Lucy McBath, a WFP social-justice activist affiliated with M4BL, would defeat the incumbent Republican Karen Handel to become the Congresswoman from a predominantly White district once held by

Newt Gingrich!

A new generation of activists/organizers imagined it and as a result Democrats retook control of the House of Representatives and progressives and liberals captured governorships, state and local offices across the land. In Wisconsin, the dreaded Scott Walker was finally ousted by Tony Evers whose running mate, Mandela Barnes, a member of the WFP, will become the first African American elected to statewide office in that State. Moreover, the popular vote in the Congressional races exceeded Hillary Clinton's lead over Trump in the 2016 election by millions of votes.

Taken in its totality it was a resounding victory, a "blue wave" that in many respects was a women's wave, spearheaded by women of color in general and African American women in particular. Now the task is to harness this amazing energy and the fruits of the labor. Unlike Rev. Jesse Jackson's campaigns or Bernie Sanders' campaign, the progressive movement cannot afford to miss the opportunity of the moment. The season is ripe for the creation of an independent, progressive, third force in American politics. And, an emerging structure is in place to advance this goal, the Working Families Party under the leadership of a young, energetic, African, activist/organizer, Maurice Mitchell.

Over the years I have suggested that Rev. Jesse L. Jackson's National Rainbow Coalition offered the greatest opportunity for transformative change in the U.S. since the Populist Movement of the late 19th century. In that era, for a brief moment, Black farmer and worker alliances joined White farmer and worker alliances to mount a serious challenge to the new White power structure in the South. The Populist Movement came "dangerously" close to succeeding; so much so that the new rulers played the "race card" to induce the White leaders of this insurgent movement to abandon their erstwhile Black allies. The divide and conquer strategy worked. The alliance was shattered. The leaders in the power structure breathed a sigh of relief and "rewarded" White poor and working-class people by instituting a system of psychological and material benefits called "Jim Crow" to ensure that Blacks and Whites in the South would never again "unite and fight" the ruling class. The Populist Movement was permanently defanged!

I cite this history because it is instructive for how a successful third force must be constructed if it is to attract substantial numbers of people of African descent and other people of color. The National Rainbow Coalition worked because, unlike the Populist Movement, it emerged out of the Black community with the issues of civil rights/human rights for Black people at its core. From this base, Rev. Jackson brilliantly crafted an "economic common ground" message and platform to reach out to and include Latinos, Asians, Native Americans, Arab-Americans, White farmers, workers and predominantly White progressive organizations and constituencies to create a Rainbow Coalition. Unlike the Populist Movement, with this formulation it was highly unlikely that the interests and aspirations of Black people would be abandoned or betrayed.

Putting it bluntly, there is a long and justifiable history of skepticism in the Black Freedom Struggle about joining or building coalitions with predominantly White or White led progressive organizations and movements. Therefore, I believe that the centrality of race, racism and the leadership of people of color must be at the core of any progressive third force that will gain substantial support from people of African descent and other people of color. This is why the cross-generational transfer of leadership to Maurice Mitchell to become the National Director of the Working Families Party is of fundamental significance.

While there are certainly other Parties and formations in the progressive landscape that might take on the task at hand, Maurice Mitchell assumes the mantle of leadership at WFP coming directly out of the M4BL where he has deep roots and is widely respected. This is the decisive difference that can potentially set WFP apart from other progressive Parties and formations. What M4BL can bring to the table is an unquestioned and uncompromising commitment to ensuring that all Black lives matter and that the interests of Black people will always be at the center of any coalitional effort, alliance or Party they support. I believe Maurice Mitchell shares that commitment, and from that vantage point will be able to effectively attract and engage people of African descent in WFP and effectively reach out to other people of color and predominantly White progressive Parties, formations and constituencies. His reputation for collaborative work will be extremely helpful in this regard. And, unlike the Rainbow Coalition, Maurice Mitchell brings the collaborative, facilitative, collective leadership orientation of M4BL to his role as National Director of WFP. These are indispensable starting points for WFP to become the progressive third force in American politics.

The WFP also has other critically important assets. Maurice Mitchell has signaled his intent to deepen the Party's commitment to civic participation and engagement, community-based political education, organizing around issues, movement and institution-building as a way of touching people's lives on a day to day, month to month basis in between election cycles. This people and community-centered, multifaceted process is essential to advancing a vision and program of genuine "participatory democracy" and motivating increasing numbers of people to engage in the electoral process to enable progressives to seize the reins of power at all levels of government. Campaigns do not equal democracy; they are an important dimension of democracy.

Participation is the essence of democracy, and the election of persons to hold public office should be the outcome of people and community-based participatory processes. WFP is correct to adopt this approach as a centerpiece of its work. It will establish WFP as a "Party of a new type" in American politics.

Fusion is another incredibly important asset which WFP can utilize as a potential third force. Fusion allows for the cross endorsement of candidates which facilitates a third party acquiring the number of votes required to maintain ballot status. A party can also run its own candidates irrespective of whether they are endorsed by another party. For example, in New York, instead of voting for Governor Andrew Cuomo on the Democratic line, I voted for him on the WFP line. WFP already has ballot status in New York, Connecticut, Oregon and South Carolina and is actively working to secure ballot status in scores of states around the country. Fusion is a powerful tool which will enable the Party to institutionalize itself as a force to be reckoned with at all levels of government.

Though there are a number of other ballot access, voter registration and election reforms that WFP and progressives should push to enact, there is no more important reform than Instant Run-off Voting or Ranked Voting to open space for a progressive third force to thrive. Instant Run-Off Voting (IRV), which has been adopted in Maine, allows voters to select their first choice for a political office and a second choice for the same office if they so desire. In practical terms, IRV removes the dilemma some progressives face of choosing between a candidate they truly believe in and another candidate who may be less desirable. However, that less desirable candidate may have a better chance of defeating a candidate from another Party who is perceived as a much worse alternative.

The most recent example of how IRV may have made a difference under these circumstances was in the battleground States of Wisconsin, Michigan and Pennsylvania in the 2016 presidential election. Hillary Clinton loss to Trump by narrow margins in each of these States. The Green Party Candidate Dr. Jill Stein amassed more than enough votes to overcome Trump's margin of victory. If IRV had been in effect, a large enough number of Dr. Stein's supporters may have chosen Hillary Clinton as their second choice thereby blocking Trump's path to the presidency via the Electoral College map.

Dr. Stein and the Green Party should not be blamed for electing Donald Trump President. The blame lies with a system which does allow people to vote for who they believe in if the person is a third-Party candidate without being labeled a "spoiler." The adoption of IRV across the country will go a long way towards alleviating this issue. Therefore, it should be at the forefront of WFP's electoral reform agenda.

Ultimately, these efforts will be for naught if WFP does not have a platform and messaging that motivates its core constituencies to engage in protests, demonstrations, policy advocacy, institution-building and elections. I am confident that WFP will be at the cutting edge in this regard. However, I would offer this cautionary note. Blacks have been the most reliable supporters, the backbone of the Democratic Party for decades, and yet we have seldom been rewarded in proportion to our support or concerns/issues/needs. Even President Obama was unwilling to explicitly advance policy proposals that addressed the deep crises in America's "dark ghettoes." This reluctance to affirmatively respond to a Black Agenda is grounded in the fear of alienating White voters, particularly White poor and working- class constituencies because of the use of "identity politics."

WFP must resist this tendency and boldly articulate a platform which addresses issues of vital concern, particularly to marginalized

Black communities. A Domestic Marshall Plan aimed at healing Black communities from the ravishes of the "War on Drugs" and decades of blatant neglect, disinvestment and deindustrialization is a long-proposed idea worth fighting for. Advocating for reparatory justice policies will also have resonance. However, there is no contradiction between addressing the needs of marginalized Black communities and marginalized White communities.

This is precisely what Rev. Jesse Jackson was able to accomplish with the principles and strategy of his economic common ground platform during the 1984 and 1988 presidential campaigns and via the Rainbow Coalition. He effectively connected White farmers facing foreclosures and workers affected by plant closings with Black constituencies from marginalized communities in urban areas. WFP and progressives in general should revisit Rev. Jackson's successes in this regard.

Though I have re-emphasized the urgent need for WFP to address issues of concern to people of African descent, I also reaffirm my confidence that to the degree that the Party is deeply engaged with M4BL and other progressive forces in the Black community, the Party will avoid the past errors of the Democratic Party and other progressive movements. Indeed, in the end, WFP must clearly identify with and incorporate the issues and concerns of all of its core constituencies into the platform and messaging of the Party. And, this can best be done by the equitable inclusion of representatives of the core constituencies into the leadership of WFP.

Moving forward, it would be awesome if Tracey Abrams, Andrew Gillum and Beto O'Rouke would openly identify with the WFP, but far more important is the reality that the Party has its own homegrown "stars" in the persons of leaders like Congresswoman Lucy McBath and Lieutenant Governor Mandela Barnes to bolster its stature. And, its greatest strength will be the hundreds, if not thousands of grassroots activists and organizers who agree to join and work to build WFP. The structure and the process are far more important than personalities.

The victories for progressives in the 2018 mid-term elections have created an enormous opening to build a third force in American politics. I cannot emphasize enough that what is urgently needed is a vehicle, a structure to seize the moment, to harness the incredible energy of the "Rainbow wave" from this election to achieve this objective. I believe that WFP has the potential to be that vehicle. It will take massive resources to build the necessary infrastructure and capacity to seize the moment. Labor unions and Progressive funders would be wise to invest heavily in WFP until the Party can build a base of millions of small donors to sustain itself long term. This will genuinely make WFP the "people's Party."

We cannot afford to miss this moment. "There is a tide" in the affairs of men and women, which "if taken at the flood," will lead to victory. "When spider webs unite, they can tie up a lion." The time to establish an independent, progressive, third force in American politics is now!

The Vision, Mission and Prospects for the Institute of the Black World 21st Century

T he articles and essays in this volume provide a window into my worldview, ideological orientation, vision and values as a scholar/activist/organizer and perspectives on topics and is-sues I view of vital concern to Black America, the Pan African world and humanity. As such, they permeate various facets of the program-matic work of the Institute of the Black World 21st Century (IBW) as my chosen legacy project.

You may recall that a Black-oriented "think tank" was one of the projects that activists in AAPAN had agreed to work on in the initial meeting in 1989. However, the decision to make the creation of an entity like a new IBW, my legacy project was largely a result of dissatisfaction, disappointment and frustration with my support for and work on some of the major initiatives of the eighties and nine-ties. As an activist/scholar, the vast experiences acquired building

Freedom, Inc. of Youngstown and the Midwest Regional Coalition and the leading roles I subsequently played with the African Liberation Day Movement, the National Black Political Assembly and the National Black Independent Political Party equipped me to be a valuable "movement resource;" someone with a rich variety of experiences and skills that could be called upon to assist/support leaders and organizations in organizing/promoting various initiatives, projects and movements. I was quite willing, even eager to play that role, and I did.

I could write an entire volume on my ultimate disappointment with the failure of Rev. Jesse L. Jackson to transform his 1984 and 1988 Campaigns into a permanent, mass-based, progressive third-force in American politics by institutionalizing the National Rainbow Coalition; Rev. Benjamin F. Chavis's ill-fated tenure as Executive Director of the NAACP and Convener of the National African American Leaders Summit; and the Honorable Minister Louis Farrakhan's inability to translate the miracle of the Million Man March and Day of Absence into a sustained, grassroots base for Black empowerment, and perhaps one day I will. Suffice it to say here that these great lapses of leadership on milestone projects with which I played a supportive role, were decisive in persuading me that I should focus my energies on painting my own canvas.

As noted in the Autobiographical Acknowledgements, this project stands in the legacy of the incredible work and achievements of the original Institute of the Black World. Established in 1969 in the wake of the assassination of Dr. Martin Luther King, IBW began as a project of the Martin Luther King Center for Non-Violent Social Change. Such notable visionaries and scholar/activists as Dr. Vincent Harding, Bill Strickland, Rev. C.T. Vivian, Dr. Howard Dodson, Walter Rodney, Jan Douglas, Beni Ivey, Dr. John Henrik Clarke, Julius Lester, CLR James, Robert Hill, Haki Madhubuti and Pat Daly were among the Founders and Associates of this amazing institution. IBW was also inspired by Lerone Bennett, Jr.'s book, *The Challenge of Blackness,* which encouraged Black people to confront America's white supremacist institutions from a position of black power.

Accordingly, IBW engaged in scholarly research to advance policies designed to positively affect the interests of Black people in the U.S. and the world. It also convened important symposia to discuss policy issues, produced major publications, conducted programs to train young scholars and emerged as the major resource center for the movement to establish Black Studies Departments at Colleges and Universities. IBW was unquestionably one of the most influential institutions of its time. It eventually ceased operations in 1983 for lack of adequate funding to sustain its work at a high level. As those of us who were seeking to create an action-oriented, Black "think tank" searched for a model and name for a new entity, we decided on IBW, but with a more encompassing programmatic mission. We added "21st Century" to distinguish it from the original IBW. My hope is that the Institute of the Black World 21st Century will have the kind of impact in this era that renders it worthy of the adoption of the name of the original IBW.

* * * * *

The conceptual foundation for the new version of IBW can be traced to a presentation I made at the initial gathering of activists, organizers and scholars who were convened to consider forming the African American Progressive Action Network (AAPAN). In that meeting I shared feedback from my travels to numerous cities during the 1988 Jackson for President Campaign and thereafter. I encountered activists and organizers in every locale who were engaged in serious organizing around issues and concerns in their communities, e.g., police brutality, environmental racism, inequities in education, housing and healthcare, unemployment/joblessness. However, almost universally what I heard were complaints about how the "White folks" and the power structure in each community were the worst in the country, and laments that there was not a "movement" like that of the 60's.

I extracted two lessons from these conversations: There were organizing, campaigns and movements in all of the communities I visited, but they were not connected to each other in any meaningful way, i.e., people doing the same work in the same cities were doing it separately and apart from each other. Equally important, people doing work in the issue areas cited above were largely disconnected from folks doing the same or similar work in neighboring communities or cities in the state and across the country.

My conclusion was that Black communities across the country were suffering from internal disconnection, fragmentation and disorganization, but that the notion that there was "no movement" was incorrect. I advanced the proposition that there was a multiplicity of "movements" in cities and locales across the country. The problem was that these "movements" were not connected; that there was a "movement" in the country, but it was "not in conversation with itself." Therefore, a very basic task was to find ways to overcome the disconnectedness, fragmentation and disorganization retarding the capacity/power of Black communities to address issues and concerns more effectively. The prescriptions to achieve this task were/are also very basic: To recognize that we as people of African descent, Black people, are our greatest asset, that by networking, information-sharing and cross-fertilization of ideas we can learn from each other and empower ourselves to be the principal actors in our own liberation. Secondly, to recognize the urgent need to intentionally and actively promote and facilitate cooperation, collaboration and joint work among leaders, organizations, projects and movements to heal and empower Black families, communities and nations.

The Biblical parallel to the condition of Black communities and prescription for restorative change is found in Ezekiel 37, the Parable of the Valley of Dry Bones. Ezekiel asks the Lord, "can these dry bones live?" The bones are scattered, disconnected and lifeless. In effect, the response from the Lord is first there must be a spirit which permeates the bones to spark an awakening. Then the revived, live bones must be connected such that the vital organs and systems that constitute the body come to life as a healthy/wholesome being! And, so I believe it must be with marginalized, underdeveloped and underachieving Black communities.

First there must be a spiritual and cultural awakening. A people battered, bruised and traumatized by centuries of enslavement and generations of oppression under a white supremacist system must become self-aware, revived and healed. Then the leaders we raise and the institutions, projects, programs we build must be connected in ways that enhance our collective capacity/power to achieve self-determination and the creation of just and humane communities and nations. The spiritual/cultural awakening/revival and desire to collaborate are essential to the healing, restorative process. Binding the disjointed, disconnected leaders, organizations and movements together gives renewed vitality to and strength to the system/community. We as African people can be healed, empowered and restored. Black people can/will "live."

These basic observations, conclusions and prescriptions are not new or particularly profound. But, it was/is my conviction that undertaking this basic work is critical to finishing the unfinished Black freedom struggle in the U.S. and beyond. So, rather than heed the call of some supporters that I run for President again as an independent candidate or join with others to launch yet another national movement, I decided to devote the balance of my days working to create a basic structure dedicated to promoting and cultivating a culture of collaboration to enhance the capacity and power of Black communities and nations to achieve full freedom, to live!

* * * * *

As envisioned, the Institute of the Black World 21st Century (IBW) is an African-centered, progressive, action-oriented Resource Center that promotes and facilitates collaboration though its programmatic work. IBW is African-centered in that its vision, mission and work are grounded in the humanistic principles and values of the traditional way of life of African people. These African-centered principles and values are central to our efforts to maintain or restore Black families, communities and nations. As a progressive formation, IBW is firmly committed to ending all forms of oppression based on race, ethnicity, gender, sexual orientation, culture, religion or class.

Properly understood, IBW is a resource center and catalyst for effective action. IBW's Board and Staff are comprised of highly-skilled and experienced facilitators/conveners, organizational specialists, scholars, activists, organizers and policy advocates with extensive history in the civil rights/human rights, nationalist, Pan-africanist and internationalist movements. Utilizing our human and material assets, IBW actively functions to encourage leaders, organizations and movements to cultivate a culture of collaboration to heal and empower Black families, communities and nations. This definition and description of IBW is reflected in our Mission, Values and Strategies for Implementation Statements:

- **Mission:** The Institute of the Black World 21st Century is committed to building the capacity/power of Black communities in the U.S. to work for cultural, social, economic and political upliftment, the development of the global Black community and an enhanced quality of life for all marginalized people.

• **Values:** IBW's vision is rooted in the values of cooperation, community and mutual respect. It is founded on the principles of self-determination, African humanism and social justice. The struggle for social transformation through the creation of new relationships and institutions is central to this task. The objective of our work is to create greater unity among people of African descent, to acquire and maintain power to reconstruct our communities and to build viable and vital nations, inspired by the idea of a new, non-exploitative social order.

• **Strategies for Implementation:** IBW will implement its mission by working with individuals, organizations, institutions, and movements that aspire to transform and reconstruct communities of African descent. The Institute is catalyst and facilitator as well as analyst and policy maker. Creating networks, facilitating linkages and fostering communications among individuals, between organizations and communities is an essential part of our mission. The Institute does not necessarily seek to implement projects alone but prefers to provide access to information and resources which allow local groups to initiate projects and build linkages with others doing similar work. Strategic partnerships and local support committees will also be vehicles for the collaborative implementation of IBW projects and initiatives.

The charge to "cultivate a culture of collaboration" is fundamentally important to IBW's approach to healing and empowering Black families, communities and nations. Culture is simply the way of life of a particular group of people. We believe cooperation, networking, information-sharing, cross-fertilization of ideas, learning from each other, specialization and division of labor, operational unity, joint work—collaboration must become the norm, the "way of life" for people of African descent. This is consistent with the Principles of Ujima (Collective Work and Responsibility) and Ujamaa (Cooperative Economics) as elaborated in the Nguzo Saba (Seven Principles of the Black Value System) devised by Dr. Maulana Karenga.

The concept and commitment to collaboration is in my DNA as an activist-scholar, organizer and institution-builder. I developed a strong affinity for this approach as Chairman of Freedom, Inc., the organizations I founded in Youngstown, Ohio in 1967. Freedom, Inc. was constantly involved in promoting the kind of "united front" work called for by Kwame Ture and Dr. Maulana Karenga; efforts to pull leaders and organizations together to encourage them to work together on issues of mutual concern based on the concept of Operational Unity. The underlying assumption of Operational Unity is that Black people are not monolithic; we do not have a single ideology, strategy or tactical approach to dealing with immediate issues or ultimate objectives in terms of achieving freedom, equality or self-determination. Therefore, achieving total unity is impractical as a starting proposition.

Operational Unity posits that leaders and organizations from differing ideologies, strategic and tactical approaches should create or become part of a united front to identify issues, projects, programs and concerns of common interest and devise mutually agreed upon strategies and tactics to collectively address them. Leaders and organizations that join a united front do not relinquish their status, surrender their organization's institutional sovereignty or forego the right to continue work on particular issues, initiatives or projects.

There is simply an agreement to join hands with other leaders and organizations to work on mutually agreed upon issues, initiatives or projects in the interest of improving the lives of Black people. Dr. Karenga characterizes this practical approach as "unity without uniformity."

The notion is that the road to more comprehensive unity can be achieved by leaders and organizations getting to know each other and building relationships while working together/collaboratively on issues of mutual concern. As a practical matter, collaboration via Operational Unity can yield positive results in terms of productive work on concrete issues, initiatives, programs and projects in Black communities. As such, it is a community-building, nation-building process. IBW's work is grounded in the conviction that collaboration based on the concept of Operational Unity is an invaluable, even essential, undertaking to heal Black families, communities and nations.

Despite the fact that Freedom, Inc. was a nationalist/Pan-africanist organization, our style of work was such that we were trusted to convene leaders and organizations across the ideological spectrum for planning retreats. In these retreats Black elected officials, educators, agency heads, faith, labor, business, professional leaders and representatives of community-based organizations would identify issues and devise strategies for action. These retreats were exercises in collaboration through Operational Unity. The Chairman of Freedom, Inc. was the Facilitator of these extraordinary sessions.

My belief in collaborative structures and processes was further strengthened by my participation in the Youngstown Leadership Conference, a weekly breakfast meeting of Black male political, business and professional leaders at the downtown (mostly White) YMCA. Elected officials, lawyers, doctors, funeral directors, businessmen, agency heads, the Black male elite of the city comprised the membership of the Youngstown Leadership Conference (YLC). There were no women (which unfortunately was a sign of the times) or grassroots/community-based organizations at the table which was a sign of the times. I was eventually invited to attend YLC meetings because of the influence, reputation and accomplishments of Freedom, Inc. in the community.

YLC's weaknesses notwithstanding, it was a very effective vehicle for identifying issues or concerns of interest to Black people and developing plans to act on them. YLC was definitely committed to advancing and defending the interests of the Black community. There would be discussions on how to persuade mayoral administrations to appoint more Black people to positions in municipal agencies and promote those already in office to higher positions; how to address a particular crisis that may have flared up; and, generally how to secure more economic and political power for Black people. Behind closed doors, strategies would be developed and specific assignments made for implementation. YLC was not always successful in achieving the desired outcomes, but more was accomplished because of the collaborative process and collective strategizing than was likely if the leaders at the table had acted in a disjointed manner. YLC was a living example of Operational Unity and collaborative action. I viewed YLC, with revisions and improvements (inclusion of women and community based/grassroots leaders and organizations), as a model structure that should be replicated in Black communities across the country. Indeed, the concept of Leadership Conferences or Summits was incorporated into the Black Community Development Plan which I have advocated for decades [See Appendix 1].

The penchant and passion for collaboration was also reflected in my tenure as Executive Director of the Center for Constitutional Rights (CCR). The same fragmentation and disjointedness that plague Black communities is also an affliction which hampers social movements including those on the left. Police brutality, killings and misconduct was one of the major issues CCR was being called upon to address by numerous organizations and leaders in New York City. However, there was no overarching vehicle to bring the disparate leaders and organizations together to explore comprehensive, coordinated strategies for action. To address this weakness, I proposed the creation of a Movement Support Resource Center (MSRC) to convene the various leaders and organizations dealing with police brutality and misconduct in the City on a regular basis. While CCR is primarily a public interest legal organization, MSRC provided a vehicle for leaders and organizations to engage in coordinated education, mobilizing and organizing around issues and incidents of police brutality and misconduct. In some instances, MSRC actions were in support of existing CCR legal cases. In other instances, MSRC served as a place to discuss new cases that CCR might file to seek justice through litigation.

MSRC also connected social and political activists and people's lawyers from cities across the country via regular conference calls. Among the highlights of the collaborative work of MSRC was the Convening of a Congressional Black Caucus Hearing on Police Brutality and Misconduct in New York Chaired by Congressman John Conyers; a National Emergency Conference on Policy Brutality and Misconduct which brought together leaders and organizations from around the country to discuss an action agenda; and, a National Emergency March Against Police Brutality and Misconduct in Washington, D.C. that was covered live by C-SPAN. The March was influential in persuading President Bill Clinton to convene and National Roundtable on Police Misconduct at the Justice Department. These achievements were the result of collaboration and joint work by leaders and organizations practicing Operational Unity.

I cite this background to emphasize that collaboration and all that is entailed in achieving it, is foundational to my conception of the vision and mission of IBW. Beyond the theory and aspiration, however, the practice of collaboration with multi-leader, multi-organization formations or coalitional projects and initiatives requires the ability of an individual and/or institution to function as a "good faith" facilitator or convener. Accordingly, we say that IBW "promotes and facilitates collaboration." Promoting collaboration necessitates more than getting folks together and asking, "can we all get along." Creating viable collaborations requires serious work and there is an art and "science" to it.

*   *   *   *   *

It would take more space than I have in this volume to fully discuss the ingredients for effectively facilitating collaborations. However, I can list some of the more important elements this space:

• To be a "good faith" facilitator, a leader or institution must be trusted. The leaders and organizations that are being asked to collaborate must believe in the honesty, integrity and intentions of the facilitator; that the facilitator is not simply self-interested or advancing the idea for his/her or its own benefit. Leaders and organizations must believe that the collaboration is for a worthwhile cause which is mutually beneficial.

• It is important to provide ample opportunity for all of parties in the collaboration to shine, to share ideas, receive credit for their work and be empowered rather than overshadowed by the facilitator. The willingness to share "leadership" and opportunities for recognition is crucial to creating and sustaining collaborative structures or initiatives.

• The facilitator must not be perceived as potentially competing with members of the collaboration for resources, e.g. grants and financial awards. Protection of "turf" around resources is one of the major obstacles to building collaborative structures. It is extremely difficult to pull leaders and organizations together if there is a perception that the facilitator may take away resources from the participants in the collaborative.

I can say without fear of contradiction that IBW has emerged as a good faith facilitator and convener promoting and cultivating a culture of collaboration as a corrective for the fragmentation, disorganization and disjointedness that hampers the capacity for the healing and empowering Black families, communities and nations. The validity of this contention is reflected in our programmatic work. Over the past 17 years, IBW has consciously launched or facilitated the development of major projects, programs and initiatives calculated to be models of the principles and practice of Operational Unity and collaboration; models designed to address and overcome fragmentation and disorganization in ways that enhance the collective capacity/power of Black people to heal Black families, communities and nations. IBW's Drug Policy Reform Initiative, Black Family Summit, Pan African Unity Dialogue, Reparations Initiative and State of the Black World Conferences are illustrative of this crucial work.

* * * * *

Educating, mobilizing and organizing to end the "War on Drugs," police brutality and racially biased criminal justice policies that have severely damaged Black families and communities have been a major part of IBW's work over the past several years. As we assessed the crises afflicting Black communities in the U.S, it became increasingly clear that the War on Drugs was/is "a war on us;" a policy and strategy primarily targeting Black people; a policy and strategy put in place as a substitute for the massive investment required to finish the unfinished civil rights/human rights agenda of healing Black families and communities from centuries of enslavement and generations of racially-exclusive policies and practices. For IBW, ending the War on Drugs is not the end, but a means to an end—the healing, empowering, rebuilding, restoring and sustaining Black families and communities. Therefore, from the outset the Call to Action for the Drug Policy Reform Initiative has been "end the War on Drugs, invest in America's dark ghettos."

Our initial approach was to simply undertake a series of Town Hall Meetings to create greater public awareness in Black communities about the devastating damage of the War on Drugs. Working with broadly representative local planning/implementation committees, we convened highly successful Town Hall Meetings in Washington, DC, Pittsburgh and Baltimore; cities where IBW Board members already had a history of some work and good relationships with a sufficient number of leaders and organizations to assist with the mobilizing/organizing process.

In each of the cities, collaboration and joint work among organizations engaged in police and criminal justice reform or anti-violence work was rare. The condition of fragmentation, disjointedness was the order of the day among organizations doing good work around issues of concern to Black people. Not content to settle for simply convening Town Hall Meetings on the War on Drugs, we asked leaders and organizations that comprised local planning committees if they would be willing to continue working together after the event. In all instances, they agreed. Local planning committees were also asked to selectively identify other leaders and organizations who might be willing to make the same commitment. Finally, the educating and mobilizing leading up to the Town Hall Meetings included the challenge to leaders and organizations to come together after the event to discuss creating a structure to continue the process of working collaboratively on criminal justice issues.

It was out of this process that Drug and Criminal Justice Policy Reform Collaboratives (Justice Collaboratives) were formed in Washington, DC Pittsburgh and Baltimore with IBW as the facilitator [See Appendix 2: Justice Collaborative Mission Statement]. A Justice Collaborative was also established in Philadelphia after a Town Hall Meeting on the epidemic of violence and fratricide in Black communities in that City. It is important to note that from the outset formerly incarcerated persons/returning citizens have played a central role in creating and maintaining the Justice Collaboratives. [The effort in Baltimore has not been as successful as in the other cities. However, IBW maintains an office in Baltimore and remains committed to building a Collaborative type structure there]

I believe that building these Justice Collaboratives represents some of the most important organizing in Black America as a corrective for the fragmentation, disjointedness and disorganization that plagues our communities. In Pittsburgh, Washington, DC and Philadelphia, 15-25 leaders and organizations meet quarterly to share information and discuss issues of common concern. The entry point for the discussion is drug, police, criminal justice reform and the violence and fratricide in our communities. But, once the discussion begins all manner of social, economic and racial justice issues might surface for deliberation and action. In that sense, these entities have evolved into racial justice collaboratives with the potential to address a range of issues that impact Black communities.

As it specifically relates to drug and criminal justice reform, however, the Justice Collaboratives have an impressive record of accomplishments. In addition to ongoing activities to create greater public awareness about the War on Drugs and racially biased policing and criminal justice policies each Justice Collaborative has developed a local policy agenda. The Pittsburgh Justice Collaborative (PJC) helped to spearhead the effort to have City Council enact Ban the Box legislation to remove a barrier to employment by formerly incarcerated persons. The Washington, D.C. Justice Collaborative successfully mobilized faith leaders to support Initiative 71 to legalize recreational Marijuana utilizing a social justice, racial justice, reparatory justice framework. The Philadelphia Regional Justice Collaborative (PRJC) has emphasized a broad racial justice policy agenda including advocating for the restoration of the African American Advisory Committee to the Child Protective Services Agency; educating and organizing to address the crisis of violence and fratricide in the community; and, economic development/entrepreneurial development for youth/young people. The adaptation of the Law Enforcement Diversion Program (LEAD) which was innovated in Seattle, Washington has also been priority of each of the Justice Collaboratives. This program permits police officers to divert persons who commit certain offenses to program where they receive wrap-around services for rehabilitation rather than arresting them.

Through periodic conference calls and education/orientation retreats, IBW also facilitates connectivity, cross-fertilization of ideas and joint action between the Justice Collaboratives. Key leaders from Collaboratives have gotten to know each other and built relationships to create a kind of Justice Collaborative Family! This connectivity led to the Collaboratives spearheading a Day of Direct Action March and Rally at the White House demanding an end to the War on Drugs and racially biased criminal justice policies; providing support for a National Rally to Free Incarcerated Women; and, support for a

National Rally Against Murders in Black Communities. In addition, the three Justice Collaboratives are undertaking the task of educating leaders and organizations to access and utilize the Victims of Crime Act (VOCA) to secure resources to better serve victims of crime and empower them to become advocates to address the conditions breeding violence and fratricide in marginalized Black communities across this country.

The establishment and maintenance of Justice Collaboratives is illustrative of IBW's fundamental commitment to cultivate a culture of collaboration to heal Black families and communities, functioning as a trusted, good faith facilitator. These collaboratives stand as a model worthy of emulation in Black communities across the country.

* * * * *

The Black Family Summit (BFS) is a configuration of 27 socially-conscious Black professional organizations, which have thousands of members nationwide. Many of them are counseling and "healing organizations" e.g., National Association of Black Social Workers, Black Psychiatrists of America, Association of Black Psychologists, Black Administrators in Child Welfare, All Healers Mental Health Alliance, Community Healing Network, National Medical Association, National Association of Black Nurses, National Dental Association, which have thousands of members nationwide. Under the leadership of Leonard Dunston, IBW Board Member and President Emeritus of the National Association of Black Social Workers, BFS addresses a broad range of issues related to preserving and strengthening Black families as a foundation of Black communities. [See Appendix 3— BFS Mission Statement]

The BFS was conceived during the 10th Anniversary of the Million Man March. The Honorable Minister Louis Farrakhan asked

Leonard Dunston to convene a summit of leading Black professional organizations to present their policy agendas for Black America and ways that they might cooperate to improve conditions in the Black community. More than 30 organizations came to the Table in a rare display of collective sharing and strategizing. At the conclusion of the session, it was agreed that IBW would serve as the Convener of this outstanding assembly of organizations. The task was consistent with IBW's Mission and role as facilitator/convener, and under the leadership of Leonard Dunston, BFS has demonstrated the value of "collective work and responsibility."

As an umbrella formation, IBW's BFS has been particularly effective in providing culturally appropriate counseling and healing services in Black communities, which have suffered natural and man-made disasters. This process began when BFS organizations undertook a mission to New Orleans to serve distressed Black families after Hurricane Katrina. While BFS was successful in providing healing services, one of the issues which it encountered was the inability to put Black healers on the ground to provide counseling services due to a maze of restrictive state regulations. The Katrina Initiative marked the beginning of a concerted effort by BFS to break through these barriers. A significant step in this direction was taken when BFS emphatically raised the issue of the treatment of Katrina survivors at an African American Leadership Summit convened by the Federal Emergency Management Agency(FEMA) at its office in Washington, DC.

As a result of that meeting, Craig Fugate, FEMA Administrator, sought to find ways to positively engage with BFS. Ultimately, IBW/BFS and FEMA signed a unique Memorandum of Understanding designed to facilitate access to distressed Black communities by BFS healing organizations after disasters. This constructive relationship with FEMA proved very beneficial when the All Healers Mental Health Alliance convened BFS healing organizations to provide counseling services for African Americans, many of whom were elderly, who were simply stranded in Coney Island and Far Rockaway after Hurricane Sandy struck. The effective division of labor developed to successfully provide urgently needed services in these communities has become a model which has been adapted for use in other communities after disasters. In fact partnering with local organizations and agencies, BFS organizations sprang into action to provide services in Houston, Port Arthur and Beaumont, Texas and communities in Florida after Hurricane Harvey. And, after the devastating Hurricane Irma struck the Caribbean, BFS extended its reach to the U.S. Virgin Islands and other Caribbean islands to provide counseling and healing services. BFS has also been directly engaged in providing advice/counsel to organizations in Flint during the lead-contamination water crisis. The remarkable success of BFS is another example of what can be accomplished when organizations collaborate and utilize their collective resources to achieve common objectives.

*   *   *   *   *

Promoting Progressive Pan Africanism is a cornerstone of IBW's mission and work internationally. We also believe that it is critically important to promote and practice Pan Africanism in the U.S. The fact that people of African descent from the Continent, Caribbean and Central and South America now occupy the same space in increasingly diverse Black communities across the U.S. does not mean that we are relating to each other or working together on issues of mutual concern. Instead, we may simply be residing in separate ethnic and cultural enclaves passing by each other without working with each other to maximize Black power as an African Diaspora in the U.S. and internationally. Worse still, there may be open competition and hostility between more recently arrived immigrants and "African Americans."

Accordingly, acting as a good faith facilitator/convener, a few years ago IBW called together a group of 60 selected Continental African, Caribbean American, Afro-Latino and African American leaders in New York to form the Pan African Unity Dialogue (PAUD) in honor of Marcus Mosiah Garvey. IBW proposed that the leaders agree to meet at least four times a year to share information on organizational projects, programs and activities; receive updates on events and issues from around the Pan African world; engage in cultural exchanges; and, explore areas for joint work/collective action as necessary. [See Appendix 4—PAUD Mission Statement].

It has been a rich and rewarding experience. Forty to 60 leaders (sometimes more) meet quarterly for up to three hours for very informative, productive and action-oriented discussions on issues that affect people of African descent in the U.S. and globally. In that regards, PAUD played an active role in disseminating information to ensure that immigrant communities were fully represented in the 2010 Census; supported efforts of Muslim Imams to expose the New York Police Department/FBI/CIA illegal surveillance of Muslim Mosques; adopted and advocated for immigration policy reform that is inclusive and protects the interests of people of African descent; consistently discussed and supported strategies for Black economic development in New York and beyond; hosted an Afro-Descendant Summit with President Nicolas Maduro of Venezuela; supported the demand for massive resources to overcome the Ebola crisis in Africa; discussed the new "scramble for Africa" and began discussions on Criteria for Foreign Investment in Africa; conducted discussions on principles of democratic governance in Africa; and, devoted considerable time to identifying crisis points in Africa and exploring strategies for PAUD and the Diaspora to contribute to resolving them.

It is an amazing sight to witness an array of leaders from the Continental African, Caribbean American, Afro-Latino and African American communities gathered around the Table sharing information, discussing issues of concern to people of African descent and adopting strategies for collective action; proof positive that operational unity and collaboration work in promoting and practicing Pan Africanism in the U.S.

∗   ∗   ∗   ∗   ∗

The National African American Reparations Commission is at the center of the growing U.S. and global Reparations Movement. It is convened and administered by IBW and represents another example of Operational Unity and collaboration as effective means of promoting and defending the interest of people of African descent. The demand for reparations has been a constant thread in the Black Freedom Struggle ever since the formal end of enslavement, ebbing and flowing in intensity based on circumstances in various periods. In the latter part of the 20th Century, the National Coalition for Reparations for African Americans (NCOBRA) was unquestionably the leading formation driving the U.S. Reparations Movement. However, with the passage of its veteran leadership, the national hysteria after the 9-11 terrorist attack and the election of Barack Obama as the country's first African American President, the reparations movement experienced a lull.

To the degree that a movement still existed, it was largely fragmented and not functioning as a unified force. However, dramatic developments in the Caribbean served as a catalyst to revitalize the Reparations Movement in the U.S. and the Pan African World;

developments which afforded an opportunity for IBW to once again utilize its experience and commitment to Operational Unity and collaboration to propose an umbrella structure to advance aspects of a reparations agenda in the U.S.

In 2013, the Heads of State of the 15 nations which comprise The Caribbean Community (CARICOM), a body that promotes regional cooperation, voted unanimously to demand reparations from the former European colonizers for Native genocide and African enslavement! This was a huge development because not only were scholars, activists and organizers in the Caribbean demanding reparations, now the Heads of State of governments across the political spectrum had joined in issuing the call! While serving his turn as the rotating Chairman of CARICOM, Dr. Ralph Gonsalves, Prime Minister of St. Vincent and the Grenadines led the charge. A brilliant address to the body by Professor Sir Hilary Beckles, who was Vice-Chancellor (President) of the University of the West Indies Cave Hill Campus in Barbados at the time, set the stage for Dr. Gonsalves to urge leaders of CARICOM to act. In response, a CARICOM Reparations Commission (CRC) was established with Professor Beckles as its Chairman. CRC was given a mandate to encourage the creation of Reparations Commissions in each of the member nations and to devise a Reparations Program with specific proposals/demands to be presented to the former colonial powers to repair the damages resulting from the crimes of Native Genocide and African enslavement.

Against the backdrop of the "lull" in the movement, at the Reparations Issues Forum, convened by Congressman John Conyers at the 2013 Congressional Black Caucus Foundation, Inc. Annual Legislative Conference, a group of reparations activists, including Rev. JoAnn Watson, Atty. Nkechi Taifa and Dr. Julianne Malveaux, huddled to discuss ways to re-engage leaders, organizations and constituencies to advance the demand for reparations. I recommended that we use the dramatic developments in the Caribbean as a reference point to spark renewed interest in the reparations movement in the U.S. In addition, the group took note of the enormous impact of Ta-Nehisi Coates' highly influential article The Case for Reparations in the Atlantic Monthly magazine. A generation of young people who had not been aware of the struggle for reparations or were pessimistic about its prospects, now seem receptive to becoming involved.

Based on these factors, our little planning group agreed on the first phase of a strategy that would entail holding Town Hall Meetings in various cities across the country to familiarize Black people with the CARICOM Reparations Commission and its 10 Point Reparations Program as a means of sparking renewed interest in the Reparations Movement in the U.S., including HR-40, the Reparations Study Bill. Dr. Ralph Gonsalves or Professor Sir Hilary Beckles would be invited to be the Keynote Speaker at these Town Hall Meetings. As the Moderator for the Issues Forum and President of IBW, I agreed to utilize our experience and reputation as good faith conveners/facilitators to organize at least one such Town Hall Meeting in the coming year.

The planning/strategy meeting at the 2013 Reparations Issues Forum proved to be a decisive turning point in the U.S. Reparations Movement. Since that time, with IBW functioning as the lead organizer and facilitator and with the support of a cross-section of reparations advocates and leaders, the Reparations Movement in the U.S. has taken on new life.

Based on relationships with longtime friends and allies, IBW selected Chicago as the site for a major Town Hall Meeting on "Revitalizing the Reparations Movement." Working in concert with Dr. Conrad Worrill, veteran scholar/activist and Chairman Emeritus of the National Black United Front, and Dr. Iva Carruthers, General Secretary of the Samuel DeWitt Proctor Conference, a major Town Hall Meeting was convened at Chicago State University in April of 2014. Moderated by Judge Lionel Jean Baptiste, an audience of more than 800 people were brought to their feet time and time again by highly informative and inspirational presentations on the urgent necessity to strengthen the U.S. and global Reparations Movements. Speakers included: Rev Dr. Jeremiah Wright, Dr. Worrill, Dr. Carruthers, Councilwoman Rev. JoAnn Watson, Kamm Howard of NCOBRA, Congressman John Conyers, Don Rojas, IBW's Director of Communications, Special Guest Professor Sir Hilary Beckles and the Honorable Minister Louis Farrakhan. It was an electrifying gathering that was viewed by more than 10,000 people from across the U.S. and the Caribbean. This amazing Town Hall Meeting set the stage for a series of powerful events that have generated incredible new interest and action on the issue of reparations for African Americans.

After the Chicago Town Hall Meeting, the IBW team collaborated with the staff of Congressman John Conyers and key leaders of the CARICOM Reparations Commission to organize what the Congressman called the most successful Reparations Issues Forum since HR-40 was first introduced in in 1989. The 2014 Reparations Issues Forum featured a high-profile Panel with Ta-Nehesi Coates; Camillo Gonzales, Foreign Minister of St. Vincent and the Grenadines; and Professor Sir Hilary Beckles, Chairman of the CARICOM Reparations Commission. They addressed a jam-packed audience on aspects of the U.S. and global Reparations Movements. Everyone on the Panel praised Congressman John Conyers for his steadfast support of the reparations movement and stressed the importance of HR-40. It was a very informative and inspiring Reparations Issues Forum; another step in revitalizing the U.S. Reparations Movement.

Building on the success of the Chicago Town Hall Meeting and Reparations Issues Forum, Don Rojas and I proposed to Professor Beckles that Members of the CARICOM Commission come to the U.S. for a national/international Reparations Summit. We argued that such an event would accelerate the momentum sparked by the Chicago Town Hall Meeting and Reparations Issues Forum and contribute to the momentum of the global Reparations Movement. To maximize the potential impact of the proposed Summit, IBW moved to organize a U.S. Reparations Commission as a parallel body to the CARICOM Commission. Consistent with the principles of Operational Unity and IBW's commitment to collaborative processes, it was imperative that the work of organizations and leaders like NCOBRA, National Black United Front, December 12th Movement and the Nation of Islam be recognized and respected. Accordingly, we reached out to representatives of these organizations and constituencies to discuss the proposed Commission first and invited them to designate representatives to serve. We also felt it was important to establish a Commission which was diverse and representative of leaders and constituencies beyond the long-time proponents of reparations to broaden the base of support and engagement for the concept and movement. This outreach resulted in IBW establishing the National African American Reparations Commission (NAARC). [Appendix 5 See listing of the initial NAARC Commissioners].

The primary Mission of NAARC was to devise a Preliminary 10 Point Reparations Program and convene area/regional hearings and other means of educating and enlisting the support of people of African descent to mobilize/organize to compel the U.S. Government and other institutions to respond to its demands. The creation of NAARC also set the stage for a dynamic synergistic relationship with the CARICOM Reparations Commission to enhance the growing

U.S. and global Reparations Movements.

In April of 2015, IBW convened a National/International Reparations Summit in New York, which was attended by delegations from 22 nations and territories from the Caribbean, Central and South America, Africa, Canada and Europe. The highlight of the Summit was an extraordinary interface between NAARC and representatives of the CARICOM Reparations Commission. The Summit was a resounding success! The Communique from the proceedings reverberated across the Black world and served as catalyst of encouragement for advocates from the participating countries and territories to form Reparations Commissions.

Immediately after the Summit, NAARC Commissioners adopted a Preliminary Reparations Program and, with the consent of Congressman Conyers, revised HR-40 from a bill to study slavery and make recommendations about same to one which focuses on remedies. As of this writing, the steady progress continues. The revised version of HR-40 was introduced in 2017, as a bill to create a Commission to Study Reparations Proposals for African Americans; two highly successful Area/Regional Hearings/Town Hall Meetings have been convened in Atlanta and New Orleans where leaders, organizations and constituencies reviewed NAARC Preliminary 10 Point Reparations Program and offered comments and recommendations for possible inclusion in the Final Program. Both Hearings/Town Hall Meetings were proceeded by weeks of interviews and discussions on Black talk radio, which contributed to public awareness about the definition of reparations, history of the U.S. Reparations Movement, historical precedents for awarding reparations and the current status of the Movement. Additional Hearings/Town Hall Meetings are planned for Los Angeles and the Bay Area in California, Washington, DC and Detroit before NAARC adopts a Final Reparations Program.

NAARC has established a Task Force on Colleges and Universities that Benefitted from Slavery with the objective of assisting students and community groups to hold these institutions accountable; a very productive relationship has been developed with the Movement for Black Lives (M4BLs), which has a Policy Platform that includes a major section on reparations; the relationship and synergy with the CARICOM Reparations Commission is strong as joint work on the U.S. and global Reparations Movements continues; and, finally, IBW has created the most extensive online Reparations Resource Center in the world—which is available to scholars, reparations advocates and anyone who wishes to learn more about the righteous struggles of peoples of African descent to secure reparations to repair the damages of the holocaust of enslavement, the brutal exploitation and oppression of colonialism and the ongoing oppression of post-emancipation.

I have taken time to elaborate on IBW's role in contributing to the revitalization of the U.S. Reparations Movement because it is an illustration of our role as a good faith convener/facilitator skillfully utilizing the principles of Operational Unity and collaboration to achieve positive results. The achievements from the Reparations Issues Forum at the CBC in 2013 where a small group huddled to outline an initial strategy to re-energize the U.S. Reparations Movement to the amazing events leading up to the formation of NAARC, the formulation of the Preliminary 10 Point Reparations Program and the introduction of revised HR-40 are nothing short of remarkable; some of the best collaborative education, mobilizing and organizing in Black America in recent history; work which attests to the validity and value of the vision and mission of IBW.

✳ ✳ ✳ ✳ ✳

The largest collaborative Initiative IBW undertakes is the

convening of **State of the Black World Conferences.** One of the three major projects agreed to by the activists who met to form the African American Progressive Action Network (AAPAN) was to reinstitute the practice of holding periodic "State of Black America Conferences." At the height of the era of Black Power and Black Nationalism, these gatherings pulled together leaders, activists and organizers from various organizations and concerned sisters and brothers to discuss the current state and future of people of African descent in America and the world. The Black Power Conferences of 1967 and 1968 and the Congress of African People in 1970 were in this same spirit.

AAPAN moved to resume these types of conferences as inclusive gatherings of a broad cross-section of leaders and organizations in Black America. As such, they were intended to be gatherings of the "Black Nation" as a whole rather than a convention of a particular organization, e.g., NAACP, SCLC, Urban League, Black Social Workers, etc. AAPAN initiated the process of reinstituting these gathering by convening State of the Race Conferences in Baltimore in1994 and 1997. Based on the lessons learned from the State of the Race Conferences, AAPAN convened the first State of the Black World Conference in Atlanta in 2001. And, as previously noted, the call for the establishment of an African-Centered Institute was issued at the first State of the Black World Conference.

SOBWCs are envisioned as collaborative undertakings which exemplify IBW's commitment to the concept of operational unity. Ideally, the Conferences are convened every four years to avoid the appearance of competing with numerous organizations that hold annual conventions/conferences. They are convened in the fall because most organizations hold their annual conventions/conferences in the spring and summer. SOBWCs are also held after presidential elections to assess the outcome of and impact of the election on Black America and the Pan African world. Typically, IBW will pull together a National Organizing Committee comprised of representatives from various national organizations, particularly the Black Family Summit, in hopes of encouraging them to mobilize their members and constituents to attend the SOBWC. The goal is to have organizations buy into the concept of SOBWCs as a united front type event. We take these steps to create an environment conducive to encouraging as many organizations and leaders as possible to support a great gathering of Black people every four years.

Philosophically IBW is a progressive, African-centered, Pan Africanist formation, but to foster Operational Unity and promote collaboration. IBW's approach is always to appeal to leaders, organizations, constituencies and ordinary people beyond the core of "true believers." A Ron Daniels axiom is that we cannot expand the base for the ideas we espouse by constantly having incestuous conversations with ourselves. We can only broaden the base for our ideas by casting a wider net and engaging in collaborative community-building, nation-building processes. State of the Black World Conferences provide the largest platform for IBW to operationalize and demonstrate the value of this foundational approach.

After Atlanta, IBW convened SOBWCs in New Orleans in 2008, Washington, DC in 2012 and Newark, NJ in 2016. Declarations of Intent and Calls to Action, which contain the projects and recommendations derived from the Working Sessions, were issued after each of these conference. In each instance, IBW reviewed the recommendations and elected to implement the ones which match our organizational priorities and capacity. Each of these Conferences served to keep alive the concept and potential of great gatherings of People of African descent as vehicles for Black empowerment utilizing the principles of Operational Unity and collaboration. In that regard, SOBWC IV, which IBW convened in Newark, November of 2016, was an extraordinary gathering of more than 2,000 participants and has been hailed as one of the most inspirational, informative and productive conferences in this period; arguably the most impressive testimony yet to IBW's credibility, experience and skill as a good faith convener and facilitator! However, the shortcoming of this incredible conference was IBW's lack of capacity to effectively follow-through to maintain the Issue Area Working Groups to continue the networking, information sharing and potential joint work long term. [Appendix 6: See SOBWC IV Declaration of Intent and Call to Action]

∗   ∗   ∗   ∗   ∗

From "Guts and Faith" to Scope, Scale and Sustainability. The Future of the Institute of the Black World 21st Century.

IBW's inability to harness the enthusiasm and momentum of State of the Black World Conference IV by facilitating the connectivity of the participants is symptomatic of the challenges we face in permanently operationalizing and institutionalizing collaboration and Operational Unity as our "theory of change" and empowerment for people of African descent in the U.S. and the Pan African world. From the Drug and Criminal Justice Policy Reform Collaboratives to the Black Family Summit, Pan African Unity Dialogue, National African American Reparations Commission to the convening of State of the Black World Conferences, IBW has demonstrated the value of cultivating a culture of collaboration to heal and empower Black families, communities and nations and its role as an effective good faith convener/facilitator utilizing the principles of Operational Unity.

But, as I have previously stated, IBW has succeeded in coming this far by "guts and faith." In part, this is because our approach is either not well understood or undervalued in foundation/funding circles. Frankly, if properly understood, funders should view IBW as a vital component of the organizational and institutional infrastructure or "ecosystem" for the sustained empowerment of people of African descent in the U.S. and the Pan African World. Therefore, we must redouble our efforts to educate prospective funders about the validity and value of IBW's approach and role as good faith conveners/ facilitators cultivating a culture of collaboration, connecting the "dry bones," to heal and empower people of African descent, Black people. [Appendix 7: See IBW Programmatic Chart as Resource Center]

In the meantime, we must continue the struggle. The good news is that IBW has also come this far by "living off the land." Most of our non-funded Initiatives have been sustained by the contributions small and large of the people, Black people, who are aware of the long history, experience, consistency of commitment and work of IBW's Officers and Board Members and believe in our vision/mission and programmatic Initiatives. The success of the historic International Reparations Summit is illustrative of this kind of people-based support. The down side is that the Summit barely broke even and therefore did not generate a surplus of resources for follow-up. Similarly, the overall volume of the contributions from our base of supporters has not been sufficient for IBW to build the infrastructure and capacity to survive and thrive and have meaningful impact long term.

Herein lies the challenge in terms of IBW achieving the scope and scale to become a dynamic resource center and engine for Black empowerment in the U.S. and the Pan African World. We've come thIS far by guts and faith, but it is not sustainable. While IBW will likely make some breakthroughs with foundations and funders, in the spirit of Marcus Garvey, our goal is to have a minimum of 50% of our operations and programmatic budget provided by donations/

contributions and in-kind services coming from people of African descent, Black people from the U.S. and the Pan AfricanWorld! Though we may find allies elsewhere, it is still the case that the most important source of our liberations is ourselves. Black people must be the primary contributors to the change we seek to make and the brighter future for our people we seek to forge.

Finally, IBW has come this far by guts and faith, evolving, emerging as a trusted, good faith facilitator/convener, persistently and relentlessly promoting collaboration and Operational Unity to heal and empower Black families, communities and nations. But, the legacy I/ we seek to leave will not be secure without the cross-generational orientation and transfer of leadership. We are charged with the obligation of ensuring historical continuity and the sustenance of this vital work through identifying and building relationships with a new generation of leaders, movements and organizations and locking arms cross-generationally to finish the unfinished Black freedom struggle and the promise of progressive Pan Africanism globally. Fortunately, IBW has a long history of cultivating cross-generation dialogue and engagement. Therefore, we are confident that our continuing commitment to this vital process will yield fruit in terms of the survival and enhanced development of IBW and the creation of a new Pan African World order!

The Epilogue

I t's been a long, tortuous, difficult, often delayed time coming but finally "The Book," the first volume is done! I sincerely hope it has shed some light on the path I've tread from the coalfields of West Virginia, to the small steel town of Youngstown, Ohio and the Hill District of Pittsburgh and beyond... the rough and rich experiences I have lived in pursuing this journey... the legions of family, friends, acquaintances and supporters as acknowledged in the special "libation" who have nourished, encouraged and inspired me to keep climbing toward the mountaintop; insights into my vision, values and political grounding as reflected in the Vantage Point Articles and Essays; and, most of all, gained a sense of my fervent dedication to building the Institute of the Black World 21st Century as an African-centered, progressive, action-oriented Resource Center and good faith convener and facilitator committed to cultivating a culture of collaboration to heal and empower Black families, communities and nations. This is my legacy project and I have penned this first book in the hope that friends, allies, supporters and people of conscious and goodwill will embrace it and contribute to fulfilling its promise toward the rescue and restoration of people of African descent, Black people in the U.S. and the Pan African World!

I'm still on this journey. "We've Come This Far by Faith" is one of my favorite gospel songs. "I Ain't No Ways Tired" is another favorite. They are both inspirational, but now at the three quarter-century mark (plus one), I confess to being just a bit weary, but I won't faint. I am invigorated by hearing the voices of the ancestors whispering in my ears "hold on just a little bit longer." I am steeled in my determination to continue cognizant that I am standing for Damu Smith, Dr. Ronald Walters, Dr. Charshee McIntyre, Wayne Thompson.......
"We've Come This Far by Faith" and, "I Ain't No Ways Tired." Still on this journey. A luta continua!

Appendices

Appendix 1
Black Community Development Plan

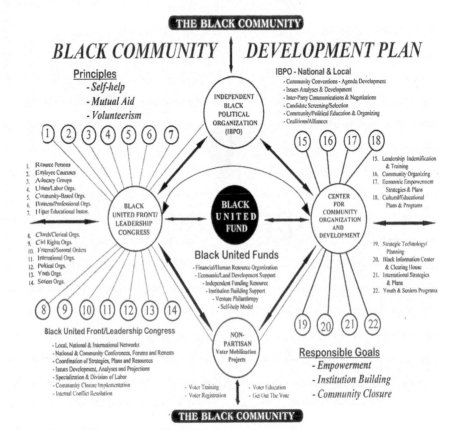

THE BLACK COMMUNITY

BLACK COMMUNITY | DEVELOPMENT PLAN

Principles
- *Self-help*
- *Mutual Aid*
- *Volunteerism*

INDEPENDENT
BLACK
POLITICAL
ORGANIZATION
(IBPO)

IBPO - National & Local
- Community Conventions - Agenda Development
- Issues Analyses & Development
- Inter-Party Communications & Negotiations
- Candidate Screening/Selection
- Community/Political Education & Organizing
- Coalitions/Alliances

(1) (2) (3) (4) (5) (6) (7)　　　　　　　(15) (16) (17) (18)

1. Resource Persons
2. Employee Caucuses
3. Advocacy Groups
4. Unions/Labor Orgs.
5. Community-Based Orgs.
6. Business/Professional Orgs.
7. Higher Educational Instns.

8. Church/Clerical Orgs.
9. Civil Rights Orgs.
10. Fraternal/Sororal Orders
11. International Orgs.
12. Political Orgs.
13. Youth Orgs.
14. Seniors Orgs.

BLACK
UNITED FRONT/
LEADERSHIP
CONGRESS

**BLACK
UNITED
FUND**

CENTER
FOR
COMMUNITY
ORGANIZATION
AND
DEVELOPMENT

15. Leadership Indentification
　　& Training
16. Community Organizing
17. Economic Empowerment
　　Strategies & Plans
18. Cultural/Educational
　　Plans & Programs

Black United Funds
- Financial/Human Resource Organization
- Economic/Land Development Support
- Independent Funding Resource
- Institution Building Support
- Venture Philanthropy
- Self-help Model

19. Strategic Technology/
　　Planning
20. Black Information Center
　　& Clearing House
21. International Strategies
　　& Plans
22. Youth & Seniors Programs

(8) (9) (10) (11) (12) (13) (14)　　　　　(19) (20) (21) (22)

Black United Front/Leadership Congress
- Local, National & International Networks
- National & Community Conferences, Forums and Retreats
- Coordination of Strategies, Plans and Resources
- Issues Development, Analyses and Projections
- Specialization & Division of Labor
- Community Closure Implementation
- Internal Conflict Resolution

NON-
PARTISAN
Voter Mobilization
Projects

- Voter Training
- Voter Registration
- Voter Education
- Get Out The Vote

Responsible Goals
- *Empowerment*
- *Institution Building*
- *Community Closure*

THE BLACK COMMUNITY

Appendix 2
Justice Collaborative Mission Statement

DRUG AND CRIMINAL JUSTICE POLICY REFORM COLLABORATIVES

Mission Statement

Consistent with our Mission and Values, the Institute of the Black World 21st Century (IBW) is committed to serving as a good faith facilitator to convene organizations and leaders in cities across the U.S. to create Justice Collaboratives to end the "War on Drugs," discriminatory criminal justice policies, mass incarceration, violence and fratricide (murders) that have devastated Black families and communities. Justice Collaboratives are grounded in the belief that by coming together in a spirit of unity, without surrendering one's organizational identity, Black leaders and organizations can collectively work to heal Black families and communities from the destructive effects of racially biased criminal justice policies.

Justice Collaboratives Function to:

• Promote information-sharing and the identification of issues/concerns of mutual interest.

• Sponsor events to educate the public about the devastating effects of the War on Drugs and discriminatory criminal justice policies on Black families and communities.

• Encourage joint action/work to enact policies that end the War on Drugs, racially biased criminal justice policies and mass incarceration with an emphasis on safe, just and humane alternatives.

• Educate, organize/mobilize to combat the epidemic of violence and fratricide (murders) in Black communities.

- Advocate for greater Black investment in Black communities, investment by private sector agencies and institutions and governmental policies which repair the damages inflicted by disinvestment and discriminatory criminal justice policies.

www.ibw21.org

info@ibw21.org

888-774-2921

Appendix 3
Black Family Summit Mission Statement

BLACK FAMILY SUMMIT

The Mission

The Black Family Summit (BFS) of the Institute of the Black World 21st Century (IBW) is a national network of primarily socially-conscious Black professional organizations, institutions and agencies committed to the preservation and strengthening of Black families, in their various forms, as the foundation for the survival, healing, restoration and development of Black communities and nations in the U.S. and worldwide. Consistent with the vision of (IBW), the mission of BFS is rooted in the values of cooperation, collaboration and collective work as reflected in the traditional way of life of people of African ancestry. Adhering to the principles of operational unity, BFS will pursue its mission through the formulation of holistic private and public programs, projects and initiatives.

Basic Programmatic Activities

• Periodic information-sharing conference calls to gain familiarity with the work of the participating organizations, institutions and agencies.

• Annual Public Policy Forum with representatives of the Congressional Black Caucus and key national civil rights/human rights organizations to review and present policy priorities to members of Congress.

• Periodic leadership dialogues with a broad range of local, national and international organizations to exchange analyses and perspectives on the state of Black America and the Pan African world. Such dialogues may include participation of leaders from civil rights/ human rights organizations, the African Union, representatives of CARICOM, scholar/activists, grass-roots/Community-based advocates, leaders from the Movement for Black Lives, elected officials and faith leaders.

• In the spirit of operational unity, joint work on programs, projects and initiatives by mutual agreement of participating organizations, e.g., convene local, state, regional or national forums to address critical issues, crises and policy concerns affecting the Black community and recommend actions to respond where appropriate; joint work in providing culturally appropriate disaster relief and preparedness training and work in response to natural and man-made disasters. Such initiatives may involve all or a sub-group of the whole.

Criteria for Membership

• Agreement to participate in at least one information-sharing conference call a year.

• Share organization's top policy priorities and good faith effort to attend/participate in the Annual Public Policy Forum.

• Honor commitment(s) to implementing BFS programs, projects and initiatives as agreed to by the organization.

Appendix 4
Pan African Unity Dialogue Mission Statement

PAN AFRICAN UNITY DIALOGUE

Background

The Pan African Unity Dialogue was initially convened by the Institute of the Black World 21st Century out of recognition of the emergence of a "new African community" in the U.S.; a community enriched by the arrival of increasing numbers of Continental Africans and people of African descent from the Caribbean, Central and South America. Residing in the same neighborhoods does not necessarily mean that these diverse African people will unite to advance their mutual interests in a society where individual and institutional racism remain barriers to Black progress.

Mission and Goal

The mission of the Pan African Unity Dialogue is to "practice Pan Africanism in the United States," the "African Diaspora," by promoting unity, cooperation and action between Continental Africans, Caribbean Americans, Afro-Latinos and African Americans. The goal is to achieve social, economic and political empowerment for people of African descent, Black people, in the U.S. and the global Black community.

Functions

To achieve this mission and goal the Pan African Unity Dialogue functions to:

• Promote cultural and historical exchanges about people of African descent from Africa, the Caribbean, Central and South America and the U.S.

- Facilitate information-sharing about the background, programmatic priorities and calendar of events of the Participants.
- Explore ways to impact local, state and national policies affecting people of African descent in the U.S.
- Provide updates on the social, economic and political status of people of African descent in Africa, the Caribbean, Central and South America and to act to ameliorate or resolve crises, promote democracy, development and Black empowerment.
- Mobilize/organize collective actions to promote and defend the interests of people of African descent in the U.S. and the Pan African World as necessary and appropriate.

Appendix 5
The First Members of the National African American Reparations Commission

NATIONAL AFRICAN AMERICAN REPARATIONS COMMISSION

Dedicated to the Memory of Queen Mother Moore

Rev. Dr. Jeremiah Wright
Pastor Emeritus, Trinity United Church of Christ, Chicago, IL

Professor Charles Ogletree
Executive Director, Charles Hamilton Houston Institute for Race and Justice, Harvard University, Boston, MA

Dr. Conrad Worrill
Director of the Carruthers Center for Inner-City Studies, North Eastern University, Chicago, IL

Dr. Ray Winbush
Director of the Institute for Urban Research, Morgan State University, Baltimore, MD

Atty. Roger Wareham
December 12th Movement, New York, NY

Dr. Iva Carruthers
General Secretary, Samuel DeWitt Proctor Conference, Chicago, IL

Rev. JoAnn Watson
Former Detroit City Councilwoman, Detroit, MI

Atty. Nkechi Taifa
Criminal Justice Reform and Reparations Activist, Washington, DC

Dr. Julianne Malveaux
Political Economist and President Emeritus, Bennett College for Women, Washington, DC

Nana Dr. Patrcia Newton
CEO, Black Psychiatrists of America, Baltimore, MD

Yvette Modestin
Founder and Executive Director,
Encuentro Diaspora and IBW Board Member, Boston, MA

Kamm Howard
National Coalition of Blacks for Reparations in America, Chicago, IL

Dr. Joyce King
Benjamin E. Mays Endowed Chair for Urban Teaching, Learning and
Leadership, Georgia State University, Atlanta, GA

Dr. V.P. Franklin
Editor, Journal of African American History, New Orleans, LA

Salim Adofo
Vice-President, National Black United Front, Washington, DC

Adebukola Ajao
Co-Founder, We Are the Ones, Blogger for Huff Post, Boston, MA

Minister Akbar Muhammad
Nation of Islam, St. Louis, MO

Convened and Administered by the
Institute of the Black World 21st Century

Ron Daniels
President, New York, NY

Don Rojas
Director of Communications, Baltimore, MD

Appendix 6
State of the Black World Conference IV Declaration of Intent and Call to Action

DECLARATION OF INTENT AND CALL TO ACTION

The Spirit, Power and Significance of an Historic Gathering

They came by the hundreds, more than two thousand in all, from the greater Newark/New York region, Black America and the Pan African World, drawn by the urgent impulse to connect, network, bond, share and unite in the wake of one of the most hate-filled, demagogic and divisive presidential elections in decades; an election which produced a presidential regime, elected by less than a majority of the popular vote; a regime imbedded with racism, white nationalism and Islamophobia. It is one of the most threatening moments since the arrival of Africans on these hostile American shores.

November 16-20, 2016, Africans from the far reaches of the U.S. and the Pan African World—South Africa, Nigeria, Ghana, Ethiopia, Uganda, Cameroon, Republic of Congo, Haiti, Jamaica, Barbados, Trinidad, Costa Rica, Columbia, Venezuela, Brazil, Canada and Europe converged on Newark, New Jersey, one of the great historical epicenters of Black Freedom Struggle, for State of the Black World Conference IV—responding to the Call. It's Nation Time Again!

In yet another hour of grave crisis, people of African descent, Black people, came seeking to be inspired, revitalized, informed and armed to intensify the essential, continuing struggle to defend and promote the dignity, survival, development, interests and aspirations of Africans, Black people, in America and the Pan African World.

As the words "it's nation time" reverberated throughout the gathering, a spirit of Black love, sharing, bonding, healing, collaboration, resistance, self-determination and renewed commitment to build and strengthen Black institutions, to control the politics and economics of Black communities, territories and nations permeated the deliberations.

While it is impossible to capture the full meaning of the words of the formidable array of more than one hundred Speakers, Panelists and Resources People who shared their insights, knowledge and wisdom with this remarkable gathering, these paraphrased expressions are illustrative of the powerful tenor of the deliberations and proceedings:

- Prior to one of the Empowerment Plenary Sessions, Atty. Faya Rose Toure came to the stage and led the assembly in a rousing rendition of the Freedom Song, "Ain't Going Let Nobody Turn Us Around."

- Paramount Chief Dr. Leonard Jeffries spoke on the significance of the gathering and recited a roll call of courageous African leaders to whom we should look for inspiration in this time of crisis. As he has taught so often, Dr. Jeffries stressed the urgency of using a "systems analysis" to successfully confront and defeat a U.S. and global system of white supremacy.

- An impassioned Danny Glover expressed the feelings of many Participants when he said, we needed this conference, we needed to be together at this moment. He encouraged a spirit of constant struggle by Black people, people of color and the oppressed to resist White supremacy and neo-liberal schemes of domination, propagated by the U.S.

- Rev. Waltrina Middleton graphically illustrated the contradictions and moral bankruptcy of the U.S. presidential election by pointing out that the Rev. Dr. Jeremiah Wright was viciously denounced for simply condemning the hypocrisy of U.S. domestic and foreign policy, while Donald Trump waged a campaign of flagrant and inflammatory insults to people of African descent/Blacks, Mexicans, immigrants, Muslims and women and could be elected President of the United States.

- In discussing the shocking results of the U.S. presidential elections and the rise of white nationalist and xenophobic movements in the U.S. and Europe, Professor Sir Hilary Beckles firmly declared that we are not going back to the days of white supremacist domination; that the determined quest for reparatory justice will be the dominant movement of the 21st Century.

- George Fraser sternly reminded the gathering that White folks will not save us; they are too busy taking care of their own; they aren't even thinking about us; no one will save us but us!

- South African Counsel General Mathula Nkosi was so moved by the spirit of the discussions that she spoke passionately about the similarity of our struggles. She recounted the role that Africans in America played in shattering apartheid and spoke to the urgent need to finish the struggle for genuine self-determination by achieving economic independence.

- Susan L. Taylor reminded us of the resilience of African people as the survivors of the holocaust of enslavement and shared an inspiring illustration of how love, compassion and culturally-relevant education and mentoring can rescue/save thousands of our youth/young people who have been marginalized under an oppressive system.

- The brilliant poet Lady Brion brought the gathering to its feet with an inspiring spoken word oration on the vital, indispensable role of women, of sisters, as leaders and partners in the struggle for the liberation of Black people!

- The Conscious Ones of the Lola Louis Creative and Performing

Arts Studio treated the assembly with an inspiring, dramatic presentation of Maya Angelou's And Still I Rise!

• Dowoti Desir opened the Closing Ndaba/Plenary with an inspiring traditional African religious Invocation in which she evoked the memory of Boukman, the Haitian spiritual leader whose prayer ignited the Haitian Revolution. That same spirit and power will arm this generation for the awesome battles ahead.

• In an instructive and inspiring lecture Dr. Maulana Karenga reaffirmed the value of the principles of the Nguzo Saba as a foundation and guide at this critical moment in our history and proclaimed that fundamental to the struggle for reparations is the repair and restoration of ourselves as African people, that when we repair ourselves, we repair the world!

• Honorable Minister Louis Farrakhan challenged and charged the assembled Participants to rededicate ourselves to building independent Black institutions to achieve social, economic and political control over the spaces and places where we live, to create national/international structures of self-governance and reach out to other people of color nationalities and ethnicities to build a new Nation, one so splendid in its humanity that people of all races will feel compelled to follow.

There was a spirit so strong, so pervasive among the Participants that you needed to be present as an eyewitness at this awesome assembly to feel the power of SOBWC IV.

It is also impossible to capture the breadth, depth and scope of the deliberations of this powerful gathering and the resolutions, recommendations, projects and initiatives discussed in the Issue Area Working Sessions in this Declaration. In composite, they will be posted on the IBW web site www.ibw21.org along with how each Session assigned responsibility for implementation.

About the Declaration

The purpose of this Declaration is to articulate IBW priorities for Racial Healing and Collaboration for Black Empowerment in terms of our work leading up to State of the Black World Conference IV and as an outgrowth of the proceedings. As such this Declaration marks a continuation of the work outlined at State of the Black World Conference III which was organized around the Theme: State of Emergency in Black America: Time to Heal Black Families and Communities.

IBW'S PRIORITIES AND PRESCRIPTIONS FOR ACTION

Resisting a Racist Regime

We encourage people of African descent to assume a posture of permanent resistance against the regime which will occupy the White House/Presidency on January 20th as a fervent expression of opposition to white supremacy, sexism, racism, white nationalism, Islamophobia and xenophobia; and to advance a vision of social, economic and political transformation as an expression of our collective resolve to achieve self-determination and a just, humane and peaceful society for African people, other people of color and the oppressed/marginalized people of all races, ethnicities and nationalities.

Towards A Domestic Marshall Plan for Black Communities

Reaffirm support for the demand by Mayor Ras J. Baraka, the National Urban League, the Center for Nu Leadership for Urban Solutions and Harvard University's Charles Hamilton Houston Institute for Race and Justice for a Domestic Marshall Plan type program for massive re-investment by the federal government to rebuild oppressed and marginalized Black communities across the nation.

Ending the War on Drugs and Mass Incarceration

Continue the relentless struggle to end the devastating "War on Drugs" in all its destructive manifestations; end police occupation, violence and killing of Black people and mass incarceration. And work for the decriminalization of drugs within the context of a racial, social, economic justice and public health framework; advocate for pre-arrest diversion programs like the Law Enforcement Assisted Diversion (LEAD) initiative; mobilize/organize victims of crime to become a constituency for criminal justice reform and de-incarceration; assist formerly incarcerated persons/returning citizens to empower themselves as a constituency for social justice and social change; consolidate existing Justice Collaboratives and expand to other cities (within the limits of IBW's capacity) to advocate for drug and criminal justice reform; and, strengthen the Police Reform and Accountability Task Force as a Resource Center to promote models of police restructuring to enable Black people to establish control over the police/law enforcement to create safe, just and wholesome communities.

Enhancing the Black Family Summit

Further strengthen and empower the Black Family Summit (BFS) as a resource to implement vital programs like the Emotional Emancipation Circles; to increasingly function as well equipped first responders to mediate and address crises in Black communities through the development of Trauma Centers; and, strengthen the capacity of BFS organizations to employ culturally-appropriate approaches to disaster prevention and relief, utilizing principled and effective relations with the Federal Emergency Management Agency (FEMA) and similar federal, state and local agencies.

Creating a Black Research Consortium

Continue the effort to operationalize IBW's Research Consortium to attract a critical mass of African-centered scholar activists to become a collective resource to undertake theoretical and applied research in support of programs, projects and initiatives by people of African descent in the U.S. and the Pan African world.

Black Dollars as a Weapon and Asset
in the Black Freedom Struggle

Encourage the use of the 1.5 trillion dollars of Black consumer power as a weapon to advance the social, economic and political interests and aspirations of people of African descent in the U.S. and the Pan African world by utilizing coordinated, strategic and collective Economic Sanctions/Boycotts to compel businesses/corporations and banks/financial institutions that thrive on Black dollars to reinvest in Black communities, agencies and institutions; to oppose and repeal racially biased public policies targeting Black people and to support policies that promote and protect Black interests. Equally important, to consistently encourage the mobilization/organization of the 1.5 trillion dollars in Black consumer power as the major asset to nourish models of economic and community development to stimulate socially responsible wealth generation and the building of a solid, stable and sustainable internal economy.

Building Labor/Community Solidarity

Continue to build strong bonds of labor/community solidarity as a means of combating the onslaught by the corporate/capitalist class against unions and labor organizations; a war on labor calculated to irreparably cripple the organized vehicles that promote and defend the interests of workers, the struggling middle class and the poor.

Accordingly, IBW will request that the Pan African Unity Dialogue in New York convene a Labor/Community Solidarity Summit to discuss and devise strategies for mass, popular education and action in defense of labor. Similar Summits should be convened by Black led organizations in cities across the country.

Intensifying the U.S. and Global Reparations Movement
Work to intensify the U.S. and global struggle for reparations within the context of the Durban Declaration and Program of Action and the U.N. Decade for People of African Descent. To that end, IBW will:
• Strive to strengthen the National African American Reparations Commission (NAARC) as a co-partner with the CARICOM Reparations Commission in expanding the global Reparations Movement.
• With the consent of Congressional John Conyers, finalize the revision of HR-40 from a "Study Bill" to a "Remedy Bill" to be introduced in the next Congress of the United States as a tool for mass public education, mobilizing/organizing and action to advance the struggle for reparations.
• Encourage the creation of Reparations Studies Curricula at Historically Black Colleges and Universities in collaboration with the University of West Indies Mona Campus in Jamaica.
• Support the convening of Reparations Summits in Africa and Columbia in 2017.

Continuing Cross-Generational Dialogue
and Engagement
Continue the Cross-Generational Dialogue initiated at SOBWC IV working collaboratively with the Movement for Black Lives and the Conveners/Facilitators of the Hip Hop/Cultural Workers Plenary and Working Sessions. Accordingly, based on the recommendations

from the Cross-Generational Dialogue IBW will:

• Establish safe "Teaching Spaces" for frank/honest cross-generational learning, sharing, exchange of perspectives, constructive critique and devising strategies to strengthen cross-generational engagement.

• Convene a session on the implications and lessons of Cointelpro for the current generations of activists/organizers associated with Black Lives Matter, Movement for Black Lives and similar formations.

Addressing Key Issues in Africa, the Caribbean, Central and South America

Based on the deliberations and documents developed by the Pan African Unity Dialogue convened by IBW in New York, work to mobilize mass based, popular support for:

• African-centered Principles of Democratic Governance in Africa and the Caribbean.

• Guidelines for Addressing and Resolving Crises in Africa and the Caribbean.

• Principles and Guidelines for Foreign Investment in Africa to counter the "new scramble for Africa."

In addition, continue efforts to strengthen the capacity of the Diaspora to impact U.S. policy toward Africa, the Caribbean, Central and South America; strengthen bonds of solidarity and action with Afro-Descendant communities in Central and South America; and intensify efforts to develop mutually beneficial business and commercial relations between Africa, the Caribbean, Central and South America and the Diaspora in the U.S.

Newark as an African Model City

In the spirit of "It's Nation Time" and in a collective expression/act of Kujichagulia, Self-Determination, we Declare Newark, New Jersey, under the leadership of Mayor Ras J. Baraka, an African Model City.

• We call on sisters and brothers from the U.S. and the Pan African world with resources, expertise and skills from all sectors of our communities to embrace this community-building/nation-building Pan African Project.

• Dr. Ron Daniels has requested that Dr. George Fraser tap the resources of the vast network of 65,000 socially conscious Black professionals, business owners and community development specialists affiliated with Fraser Net, Inc. to contribute to this major undertaking.

• With the consent and collaboration of Mayor Baraka, IBW is tentatively calling for an Economic and Community Development Planning Summit in Newark April 4, 2017, the date of the martyrdom of Dr. Martin Luther King, Jr. We wish for God and the Ancestors to bless this monumental endeavor.

The Road Ahead: Implementation with Capacity

Given the tremendous demand that IBW not wait four years to convene another State of the Black World Conference, capacity permitting, we propose the following:

• Based on the urgent need to implement the Economic Priorities outlined in this Declaration, IBW proposes the convening of day and a half Economic Development for Black Empowerment Mini-Conferences in selected cities/areas over the next 18 months beginning with the Northeast Corridor. These Mini-Conferences will be structured in a manner similar to the Plenary and Working Sessions at SOBWC IV and utilize the models showcased at the Conference as the basis for education, organization and action.

• Returning to Newark to convene State of the Black World Conference V in November 2018 to assess the implications of the crucial

Mid-Term Elections on Black America and the Pan African World and review progress on the resolutions, recommendations, initiatives and IBW Priorities advanced at State of the Black World Conference IV.

• Implementing the Proposals above are totally contingent on enhancing IBW's capacity as a Good Faith Convener/Facilitator.

Enhancing/Building IBW's Capacity

The Seventh Goal of State of the Black World Conference IV states: "Strengthen the Institute of the Black World 21st Century as a Good Faith Facilitator and Resource Center Promoting a Culture of Collaboration for Healing and Black Empowerment."

In his Keynote Presentation Dr. Ron Daniels stressed that for far too long, IBW has achieved stunning successes with limited financial resources and infrastructure. He shared that IBW did not have the resources to undertake SOBWC IV but made the decision to move forward because the tenor of the times dictated the need for a significant global gathering of people of African descent. By "guts and faith" the efforts of IBW proved providential in terms of the timing and response from the Participants. However, he indicated the "guts and faith" approach is not sustainable if IBW is to function as a good faith facilitator to convene gatherings like SOBWC IV and effectively implement the Priorities of the Declaration. He made an urgent appeal to the Participants to assist IBW to fulfill its mission by becoming sustaining contributors.

Dr. Haki Madhubuti's Contribution
and Challenge

At the conclusion of Dr. Daniels' Keynote Presentation, Haki Madhubuti strongly affirmed the value of the work of IBW and urged the

Participants to assist the organization to build the capacity/infra-structure to effectively continue its vital role as a Convener/Facilita-tor and Resource Center for Africans in America and the Pan African World. He asked as many Participants who could afford it to pledge a minimum of $25 a month to support IBW. Scores of Participants raised their hands to make pledges in response to Haki's appeal. Haki set the tone by making a major donation and pledged that there is more to come.

Minister Farrakhan's Contribution and Pledge

During the Closing Ndaba/Plenary, where he delivered the Closing Charge as the Keynote Speaker, The Honorable Minister Louis Far-rakhan made a major donation and pledged substantial resources to move the gathering beyond the State of the Black World Conference stage to the implementation stage. The Minister urged IBW to create independent ministry type structures to serve the needs of African people and fortify our self-determination as a Nation.

The Stage is Set for Sustaining Contributions
for Capacity-Building

With the outpouring support at SOBWC IV the stage is set for Par-ticipants to join the effort to build IBW's infrastructure and capacity. You can respond to Haki Madhubuti's Challenge and Minister Far-rakhan's Charge by becoming a Member of the Gregory Griffin Cir-cle of Sustaining Contributors via a monthly donation of $25 ($300 a year). Visit the website www.ibw21.org to sign-up and spread the word to family, friends and associates to join you. You can also make arrangements to pay an annual donation via check or money order by calling 888-774-2921.

Racial Healing and Collaboration for Black Empowerment
A Luta Continua... The Struggle Continues

Nataki Kambon, the visionary Spokesperson for the Let's Buy Black 365 Movement, summed up the feelings and feedback expressed by scores of the Participants of State of the Black World Conference IV. She said that to join with and witness hundreds of Black people standing in unison, chanting "It's Nation Time, Harambee," to close this historic gathering was one of the most moving and inspiring moments of her life.

Now the real work begins as we collectively strive, with the blessing of God and the Ancestors, to fulfill the promise of one of the great gatherings of people of African descent in the 21st Century, to by our sheer collective will, energy, contributions, sustained struggle and triumphs transform this moment in time into a decisive turning point in reclaiming our just and righteous role at the forefront of human civilization. "Up you mighty race, you can accomplish what you will." It's Nation Time!

Appendix 7
IBW Programmatic Chart as Resource Center

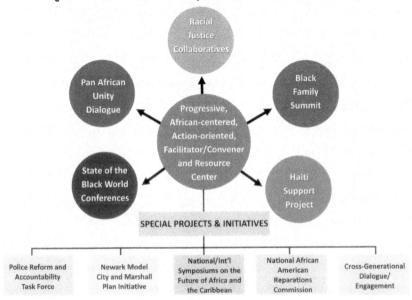

Institute of the Black World 21ˢᵗ Century

Cultivating a Culture of Collaboration to Empower and Heal Black Families and Communities

Racial Justice Collaboratives

Pan African Unity Dialogue

Black Family Summit

Progressive, African-centered, Action-oriented, Facilitator/Convener and Resource Center

State of the Black World Conferences

Haiti Support Project

SPECIAL PROJECTS & INITIATIVES

Police Reform and Accountability Task Force

Newark Model City and Marshall Plan Initiative

National/int'l Symposiums on the Future of Africa and the Caribbean

National African American Reparations Commission

Cross-Generational Dialogue/ Engagement